POWER
FOODS
FOR
DIABETES

Cooking Light.

American Diabetes Association.

POWER FOODS FOR DIABETES

The Top 20 Foods and 150 Recipes for Total Health

Oxmoor
HOUSE.

Contents

What Can I Eat Now?

Once you've been diagnosed with type 1 or type 2 diabetes, knowing what foods are good for you and how to incorporate them into your lifestyle is essential. In this chapter, *Cooking Light* and the American Diabetes Association give you meal planning and lifestyle advice, practical answers to everyday questions, and an easy-to-understand glossary of the top Power Foods.

WHEN YOU EAT A MEAL, the levels of glucose in your blood naturally rise because of the sugars and starches in the food. In response to the elevated glucose, the pancreas secretes insulin, a hormone that tells the body's cells to absorb the extra glucose. In type 1 diabetes, an autoimmune disease that occurs most frequently in young people but can be diagnosed at any age, the cells that produce insulin are destroyed and the body stops or greatly reduces the amount of insulin produced. With type 1 diabetes, you must inject or pump insulin daily.

In type 2 diabetes, the body does not produce enough insulin, is unable to use insulin to adequately lower blood glucose, or both. Ninety to 95 percent of people with diabetes have type 2 diabetes. A healthy diet and physical activity are major components of successfully treating and managing type 2 diabetes. In addition, people with type 2 diabetes may take medications, including insulin, to lower blood glucose levels.

An eating plan that includes lean protein, fruits and vegetables, beans, healthy fats, and fat-free dairy foods—all of which are Power Foods—can help control blood glucose levels and help prevent or control other complications of diabetes, such as heart disease and eye, kidney, and nerve damage.

To get started with making healthful changes, work toward incorporating the following eight essentials for good health into your daily life. But remember to be patient with yourself. It takes time for changes to your lifestyle to become habits, so focus on achieving one objective at a time.

8 Healthy Living Basics

1 INCORPORATE POWER FOODS INTO MEALS.

Power Foods are nutrient dense, meaning they are an excellent source of nutrients such as protein, heart-healthy fats, vitamins, minerals, and antioxidants. Power Foods are natural foods that have not undergone excessive processing that removes fiber or other nutrients. Once you know what the Power Foods are (they start on page 22), they can form the foundation of meals you prepare at home as well as those you enjoy with family and friends away from home. As with all foods, enjoy Power Foods in serving sizes that fit into your personal eating plan. With each Power Food, you'll find a list of recipes in the book that use the ingredient in a variety of great-tasting dishes.

2 CHOOSE "SMART CARBS."

Whole grains, beans, and sweet potatoes are all high-carb foods, but they are "smart carbs" because they contain fiber, vitamins, minerals, and phytochemicals that are beneficial to your health. "Smart carbs" are nourishing, high-carbohydrate foods that are whole foods or minimally processed.

As an example, ⅓ cup of brown rice has about the same amount of carbs and calories as ⅓ cup of white rice. But brown rice is a "smart carb" because it has more fiber and is rich in B vitamins and trace minerals contained in the outer hull, bran, and germ, which are removed when white rice is produced.

Other "smart carbs" include fresh fruits; whole grains such as oats, quinoa, and wild rice; and 100% whole-grain breads and pastas. Serving size is still important, even for "smart carbs": ⅓ to ½ cup is a typical serving size, depending on the food.

3 MINIMIZE ADDED SUGARS.

Sugary foods, such as cakes, cookies, pies, and brownies, should be occasional treats when you have diabetes since they cause blood sugars to spike. In addition to sugar, desserts usually contain butter or oil as well as other carbohydrates from white flour, making them high-calorie, low-nutrient additions to your meal.

You should, of course, sometimes treat yourself to a slice of birthday cake or a piece of pie, but you'll need to substitute the dessert for other carbohydrates in your meal. For example, if you are going to enjoy a slice of cake that has 30 grams of carbs, you'll need to eliminate a slice of bread from lunch (make your sandwich open-faced) to cut 15 grams of carbs and skip the potatoes at dinner to cut an additional 15 grams of carbs.

If sugars were only in desserts, it would be easy to track them, but they are also in many processed foods. Check labels on tomato sauce and pasta sauce, baked beans, frozen dinners, flavored instant oatmeal, flavored yogurt, and non-dairy milk (like soy milk). Sugar lurks in ingredients with names other than "sugar." Look for honey, maple syrup, agave, molasses, high fructose corn syrup (sometimes called corn sugar), and turbinado (raw) sugar in the ingredient list on labels.

Avoid sugar-sweetened beverages. They have been linked to developing type 2 diabetes and worsening cardiovascular risk factors. Plus, they offer no nutritional value other than extra calories. Instead of drinking sugar-sweetened soft drinks, energy drinks, tea, and sports beverages, opt for artificially sweetened or unsweetened beverages or water.

4 BOOST FIBER.

Fiber is the indigestible part of fruits, vegetables, beans, and grains. All dietary fibers are either soluble or insoluble, and both are important for digestion, health, and preventing conditions such as heart disease, diabetes, and obesity. The difference is that soluble fiber dissolves in water, while insoluble does not. This affects how each benefits your health. Soluble fiber, found in beans, lentils, oats, apples, oranges, cucumbers, and carrots, attracts water, which slows digestion. Slow stomach emptying helps you feel full longer and may also have a beneficial effect on blood sugar levels. Insoluble fiber, found in whole grains, seeds, nuts, and vegetables, doesn't dissolve in water, so it passes through the intestinal tract almost intact. This added bulk is beneficial for intestinal health.

High-fiber meals usually require a lot of chewing, which slows you down and makes you more attuned to when you've had enough to eat. Fiber adds no calories to your diet, yet it bulks up meals, making you feel full for a longer time.

The American Diabetes Association recommends a minimum of 25 grams of fiber a day for women and 38 grams for men. Most Americans consume only about half this amount. To incorporate more fiber into your everyday meals, choose a high-fiber breakfast cereal with no added sugars; add beans or lentils to soups and top your salads with seeds, nuts, and a variety of vegetables; choose 100% whole-grain breads and pastas; and enjoy whole fruits for snacks and desserts.

5 CHOOSE HEALTHY FATS.

All fats are high in calories—there are about 120 calories in a tablespoon of any type of oil—so you'll want to keep portions small even for healthy fats. Fat is a vital component of your diet. You need fat for energy; absorption of vitamins A, D, E, and K; and for healthy hair and skin.

But for heart health, it's important to make smart choices about the fats you do include in your meals. The key is to substitute mono- and polyunsaturated fats for trans and saturated fats. (Your diabetes educator or registered dietitian will help you learn to substitute healthy for unhealthy fats.) Saturated fats and trans fats raise your cholesterol levels and having high cholesterol is a key risk factor for heart disease. Limiting these fats is particularly important for people with diabetes, since having diabetes already puts you at high risk for heart disease.

Saturated fat is found in foods such as fatty meats, chicken and turkey skin, butter, cheese, whole-milk dairy products, lard, coconut oil, palm oil, and chocolate. Trans fat is produced when liquid oil is processed to turn it into a solid fat. It's found in margarine, shortening, snack chips and crackers, commercially made cookies and cakes, and French fries. Read labels carefully. Avoid foods with the word "hydrogenated" in the ingredient list. Hydrogenated oil contains trans fat and manufacturers are allowed to list trans fat at 0 grams if the product contains less than 0.5 grams of trans fat *per serving*.

While cutting back on saturated and trans fat, you can substitute heart-healthy monounsaturated and polyunsaturated fats, and omega-3 fatty acids. For cooking oils, these include canola, olive, corn, cottonseed, safflower, sunflower, and soybean oils. They're also found in avocados, nuts, sunflower seeds and pumpkinseeds, and fatty fish. Tuna, trout, sardines, and salmon are also excellent sources of omega-3 fatty acids.

6 LIMIT SODIUM.

Eating too much sodium can raise blood pressure, which increases the risk for heart attack or stroke. In people with type 2 diabetes, the risk for heart attack and dying from heart disease is the same as in people who have already had heart attacks, so keeping blood pressure in check is vital. Aim for 2,300 milligrams or less of sodium each day. If you have high blood pressure, talk to your health-care provider about the right amount for you.

You may be surprised to find out that it's the salt found in processed foods that is the biggest source of sodium for most people. Reading labels is crucial. It's important to choose products with the least amount of sodium—the amount can vary widely between different brands of the same type of product—or, even better, make your own versions at home. Soups, broths, soy sauce, packaged seasoning mixes, and snack foods are high in sodium, but other foods you wouldn't think of as containing excess sodium can contain a surprisingly high amount, including bread, breakfast cereals, pre-marinated meats, condiments, and pasta sauces.

Cooking at home is one way to control everything that goes into your meals, but even then, it's important to be mindful of how much salt (and high-sodium foods) you're adding to your diet. If you often reach for the salt shaker to season food, try stirring in a pinch of grated lemon zest, a splash of lime juice or vinegar, or a spoonful of chopped fresh herbs to add lots of flavor and cut the amount of salt you need. When you begin to cut back on sodium, things may initially taste blander, but your taste buds will adjust, and over time, you'll need less salt in your food.

7 WORK TOWARD AND MAINTAIN A HEALTHY WEIGHT.

Being overweight is strongly correlated with having type 2 diabetes—almost 90% of people with type 2 diabetes are overweight. If you weigh more than you should, losing 7% of your body weight can reduce your risk of developing type 2 diabetes. For example, if you weigh 200 pounds, losing 15 pounds, 7% of your body weight, can help control blood glucose, improve blood pressure and cholesterol levels, and give you more energy. Losing weight is most likely to help blood glucose if you have not had diabetes for a long time.

Talk with your registered dietitian who will personalize your weight-loss goals and eating plans to help you take off pounds sensibly and safely. When you change your eating and exercise patterns, you may need an adjustment in your insulin or other diabetes medications, so involving your health-care team is essential. Your dietitian can guide you to take small, easy-to-incorporate steps toward being more active and eating fewer calories, making it more likely that the changes will become an enjoyable part of daily life.

8 GET SOME EXERCISE.

Being physically active can help lower your blood glucose, keep you at a healthy weight, and help maintain a healthy heart. Health experts recommend 30 minutes of exercise at least five days a week. If this sounds like it's more than you have time for, break it up into two 15-minute sessions when it fits into your schedule. You can do jumping jacks or jump rope while you watch TV, go for a walk, ride a bike, swim, take an exercise class, dance, or do an online workout at home.

If you have not been active, check with your health-care team before starting any strenuous exercises to make sure you're choosing activities that are safe for you. Your insulin or other diabetes medications and your food intake may need to be adjusted when you start working exercise into your daily routine. Your diabetes educator or your physician will explain what you need to do to get fit while keeping your blood glucose at a steady level.

3 Ways to Manage Your Meals

There are three methods to choose from when planning what you eat each day. Meal planning is critical for people with diabetes to help improve blood glucose levels, balance food intake with insulin or other diabetes medications (if medications are prescribed), and help you maintain or lose weight and eat heart-healthy foods.

The method you use is up to you and your health-care team based on your individual needs. Whichever plan you choose, your registered dietitian will personalize the plan taking into account your food likes and dislikes, exercise level, daily work and activity schedule, and the diabetes medications you take.

1 CREATE YOUR PLATE

This is the easiest method for meal planning for people with diabetes. You simply use a dinner plate to decide how much to eat. One caveat: Use a 9-inch plate with this method, not an oversized one, to help keep portions in check.

Fill half your plate with colorful vegetables, such as green beans, carrots, broccoli, spinach, or salad greens. Fill one-fourth of your plate with a carbohydrate-containing food such as 100% whole-grain pasta or bread, brown rice, or sweet potatoes. Fill the remaining one-fourth with a protein-rich food, such as 3 ounces of chicken, lean beef or pork, fish, or tofu.

To round out your meal, enjoy a serving of milk or yogurt or a piece of fruit for dessert, or both, if your eating plan allows. Your registered dietitian will help you determine what's right for your meals as well as snacks, based on your personal needs.

2 CARB COUNTING

Carb counting is a bit more complicated than the "create your plate" method. Your registered dietitian will tell you how many carbs you can have at each meal and for snacks if you enjoy eating between meals. Then, you decide which foods you will have based on the number of carbs they contain. Typically, the amount of carbs for meals will be somewhere between 45 and 60 grams and 15 grams for a snack.

For this method, you need to know how many carbs foods contain. You can look at the label, or if the food doesn't have a label, use a carb-counting book, website, or app. At first, it may seem time consuming, but once you learn the carb count of the foods you commonly eat, you won't have to look them up every time. Keep in mind that you need to match your serving size to the serving size on the label or in the book or app. It's easy to focus only on carbs using this method, but you'll also need to include lean protein in your meals, use heart-healthy fats, and watch calories if you are trying to maintain or lose weight.

3 FOOD CHOICES

The food choices system, previously called the exchange system, groups foods together based on their carbohydrate, protein, fat, and calorie levels. For example, starchy vegetables are grouped together, and the serving size of each one varies so that the carb, protein, fat, and calorie level for a serving is the same for the entire food list of starchy vegetables. In this category, a serving of corn is ½ cup, a serving of hominy is ¾ cup, and a serving of winter squash is 1 cup. You can make "choices" for each meal from the food lists, using the serving sizes provided.

This method is more complicated to learn, but it helps with weight control because foods are grouped not only by the amount of carbs they contain, but also by the calories they have. In addition, serving sizes for each food are given within the food lists. The food choices method also helps with heart-healthy eating, since milk and yogurt are grouped as fat-free, reduced-fat, and whole milk choices, and protein foods are grouped as lean, medium-fat, and high-fat choices.

Your registered dietitian will work with you to set up an eating plan with the number of choices from each food list for each meal and snacks if you enjoy having them.

Real-Life Questions

SHOULD I CONSIDER THE GLYCEMIC INDEX OF FOODS?

The glycemic index (GI) is a measure of the rise in blood glucose after eating a serving of food that contains 50 grams of carbohydrate compared to the rise in blood glucose after eating pure glucose (sugar) or white bread. Foods with high GI raise blood glucose more than foods with low GI. Once you have mastered carb counting, choosing foods with lower GI/more fiber may be helpful in keeping your blood glucose in control.

One of the pitfalls of using GI as a method for choosing foods to eat when you have diabetes is that serving size is not taken into account. Split peas have a medium GI of 25. If you eat ⅓ cup, that's only 14 grams of carbs, but if you eat 1 cup of them, it's a whopping 42 grams of carbs.

Another problem with using GI is that the number the food is assigned is based on a serving size that contains 50 grams of carbohydrate, which may not be a typical serving size. For example, broccoli has a very low GI of 10. But, to get 50 grams of carbohydrate from broccoli florets, you would need to eat more than 13 cups.

Yet another issue with this method is that it's based on eating single foods, not as in real life where you eat a combination of foods at once. You may know the GI of each particular food, but you don't know what the GI would be of all the foods combined in your meal in the serving sizes you consume.

In general, though not always, low-GI foods are less processed, more wholesome foods. But don't use GI as your only consideration in meal planning—you still need to take into account the grams of carbohydrate and serving sizes.

WHAT ABOUT NATURAL SWEETENERS LIKE AGAVE AND HONEY?

All added sugars (table sugar, agave, honey, brown sugar, syrup, molasses), no matter if they're natural or not, should be used sparingly. Once any of these sugars are ingested, the body digests and absorbs them the same way and they have the same effect on blood sugar levels. However, some natural sweeteners, specifically agave and honey, are inherently sweeter than cane sugar and therefore smaller amounts can produce the same sweet taste.

WILL ARTIFICIAL SWEETENERS HELP ME CONTROL MY BLOOD SUGAR LEVELS?

Foods and beverages that use artificial sweeteners may help you control your sweet tooth. These sweeteners, also known as sugar substitutes or low-calorie sweeteners, have far fewer calories and carbohydrates and are also about 100 times more intense than regular sugar, which means you can use less while still satisfying your cravings for something sweet. Here are the sugar substitutes you'll find in stores:

• Acesulfame potassium (brand names: Sunett, Sweet One)
• Aspartame (NutraSweet, Equal)
• Neotame
• Saccharin (Sweet 'N Low, Sugar Twin)
• Sucralose (Splenda)
• Stevia/Rebaudioside A (SweetLeaf, Sun Crystals, Steviva, Truvia, Pure Via)

WHAT IS A SERVING?

No matter which method you use for meal planning, you must pay attention to serving sizes in order to help with blood glucose levels, calorie intake, and heart health. If you're eating a packaged food with a label, the serving size is listed on the label with the nutrition information given for the serving. If you eat more or less of the food, account for the carbs and other nutrients accordingly.

Use books, websites, or apps to look up the nutrition information for foods without labels and enjoy the serving size given, or account for a larger or smaller portion in your meal plan. A typical diabetes-friendly serving of starchy foods such as brown rice, whole-wheat pasta, or stuffing is ⅓ cup, which has about 15 grams of carbohydrate. Examples of typical serving sizes of fruit are 1 cup of diced honeydew, a small banana (4 ounces), or ½ of a large pear (4 ounces). You can have a larger serving, but you have to count the total number of carbs in all the foods in your meal.

A heart-healthy serving of cooked meat, poultry, or fish is 3 ounces, about the size of a deck of cards. A serving of salad dressing or mayonnaise is 1 tablespoon; for an avocado, it's 2 tablespoons; and for olive oil, it's 1 teaspoon. These are much smaller servings than you are probably used to, especially when eating out.

Train your eye to estimate serving sizes by measuring or weighing servings of foods you frequently eat at home. Put the food in your plates and bowls, and after measuring foods a few times, you'll be able to estimate the correct serving size just by looking. (If you change your dinnerware, you should remeasure since amounts can look different on plates that are different sizes or shapes.) You'll soon become adept at estimating serving sizes, which can help determine how much food to eat when you are in a restaurant or in someone's home.

HOW DO I MAKE SENSE OF A FOOD LABEL?

Food labels are a wonderful resource, but they can be puzzling. Next time you check one out, use this guide to help you decipher the numbers:

• The **serving size** indicates how much food is recommended for one portion. If you eat more or less than this amount, you'll need to adjust the nutrients accordingly. (Pay special attention to the carbs!)

• Need to know how many single portions are in one jar, can, or package? Check the **servings per container**—you might be surprised at how often packages contain more than one serving.

• Food labels divide fats into **total fat, saturated fat, and trans fat** categories, but you'll want to focus on the latter two. Always stay away from trans fats—those can be harmful to your health. (They've been found to raise "bad" LDL cholesterol and lower "good" HDL cholesterol.) As for saturated fats, the American Diabetes Association recommends a daily intake of less than 10 percent of total calories. This translates to 20 grams or less for a 2,000-calorie diet and 15 grams for a 1,500-calorie diet. And lastly, you'll sometimes see monounsaturated and polyunsaturated fats' names on the label too. These are good, heart-healthy fats that should be substituted for saturated and trans fats.

• **Total carbohydrate, dietary fiber,** and **sugars** are listed together, but the key player in this section is total carbohydrate. This number indicates the grams of carbohydrate in one serving, including fiber and sugars. You want the fiber number to be high—aim for a total of 25 grams per day for women and 38 grams per day for men. Sugars can include naturally occurring sugars (like lactose in yogurt), but also could indicate high levels of added sugars (like high fructose corn syrup).

• **Protein** is a daily essential that doesn't affect your blood sugar much. According to experts, women need 46 grams a day and men need 56 grams. Most Americans easily exceed these amounts, but it's a good idea to make sure you're getting enough. If you're a vegetarian (or an occasional one), don't worry about eating certain foods together to create "complete" proteins—your body will make its own if you eat a variety of foods and a sufficient number of calories.

Nutrition Facts

Serving Size 2 Slices (57g)
Servings Per Container 10

Calories 160
Calories from Fat 20

Calories Per Slice 80
Calories from Fat 10

Amount/Serving	% Daily Value*		Amount/Serving	
	2 SLICES	1 SLICE		
Total Fat 2g, 1g	3%	2%	**Sodium** 2...	
Saturated Fat 0.5g, 0g	3%	0%	**Total Ca...**	
Trans Fat 0g, 0g			Dietary Fi...	
Polyunsaturated Fat 1g, 0.5g			Sugars 4...	
Monounsaturated Fat 0g, 0g			**Protein** 5...	
Cholesterol 0mg, 0mg	0%	0%		
Vitamin A	0%	0%	Thiamin	
Vitamin C	0%	0%	Riboflavin	
Calcium	10%	4%	Niacin	
Iron	10%	6%	Folic Acid	

Amount/Serving	% Daily...
	2 SLICE
Sodium 270mg, 130mg	11%
Total Carbohydrate 30g, 15g	10%
Dietary Fiber 1g, Less than 1g	5%
Sugars 4g, 2g	
Protein 5g, 2g	

• Vitamin and mineral amounts for **vitamins A** and **C, calcium,** and **iron** are also noted on food labels. They usually appear as percentages, which are linked to the Recommended Daily Intake for each nutrient. Percent daily values indicate how much of a daily recommended vitamin or mineral you are consuming in a certain food. Most percent daily values are for a 2,000-calorie diet, though larger food packages often provide amounts for a 2,500-calorie diet. Keep in mind that the calorie level your health-care team recommends may be less than 2,000 calories.

WHAT SHOULD I ORDER IN A RESTAURANT?

Diabetes doesn't mean your social life is over. Dining at restaurants is a normal part of life that you can enjoy; however, being prepared is key. Knowing how to order will help you dine healthfully and confidently and keep you from derailing your diet. Choose restaurants that offer a variety of dishes containing fresh fruits and vegetables and lean meats. Even many fast food establishments now offer healthier choices, so you can still make good decisions when you're on the go. Once you've wisely chosen where to eat, these tips will help you order:

• Opt for appetizers that aren't loaded with salt or fat. Veggies and hummus or a shrimp cocktail are better choices than chips and queso or French fries. If you're trying to cut down on bread or eliminate it entirely from your diet, tell your waiter upfront not to bring it to your table. If you do eat bread, plain breads are best. Watch out for cornbread, biscuits, muffins, and other breads that are high in fat, sodium, and added sugar.

• When ordering meat, poultry, or fish, choose a baked, broiled, or grilled preparation, rather than fried or breaded. Salads and sides of fresh nonstarchy vegetables are better choices than starchy foods like potatoes and white rice. However, if you opt for the latter, choose brown rice or a sweet potato and keep the portion small. Be cautious of the dressings, sauces, and gravies that might come with veggies and meats and the sour cream, butter, and cheese that come on loaded potatoes. These supplements are often heavy on sodium, fat, and calories, so ask your waiter to serve them on the side.

• A serving of fresh fruit is a smart option for dessert. Even if it's not listed on the menu, ask your waiter for a small bowl of sliced melon, berries, or citrus. If there's another dessert on the menu you'd like, order one for the table and split it. Never hesitate to ask your server questions about the menu or be afraid to ask for a substitute side that's better for your eating plan. Restaurants are generally happy to accommodate requests like preparing foods without salt as long as you ask.

AsparagusAvocadosBean
BerriesBroccoliCitrusFish
SeedGreensFat-FreeMilkM
onsNutsOatsPeanutButte
noaRedBellPeppersSoyTo
toesFat-FreeYogurtWhole
AsparagusAvocadosBean
BerriesBroccoliCitrusFish
SeedGreensFat-FreeMilkM
onsNutsOatsPeanutButte
noaRedBellPeppersSoyTo
toesFat-FreeYogurtWhole
AsparagusAvocadosBean
riesBroccoliCitrusFishFlax

TOP
20
POWER
FOODS

Asparagus

Health Benefits

These elegant stalks do more than dress up a dinner plate. Asparagus has the highest level of any vegetable of glutathione, a powerful antioxidant that helps detoxify and maintain a healthy immune system. It is a good source of folate, which is vital for making new cells, especially during pregnancy; potassium, which helps control blood pressure; and vitamin K, which helps make proteins required for proper clotting of blood. Asparagus is very low in carbohydrates, so it will not cause blood sugar to rise.

Did You Know?

Asparagus takes three years to mature from planting to the first harvest; the spears are harvested individually by hand. Because the tips are so delicate, great care must be taken to transport asparagus from the field to the packinghouse, and damaged spears must be sorted out individually. For these reasons, asparagus is one of the most expensive—yet, most delicious—vegetables.

Serving size: 1 cup raw or ½ cup cooked
Carb counting: 5 grams
Food Choice: 1 Nonstarchy Vegetable

Recipes

Asparagus and Spring Greens Salad with Gorgonzola Vinaigrette (page 103)
White Bean Salad with Shrimp and Asparagus (page 131)
Asparagus-and-Spinach Toasts with Fontina Cheese (page 158)
Asparagus with Balsamic Tomatoes (page 232)

Avocados

Health Benefits

Given their buttery texture, it's not surprising that avocados are high in fat, but the fat they primarily contain is monounsaturated fat, which helps lower cholesterol and decreases the risk of heart disease. Use avocado in place of sat fat–loaded butter on toast. Studies have shown that people who eat more unsaturated fat are less likely to develop type 2 diabetes. Avocados are a good source of fiber and vitamins C and E, as well as the antioxidant lutein.

Did You Know?

Ninety percent of America's avocados come from southern California, where they grow year round; a single tree can yield up to 500 avocados. Hass avocados, with their dark green bumpy skins and creamy flesh are the most popular variety. Botanically, avocados are a fruit, but because of their high fat content, the American Diabetes Association counts them as a fat.

Serving size: 2 tablespoons
Carb counting: 2 grams
Food Choice: 1 Fat

Recipes

Huevos Rancheros Soft Tacos (page 45)
Tomato-Avocado Dip (page 64)
Avocado BLT (page 151)
Grilled Salmon and Avocado Pitas (page 161)
Chipotle Grilled Pork Tenderloin with Strawberry-Avocado Salsa (page 201)

Beans (black, garbanzo, kidney, pinto, white)

Health Benefits

Not only are beans an excellent source of protein and fiber, but they are particularly important for people with diabetes because they have been shown to lower blood glucose levels, reduce cholesterol, and help with weight loss. Dried beans are a good source of minerals including potassium and calcium as well as folate and other B vitamins.

Did You Know?

Eating beans is one of the best ways to meet the daily fiber goal of 25 grams for women and 38 grams for men. Depending on the variety, ½ cup of beans provides 6 to 10 grams of fiber. Use them in soups, stews, and casseroles, add them to salads, or turn them into dips. When buying canned beans, choose unsalted beans, or, if you're using regular canned beans, rinse them before using to remove about 40 percent of the sodium.

> Serving size: ½ cup cooked
> Carb counting: 24 grams
> Food Choices: 1 Starch, 1 Lean Protein

Recipes

Rosemary-Garlic White Bean Spread
  (page 70)
Spicy Bean and Quinoa Salad with "Mole"
  Vinaigrette (page 95)
Coriander-Crusted Beef Salad with Black Bean
  Salsa (page 114)
Black Bean Soup (page 138)
Southwestern White Bean Pita Pockets
  (page 156)

Berries (blueberries, raspberries, strawberries)

Health Benefits

All varieties of berries are a rich source of antioxidants, which may reduce the risk of cancer, improve heart health, and aid memory. Raspberries are particularly high in fiber, with 8 grams in a 1-cup serving. Blueberries are ranked highest in antioxidants among 43 fruits and vegetables tested by the U.S. Department of Agriculture and, in one study, were found to improve insulin sensitivity. Just 8 strawberries contain more vitamin C than a medium orange. To reap the benefits of berries, include a variety of them in your meals and snacks.

Did You Know?

Berries are the perfect healthy snack or dessert for people with diabetes. They're naturally sweet, almost effortless to prepare (they just need a quick rinse under the faucet), and absolutely delicious.

> Serving size: 1¼ cups whole strawberries,
>   1 cup raspberries, or ¾ cup blueberries
> Carb counting: 15 grams
> Food Choice: 1 Fruit

Recipes

Blueberry Waffles (page 37)
Chile-Spiced Fruit Salad with Queso Fresco
  (page 80)
Crunchy Noodles and Greens Salad (page 109)
Creamy Blueberry-Chicken Salad (page 123)
Strawberry, Pistachio, and Goat Cheese Pizza
  (page 176)

Broccoli

Health Benefits

This deep green vegetable may be one of the world's healthiest—especially for people with diabetes. With very few calories and few carbohydrates to affect blood sugar, broccoli packs in the nutrients with a good amount of vitamin C, antioxidants, folate, and fiber. It contains a high amount of glucosinolates, compounds that may fight against cancer and play a role in reducing heart disease risk.

Did You Know?

Broccoli is a member of the cruciferous vegetable family that includes cabbage, Brussels sprouts, cauliflower, kale, and collards. This entire family of vegetables is associated with health benefits, but over-cooking can destroy the health-promoting components of these veggies. For the most health benefits and the best flavor, lightly steam broccoli and other cruciferous vegetables just until crisp-tender.

> Serving size: 1 cup raw broccoli or ½ cup cooked
> Carb counting: 5 grams
> Food Choice: 1 Nonstarchy Vegetable

Recipes

Broccoli Pesto Bruschetta (page 74)
Broccoli-Quinoa Casserole with Chicken and Cheddar (page 221)
Broccoli with Quinoa and Bacon (page 235)
Sesame-Broccoli Stir-Fry (page 237)

Citrus (grapefruit, lemons, limes, oranges)

Health Benefits

Of course they have vitamin C, but citrus fruits also have other antioxidants that protect the heart by reducing inflammation in the arteries and lowering cholesterol. They're also a good source of potassium, magnesium, and folate. Citrus fruits contain a moderate amount of carbohydrates, few calories, no sodium, and plenty of fiber making them an optimal choice for people with diabetes and heart disease.

Did You Know?

Oranges and grapefruit are a good source of fiber and will help you feel full longer. They are perfect for adding to salads to boost flavor and nutrients and they make an excellent diabetes-friendly snack any time of day. One word of caution: Grapefruit can interact with some heart medications, so check with your doctor about the safety of consuming the fruit. Lemons and limes are another source for a bit of citrus juice and flavor.

> Serving size: 1 medium orange or ½ of a large grapefruit
> Carb counting: 15 grams
> Food Choice: 1 Fruit

Recipes

Tomato-and-Mango Salad with Curry-Orange Vinaigrette (page 84)
Orange Salad with Arugula and Oil-Cured Olives (page 99)
Chunky Tomato-Fruit Gazpacho (page 134)
Orange and Mustard–Glazed Pork Chops (page 196)
Fresh Fruit with Strawberry Sauce (page 264)

Fatty fish (arctic char, salmon, tuna)

Health Benefits

Salmon and albacore tuna are some of the best sources of heart-healthy omega-3 fatty acids, which may decrease abnormal heartbeats, decrease triglyceride levels, slow the growth of atherosclerotic plaque, and lower blood pressure. They are excellent sources of protein and good-for-you unsaturated fat. Fish contains no carbohydrate, so it will not cause a rise in blood glucose.

Did You Know?

Mercury in fish is a concern for women who are pregnant or breastfeeding. The Food and Drug Administration recommends women in this group should limit their intake of albacore tuna to 6 ounces each week. However, salmon and canned light tuna are two of the fish recommended by the FDA for having the lowest amount of mercury. Check FDA.gov for updated information regarding fish safety.

Serving size: 3 ounces cooked
Carb counting: 0 grams
Food Choices: 3 Lean Proteins

Recipes

Mediterranean Tuna Salad (page 126)
Grilled Salmon and Spinach Salad (page 128)
Open-Faced Salmon Sandwiches with Tomato and Avocado (page 162)
Broiled Salmon with Marmalade-Dijon Glaze (page 215)
Fresh Tuna Tacos (page 216)

Flaxseed

Health Benefits

Flaxseed contains alpha-linolenic acid, a type of omega-3 fatty acid that boosts heart health. It is an excellent source of soluble fiber, which is thought to bind with cholesterol in the intestine to prevent it from being absorbed. It also makes blood cells less sticky, which may lower the risk of atherosclerosis.

Did You Know?

Flaxseed is better digested if ground before eating. If eaten whole, it may pass through the intestine undigested and you will not get its nutritional benefits. You can buy flaxseed already ground, or grind your own in a coffee grinder at home. Because of its high fat content, it will stay fresh longer if stored in the refrigerator or freezer.

Serving size: 1½ tablespoons
Carb counting: 1 gram
Food Choice: 1 Fat

Recipes

Flaxseed-Buttermilk Pancakes (page 38)
Parmesan-Rosemary Flatbread Crackers (page 71)
Turkey Cobb Salad Roll-Ups (page 171)
Confetti Rice Pilaf with Toasted Flaxseed (page 255)
Mixed Berry, Flaxseed, and Yogurt Parfaits (page 262)

Greens (kale, leafy greens, spinach)

Health Benefits

Rich in omega-3 fatty acids; antioxidants; calcium; vitamins A, B, C, and K; and fiber, leafy greens are a nutritional powerhouse for people with diabetes. One study found that consumption of these healthful greens may help lower the risk of type 2 diabetes and may protect against several kinds of cancer.

Did You Know?

Kale chips are increasingly popular, and they make a terrific low-carb snack for people with diabetes. It's best to make your own kale chips by simply tossing 2-inch pieces of kale leaves very lightly in olive oil and baking at 350° for 15 minutes. If you buy them already made, check the label first. Some varieties are fried, making them high in calories, and some brands are high in sodium.

Serving size: 1 cup raw or ½ cup cooked
Carb counting: 5 grams
Food Choice: 1 Nonstarchy Vegetable

Recipes

Cast-Iron Breakfast Pizza (page 42)
Kale Salad with Apple and Cheddar (page 107)
Thai Chicken Salad (page 116)
Quinoa-Stuffed Kale Rolls with Goat Cheese (page 224)
Spinach and Onion Couscous (page 245)

Melon (cantaloupe, honeydew)

Health Benefits

Cantaloupe is a great source of vitamins A and C as well as potassium and B vitamins. It's also a good source of fiber and contains antioxidants, which may help prevent cancer and heart disease, conditions that occur more often in people with diabetes. Cantaloupe may help lower inflammation, which can play a part in developing diseases such as cancer. Honeydew melon has less vitamin C than cantaloupe but has similar levels of other nutrients.

Did You Know?

Simple slices or cubes of cantaloupe and honeydew make healthy, delicious summer-time snacks and desserts. As a precaution, always wash the skin of melons in warm soapy water before cutting them. This removes any dirt or debris that might transfer to the flesh when you cut the melon with a knife.

Serving size: 1 cup diced melon
Carb counting: 15 grams
Food Choice: 1 Fruit

Recipes

Southwest Melon Salsa (page 62)
Prosciutto-Melon Bites (page 77)
Minty Cucumber and Honeydew Salad (page 82)
Cantaloupe Sherbet (page 270)

Milk, fat-free

Health Benefits

As an excellent source of calcium, vitamin D, and protein, fat-free milk is a great choice for people with diabetes. Having diabetes can increase the chance of bone fracture, and calcium in milk can help keep your bones strong and guard against osteoporosis, which can lead to broken bones in older adults. Including milk and dairy foods in meals can help lower blood pressure and reduce the risk of type 2 diabetes and cardiovascular disease.

Did You Know?

Surprisingly, milk contains a significant amount of carbohydrate. The carbohydrate comes from lactose, the naturally occurring sugar found in milk, and should be counted toward the carb choices for your meal or snack. Even if you choose lactose-free milk, it still contains lactose; it just has an enzyme added to help those with lactose intolerance digest the milk.

> Serving size: 1 cup
> Carb counting: 12 grams
> Food Choice: 1 Fat-Free Milk

Recipes

Bacon and Cheddar Oatmeal (page 35)
Peanut and Banana Oatmeal (page 35)
Blueberry Waffles (page 37)
White Chocolate Mousse (page 269)

Nuts

Health Benefits

Tree nuts, such as almonds, pecans, pistachios, and walnuts, contain monounsaturated fat, a heart-healthy unsaturated fat that can help lower the risk for type 2 diabetes and help lower blood cholesterol. A serving of tree nuts is a healthy alternative to chips when you're craving a crunchy snack. Walnuts are the superstars of the nut family; they are the only type that contains significant amounts of alpha-linolenic acid, the plant source of omega-3 fatty acids. Walnuts may also have a helpful effect on metabolic syndrome, a group of risk factors including obesity, high blood pressure, and high blood glucose levels that increase the risk for developing type 2 diabetes and liver, kidney, and heart diseases.

Did You Know?

Although nuts are high in calories and should be enjoyed in small amounts, they are an excellent snack for people with diabetes. A few nuts in addition to a small piece of fruit in the afternoon will provide you with the energy you need to keep you going until dinner. The fat from the nuts will help you feel full, and the carbohydrate from the fruit will give you energy. Pine nuts, which are seeds and not true nuts, also offer similar benefits.

> Serving size: 4 walnut halves, 6 almonds,
>   4 pecan halves, or 16 pistachios
> Carb counting: 5 grams
> Food Choice: 1 Fat

Recipes

Cinnamon-Raisin Waffle Sandwich (page 39)
Baby Arugula, Pear, and Gorgonzola Salad
  (page 97)
Raspberry and Blue Cheese Salad (page 101)
Kale and Beet Salad with Blue Cheese and
  Walnuts (page 106)
Sautéed Spinach with Raisins and Pine Nuts
  (page 247)

Oats

Health Benefits

Oats are known for their cholesterol-lowering abilities, but some studies have shown that they may also help reduce the risk of type 2 diabetes, control blood pressure, improve the immune system, and increase levels of appetite control hormones. Oats contain a group of antioxidants called avenanthramides, which protect blood vessels from the harmful effects of LDL ("bad") cholesterol. And they are an excellent source of beta-glucan, a soluble fiber that can help lower blood glucose levels.

Did You Know?

It's healthier if you use rolled oats or steel-cut oats instead of using pre-sweetened packages, which contain a lot of added sugar. Prepare your own oatmeal and top it with a handful of berries, a small chopped apple, or half a sliced banana to lend natural sweetness. You can also add rolled oats to dishes such as meat-loaf and pancakes to add texture and fiber.

Serving size: ¼ cup dry oats or ½ cup plain cooked oatmeal
Carb counting: 14 grams
Food Choice: 1 Starch

Recipes

Bacon and Cheddar Oatmeal (page 35)
Peanut and Banana Oatmeal (page 35)
Individual Salsa Meat Loaves (page 185)
Chewy Date-Apple Bars (page 279)

Peanut butter

Health Benefits

A smear of peanut butter on your sandwich will not only taste great, but it's also an excellent source of protein, fiber, vitamin E, potassium, magnesium, and cancer-fighting antioxidants. Consuming peanuts or peanut butter, which contain unsaturated fat, has been shown to lower cholesterol and triglycerides, which reduces the risk of heart disease. Use peanut butter in place of butter on toast or in place of chocolate for a snack.

Did You Know?

Peanuts are not a true nut but legumes that grow in their shells underground; their nutritional profile is similar to that of nuts that grow on trees. When choosing peanut butter, select a "natural" brand without added sugars. Skip "reduced-fat" brands, which include sugars and other additives. You'll only save about 5 calories in a tablespoon, and you'll take in more carbs. Peanut butter is the perfect snack for people with diabetes because it contains protein and fat, which take longer to digest and help you feel full longer.

Serving size: 1 tablespoon
Carb counting: 4 grams
Food Choice: 1 High-Fat Protein

Recipes

Peanut and Banana Oatmeal (page 35)
Curried Beef with Peanut-Coconut Sauce (page 193)
Peanut-Sesame Noodles (page 258)
Peanut Butter Ice Cream Sandwiches (page 271)
Peanut Butter-and-Jelly Sandwich Cookies (page 276)
Peanut Butter Cookies (page 278)

Quinoa

Health Benefits

Quinoa is one of the few grains that contain all nine essential amino acids that are needed by the body. Compared to other grains, quinoa has a higher amount of protein, antioxidants, and vitamin E. With 2 grams of fiber in ⅓ cup of cooked quinoa, it is an excellent source of fiber. Fiber is important for people with diabetes because it may help improve blood glucose control, helps lower cholesterol, and makes you feel full.

Did You Know?

Quinoa was grown as long as 4,000 years ago in the Andes, where this drought-resistant plant still flourishes. White and red quinoa are the most common varieties, but there are more than 120 different types. Not a true "grain," quinoa is a relative of Swiss chard and beets. Quinoa leaves, though they are not marketed in the U.S., are edible.

> Serving size: ⅓ cup cooked
> Carb counting: 13 grams
> Food Choice: 1 Starch

Recipes

Breakfast Quinoa (page 36)
Curried Quinoa Salad with Cucumber-Mint Raita (page 92)
Chicken and Asparagus in White Wine Sauce (page 207)
Kale and Quinoa Pilaf (page 239)
Quinoa with Roasted Garlic, Tomatoes, and Spinach (page 254)

Red bell peppers

Health Benefits

Low calorie and low carb, red bell peppers are an exceptional choice for people with diabetes. They are an excellent source of vitamins A and C, potassium, folate, and fiber. A medium-sized red bell pepper has double the amount of vitamin C as a medium orange, and a ½-cup serving of red bell pepper gives you almost half the vitamin A you need for the day. Bell peppers contain some of the same health-promoting sulfur-containing compounds associated with cruciferous vegetables such as broccoli and Brussels sprouts.

Did You Know?

Red peppers are nutritionally superior to green or yellow bell peppers because they are riper, so they develop more vitamins and antioxidants as they mature. This also means they are more expensive than other colors, since they stay on the plant longer to develop their bright red color.

> Serving size: 1 cup raw or ½ cup cooked
> Carb counting: 5 grams
> Food Choice: 1 Nonstarchy Vegetable

Recipes

Goat Cheese and Roasted Pepper Panini (page 154)
Smothered Pepper Steak (page 190)
Speedy Chicken and Cheese Enchiladas (page 202)
Roasted Peppers and Tomatoes with Herbs and Capers (page 242)
Bell Pepper Sauté (page 245)

Soy

Health Benefits

Soy foods such as tofu, edamame, and soy milk are linked with lower risks of breast and endometrial cancer and may help women under 65 with cognitive function. Studies on soy are inconclusive, but some researchers have found that soy may have cholesterol-lowering abilities and protective effects against obesity, diabetes, and bone and kidney diseases. Soy products supply a generous amount of protein for few calories and a modest amount of fat.

Did You Know?

Unsweetened soy milk has 7 grams less carbohydrate in a 1-cup serving than regular fat-free dairy milk. When choosing soy milk for a beverage or for cooking, choose an unsweetened variety with added calcium and vitamin D. Check the ingredients list on the package to find out if your favorite brand is fortified with these important nutrients.

Serving size: 1 cup regular plain soy milk
Carb counting: 8 grams
Food Choices: ½ Carbohydrate, 1 Fat

Serving size: 4 ounces tofu
Carb counting: 3 grams
Food Choice: 1 Medium-Fat Protein

Recipes

Edamame Salad (page 88)
Chicken, Edamame, and Rice Salad (page 125)
Succotash Burritos (page 159)
Flank Steak and Edamame with Wasabi
 Dressing (page 180)
Asian Stir-Fry Quinoa Bowl (page 222)

Tomatoes

Health Benefits

Tomatoes are an excellent source of many antioxidants, including lycopene, which help eliminate free radicals that cause damage to DNA. Lycopene is associated with decreasing cancer risk and protecting against stroke. Tomatoes contain good amounts of vitamins A and C, potassium, and fiber. They are an excellent vegetable for people with diabetes because one cup of red tomato contains only about 32 calories and 7 carbohydrates.

Did You Know?

A study from Marseille, France, found that most of the antioxidants in tomatoes are found in their skins, so don't bother peeling tomatoes. When they are sliced or chopped to put on a sandwich or use in a salad, the skins are barely noticeable anyway, so keep the nutrients and the skin intact.

Serving size: 1 cup raw or ½ cup cooked
Carb counting: 7 grams
Food Choice: 1 Nonstarchy Vegetable

Recipes

Poblano-Tomato Soup (page 136)
Thai Basil Beef with Rice Noodles (page 182)
Speedy Chicken and Cheese Enchiladas
 (page 202)
Scallops with Capers and Tomatoes (page 218)
Tomatoes Provençale (page 250)

Whole grains (barley, brown rice, bulgur, wheat)

Health Benefits

Whole grains contain the bran, germ, and endosperm—the parts of the grain that provide essential nutrients such as fiber, folate and other B vitamins, magnesium, and chromium. The fiber in whole grains is a carbohydrate, but it is not digested, so it does not raise your blood sugar. For this reason, whole grains are a superior choice over products made from processed grains, such as white flour or white rice, for people with diabetes. The extra fiber also helps you feel full longer after you eat, aids in digestion, and helps keep blood cholesterol in check.

Did You Know?

Breads, cereals, and crackers made with processed grains lose most of their nutrients during manufacturing. Food companies add back or "fortify" processed grains with vitamins including iron, folate, and other B vitamins to replace what was removed in processing.

> Serving size: ½ cup cooked bulgur, ⅓ cup cooked barley, brown rice, or whole-wheat pasta; 1 slice whole-wheat bread
> Carb counting: 15 grams
> Food Choice: 1 Starch

Recipes

Curry Chicken Wraps with Nectarine Chutney (page 163)
Grilled Zucchini Bulgur Pilaf (page 251)
Barley-Mushroom Pilaf (page 252)
Carrot-Cilantro Bulgur (page 256)
Multigrain Pilaf (page 257)

Yogurt, fat-free

Health Benefits

Yogurt is an excellent source of protein, calcium, potassium, and vitamin D. It is also a great source of probiotics, the "good" bacteria that may have health benefits ranging from boosting the immune system to helping with irritable bowel syndrome. Studies have found a link between eating yogurt and reduced risk of type 2 diabetes and high blood pressure.

Did You Know?

Greek yogurt is regular yogurt with some of the liquid whey or protein strained off. Because it is more concentrated, it has twice the protein of regular yogurt and makes a healthy snack or a rich-tasting sour cream substitute. Just be sure to read the label carefully and choose a plain fat-free yogurt with no added sugars and fortified with vitamin D.

> Serving size: 1 cup plain fat-free yogurt
> Carb counting: 18 grams
> Food Choice: 1 Fat-Free Milk

Recipes

Banana-Blueberry Smoothies (page 58)
Curried Quinoa Salad with Cucumber-Mint Raita (page 92)
Turkey Pitas with Tahini-Yogurt Sauce (page 168)
Asparagus with Lemon-Basil Yogurt Sauce (page 235)
Mixed Berry, Flaxseed, and Yogurt Parfaits (page 262)

Breakfast Quinoa, page 36

Great Beginnings

Prevent blood sugar spikes and keep your energy up with these filling and mouthwatering dishes. From quick breakfast options to casual brunch ideas, healthy options for any occasion will be right at your fingertips.

Bacon and Cheddar Oatmeal

Bacon and Cheddar Oatmeal

Satisfying oatmeal takes on a savory twist with the irresistible combination of bacon and cheddar cheese.

Hands-on Time: 2 minutes   **Total Time:** 7 minutes   **Serves:** 1

½ cup old-fashioned rolled oats

½ cup water

½ cup fat-free milk

1 center-cut bacon slice, cooked and crumbled

1 tablespoon reduced-fat shredded sharp cheddar cheese

1 tablespoon chopped green onions (optional)

Freshly ground black pepper

1 Combine first 4 ingredients in a medium microwave-safe bowl. Microwave, uncovered, at MEDIUM 5 to 6 minutes or until liquid is absorbed.

2 Add cheese, stirring until cheese melts. Sprinkle with green onions, if desired, and black pepper.

PER SERVING (serving size: about 1 cup):

Food Choices: 2 Starches, ½ Fat-Free Milk, 1 Medium-Fat Protein

Calories 239; **Fat** 6.6g (sat 2.6g, mono 2.4g, poly 1.5g, trans 0g); **Protein** 13g; **Carbohydrate** 33g; **Fiber** 4g; **Sugars** 7g; **Cholesterol** 15mg; **Iron** 2mg; **Sodium** 246mg; **Potassium** 393mg; **Phosphorus** 336mg; **Calcium** 199mg

Peanut and Banana Oatmeal

If you like softer oats, cook them up to 1 minute longer before adding the peanut butter.

Hands-on Time: 1 minute   **Total Time:** 6 minutes   **Serves:** 1

½ cup old-fashioned rolled oats

½ cup water

½ cup fat-free milk

⅛ teaspoon salt

2 teaspoons natural-style peanut butter

¼ cup sliced banana

2 teaspoons chopped dry-roasted peanuts

1 Combine first 4 ingredients in a medium microwave-safe bowl. Microwave, uncovered, at MEDIUM 5 to 6 minutes or until liquid is absorbed. Stir in peanut butter. Top with banana, and sprinkle with peanuts.

PER SERVING (serving size: about 1 cup):

Food Choices: 2½ Starches, ½ Fruit, 1 High-Fat Protein

Calories 327; **Fat** 11.6g (sat 1.7g, mono 5.4g, poly 3.4g, trans 0g); **Protein** 13g; **Carbohydrate** 45g; **Fiber** 6g; **Sugars** 13g; **Cholesterol** 2mg; **Iron** 2mg; **Sodium** 387mg; **Potassium** 473mg; **Phosphorus** 357mg; **Calcium** 155mg

Breakfast Quinoa

Like most whole grains, quinoa is surprisingly filling, but if you need more for breakfast, serve with an egg on the side.

Hands-on Time: 10 minutes   **Total Time:** 25 minutes   **Serves:** 4

½ **cup uncooked** quinoa

¾ **cup light coconut milk**

2 **tablespoons water**

1½ **teaspoons granulated brown sugar blend (such as Splenda)**

⅛ **teaspoon salt**

1 **cup sliced** strawberries

1 **cup sliced banana**

¼ **cup flaked unsweetened coconut, toasted (optional)**

1 Place quinoa in a fine sieve, and place sieve in a large bowl. Cover quinoa with water. Using your hands, rub the grains together for 30 seconds; rinse and drain quinoa. Repeat procedure twice. Drain well. Combine quinoa, coconut milk, 2 tablespoons water, brown sugar blend, and salt in a medium saucepan, and bring to a boil. Reduce heat, and simmer 15 minutes or until liquid is absorbed, stirring occasionally. Stir mixture constantly during the last 2 minutes of cooking.

2 Divide quinoa mixture among 4 bowls. Top each serving with strawberry slices, banana slices, and toasted coconut, if desired. Serve warm.

PER SERVING (serving size: ½ cup quinoa mixture, ¼ cup strawberry slices, and ¼ cup banana slices):

Food Choices: 1 Starch, 1 Fruit, ½ Fat

Calories 165; **Fat** 3.8g (sat 1.9g, mono 0.4g, poly 0.8g, trans 0g); **Protein** 4g; **Carbohydrate** 30g; **Fiber** 4g; **Sugars** 11g; **Cholesterol** 0mg; **Iron** 1mg; **Sodium** 89mg; **Potassium** 418mg; **Phosphorus** 162mg; **Calcium** 19mg

ingredient pointer

Don't skip the rinse! When time is short, you may be tempted to omit this step—but it's critical for the best flavor. Quinoa has a bitter coating that is easily removed when rinsed.

Blueberry Waffles

You can use either frozen or fresh blueberries for these waffles. If you are using frozen blueberries, do not thaw them before adding to the batter.

Hands-on Time: 5 minutes **Total Time:** 17 minutes **Serves:** 8

7.9 ounces all-purpose flour (about 1¾ cups)
1 tablespoon baking powder
Dash of salt
1¾ cups fat-free milk
3 tablespoons canola oil
2 large egg whites, lightly beaten
1 large egg, lightly beaten
Cooking spray
1 cup fresh or frozen blueberries
Additional blueberries **(optional)**
Sugar-free syrup (optional)

1 Weigh or lightly spoon flour into dry measuring cups; level with a knife. Combine flour, baking powder, and salt in a medium bowl; stir well. Combine milk, oil, egg whites, and egg in a small bowl; stir well. Add to flour mixture, stirring until well blended.

2 Coat a waffle iron with cooking spray, and preheat. Spoon about ⅓ cup of batter per waffle onto hot waffle iron, spreading batter to edges. Spoon 2 tablespoons blueberries per waffle over batter. Cook 6 to 7 minutes or until steaming stops; repeat procedure with remaining batter and blueberries. Garnish with additional blueberries and syrup, if desired.

PER SERVING (serving size: 1 [4-inch] waffle):

Food Choices: 2 Starches, 1 Fat

Calories 189; **Fat** 6.3g (sat 1.2g, mono 1.8g, poly 2.7g, trans 0g); **Protein** 6g; **Carbohydrate** 27g; **Fiber** 2g; **Sugars** 5g; **Cholesterol** 29mg; **Iron** 2mg; **Sodium** 86mg; **Potassium** 150mg; **Phosphorus** 144mg; **Calcium** 176mg

Flaxseed-Buttermilk Pancakes

These gluten-free pancakes get their nutty flavor and some nutritional heft from the flaxseed meal. The tapioca flour and potato starch keep the texture light while the brown rice flour adds some whole grains and fiber.

Hands-on Time: 20 minutes   **Total Time:** 20 minutes   Serves: 9

- **3.1 ounces brown rice flour (about ⅔ cup)**
- **1.1 ounces tapioca flour (about ¼ cup)**
- **1.3 ounces potato starch (about ¼ cup)**
- **0.9 ounce flaxseed meal (about ¼ cup)**
- **2 teaspoons measures-like-sugar calorie-free sweetener**
- **2 teaspoons baking powder**
- **1 teaspoon baking soda**
- **⅛ teaspoon salt**
- **1 cup nonfat buttermilk**
- **1 teaspoon vanilla extract**
- **2 large eggs**
- **2¼ cups fresh blueberries**

1 Weigh or lightly spoon flours, potato starch, and flaxseed meal into dry measuring cups; level with a knife. Combine flours, potato starch, flaxseed meal, measures-like-sugar sweetener, baking powder, baking soda, and salt in a large bowl, stirring with a whisk. Combine buttermilk, vanilla, and eggs; stir with a whisk. Add to flour mixture, stirring until smooth.

2 Heat a nonstick griddle or large nonstick skillet over medium heat. Pour 2 tablespoons batter per pancake onto pan; cook 1 minute or until tops are covered with bubbles and edges look cooked. Carefully turn pancakes over; cook 1 minute or until bottoms are lightly browned. Serve with blueberries.

PER SERVING (serving size: 2 pancakes and ¼ cup blueberries):

Food Choices: 1 Starch, ½ Fruit

Calories 120; **Fat** 2.4g (sat 0.5g, mono 1.3g, poly 0.6g, trans 0g); **Protein** 4g; **Carbohydrate** 22g; **Fiber** 2g; **Sugars** 6g; **Cholesterol** 41mg; **Iron** 1mg; **Sodium** 305mg; **Potassium** 143mg; **Phosphorus** 106mg; **Calcium** 96mg

ingredient pointer

For the best flavor and nutrient retention, it's best to purchase flaxseeds whole and only grind what you need right before using. Place the desired amount in a coffee grinder and pulse 10 to 15 seconds or until an evenly ground meal is formed.

Cinnamon-Raisin Waffle Sandwich

This sweetened cream cheese spread is also delicious on other breakfast breads, such as bagel thins and toast.

Hands-on Time: 3 minutes   **Total Time:** 5 minutes   **Serves:** 1

1 (1.33-ounce) frozen multigrain waffle

2 tablespoons fat-free cream cheese, softened

1 teaspoon granulated brown sugar blend (such as Splenda)

¼ teaspoon ground cinnamon

1 tablespoon raisins

1 tablespoon chopped walnuts, toasted

1 Toast waffle according to package directions.

2 Combine cream cheese, brown sugar blend, and cinnamon until well blended. Spread cream cheese mixture over waffle. Sprinkle with raisins and walnuts. Cut waffle in half. Sandwich waffle halves together with filling in center.

PER SERVING (serving size: 1 sandwich):

Food Choices: 1 Starch, ½ Fruit, 1 Lean Protein, 1 Fat

Calories 203; **Fat** 8.7g (sat 1.4g, mono 1.2g, poly 3.5g, trans 0g); **Protein** 9g; **Carbohydrate** 27g; **Fiber** 4g; **Sugars** 13g; **Cholesterol** 4mg; **Iron** 1mg; **Sodium** 412mg; **Potassium** 244mg; **Phosphorus** 292mg; **Calcium** 154mg

Breakfast is for
Champions

To get every day off to a good start, make breakfast part of your routine. Eating a healthy morning meal may help improve blood glucose levels by spreading your carbohydrate intake out over the day. And the benefits don't stop there: Studies have shown that people who eat a "carb-smart" breakfast are better at keeping pounds off and are more productive and mentally focused.

You'll also set yourself up for successful eating the rest of the day. You'll be less likely to crave fast food or a sugary treat at lunch or dinner when you've started the day with a wholesome, fiber- and nutrient-rich meal.

If you're challenged to get the recommended daily amount of fiber (25 grams for women and 38 grams for men), it's easy to include plenty of this important nutrient at breakfast. Whole-grain cereals and breads as well as fresh fruits are all good sources of fiber and are quick to grab and enjoy even if your mornings are rushed.

You can reap the benefits of eating breakfast, but only if you choose the right foods. Make heart-healthy choices that fit within the amount of carbohydrate recommended by your health-care team. If typical breakfast foods don't always appeal to your a.m. taste buds, that's no reason to skip the morning meal. Our suggestions in On the Go and Non-Traditional Breakfast Options (on the next page) provide creative choices to help jumpstart your day.

AT HOME

High-Fiber Cereal: Make sure it has at least 5 grams of fiber per serving and little or no added sugar. Shreds of wheat cereal (such as Shredded Wheat), shreds of wheat bran cereal (such as All-Bran), and high-fiber cereal (such as Fiber One) are good choices. Enjoy your cereal topped with fat-free milk, and use calorie-free sweetener, if you wish.

Oatmeal: Make quick-cooking oats in the morning. Or prepare steel-cut oats the night before, and reheat in the microwave. Top oatmeal with a handful of berries to add sweetness, texture, and fiber and a few nuts for healthy fats.

Waffle or Pancake: Top a whole-wheat waffle or pancake with a tablespoon of peanut butter or almond butter, and then sprinkle with chopped fresh fruit or berries.

Egg and Toast: This comforting and delicious favorite takes just a few minutes to make, has a good amount of protein and fiber, and fills you up. Choose whole-grain bread, and poach the egg or prepare it in a skillet with cooking spray or a few drops of oil.

ON THE GO

Egg and Veggie Wrap: Fill a small whole-wheat tortilla with sautéed vegetables like bell peppers and onions and scrambled eggs or egg whites. Wrap and go.

Cottage Cheese and Raspberries: Stir ½ cup fresh or frozen raspberries into 1 cup fat-free cottage cheese, and carry in a plastic container. Raspberries are fantastic for people with diabetes—½ cup has just 7 grams of carbs and a whopping 4 grams of fiber.

Yogurt Parfait: For a simple protein-packed breakfast, top 1 cup plain fat-free Greek yogurt with ½ cup chopped fresh fruit or berries, and sprinkle with 2 tablespoons chopped nuts.

Smoothie: Blend plain fat-free Greek yogurt with frozen unsweetened fruit and a splash of fat-free milk, pour into a travel cup, and hit the road.

Fruit and Nuts: Even on the busiest mornings, you can find time to throw an apple, orange, or small banana along with ¼ cup whole raw almonds in your bag to eat along the way.

NON-TRADITIONAL BREAKFAST OPTIONS

Soup: Heat up your favorite brand of reduced-sodium soup, or when you make soup at home, cook a double batch and freeze individual portions to reheat for breakfast.

Pizza: Spread a 6-inch whole-wheat pita with reduced-sodium marinara sauce. Top with sliced roasted red bell peppers and 1 ounce shredded reduced-fat mozzarella, and bake at 400° until the cheese melts (about 8 minutes).

Sandwich: Start with a whole-wheat English muffin, sandwich thin, or thin-sliced bread. Add 1 or 2 ounces turkey breast, lean low-sodium ham, or reduced-fat cheddar or Swiss cheese, and top with veggies like lettuce, sliced tomatoes, sliced cucumbers, or bell pepper strips.

Leftovers: Enjoy the remains of last night's dinner for breakfast. Pop leftover brown rice and vegetables, chicken and whole-wheat pasta, or meat loaf and mashed potatoes in the microwave, and you'll be going strong until lunch.

Cast-Iron Breakfast Pizza

Crushed red pepper gives this classic recipe some kick while the spinach provides color. For a crisp pizza crust, heat the skillet on the stovetop before transferring it to the oven.

Hands-on Time: 13 minutes   **Total Time:** 31 minutes   **Serves:** 8

1 (16-ounce) package commercial pizza dough
¾ cup part-skim ricotta cheese
4 center-cut bacon slices, cooked and crumbled
3 ounces shredded part-skim mozzarella cheese (about ¾ cup)
¼ teaspoon freshly ground black pepper
Cooking spray
1 (6-ounce) package fresh baby spinach
⅛ teaspoon crushed red pepper

1 Preheat oven to 450°.

2 Roll out dough to a 12-inch circle. Press dough into bottom and 1 inch up sides of a well-seasoned 10-inch cast-iron skillet. Fold edges under, and crimp.

3 Spread ricotta cheese in bottom of crust; top with bacon, mozzarella cheese, and pepper. Place pan over high heat; cook 3 minutes. Transfer pan to oven.

4 Bake at 450° for 18 minutes or until crust is lightly browned and cheese melts.

5 While pizza cooks, heat a large skillet over medium-high heat. Coat pan with cooking spray. Add spinach. Cook 1 minute or until spinach wilts, turning often with tongs. Remove spinach from pan; drain and squeeze out excess liquid. Top pizza with wilted spinach and sprinkle with crushed red pepper. Cut pizza into 8 wedges.

PER SERVING (serving size: 1 wedge):

Food Choices: 1½ Starches, 1 Nonstarchy Vegetable, 1 Medium-Fat Protein

Calories 233; **Fat** 5.7g (sat 2.7g, mono 2.4g, poly 0.6g, trans 0g); **Protein** 12g; **Carbohydrate** 30g; **Fiber** 5g; **Sugars** 1g; **Cholesterol** 18mg; **Iron** 2mg; **Sodium** 439mg; **Potassium** 219mg; **Phosphorus** 165mg; **Calcium** 162mg

small change, big result

Use a well-seasoned cast-iron skillet—it eliminates the need for extra oil to grease the pan.

Huevos Rancheros Soft Tacos

Fresh salsa tastes more vibrant than bottled and has less sodium. Corn tortillas make a good substitute for the flour variety.

Hands-on Time: 10 minutes   **Total Time:** 10 minutes   **Serves:** 2

2 large eggs
2 large egg whites
⅛ teaspoon freshly ground black pepper
Cooking spray
½ cup low-sodium refried black beans, warmed
2 (6-inch) flour tortillas, warmed
2 tablespoons shredded Oaxaca cheese
¼ cup Fresh Salsa (page 62)
¼ cup diced peeled avocado

1 Combine first 3 ingredients in a small bowl, stirring with a whisk. Heat a medium skillet over medium heat. Coat pan with cooking spray. Add egg mixture; cook 1 minute or until soft-scrambled, stirring often.

2 Spread ¼ cup beans over each tortilla; top with scrambled egg mixture, and sprinkle with cheese. Spoon salsa and avocado over eggs. Fold tortillas over filling.

PER SERVING (serving size: 1 taco):

Food Choices: 2 Starches, 2 Lean Proteins, 1 Fat

Calories 292; **Fat** 11.6g (sat 3.3g, mono 4.7g, poly 1.7g, trans 0g); **Protein** 18g; **Carbohydrate** 29g; **Fiber** 5g; **Sugars** 3g; **Cholesterol** 190mg; **Iron** 3mg; **Sodium** 429mg; **Potassium** 459mg; **Phosphorus** 261mg; **Calcium** 151mg

ingredient pointer

To soften or ripen an unripened avocado, place it in a brown paper bag with an apple or banana. These fruits produce ethylene, a gas that promotes ripening, and when stored in a concentrated area, the fruits cause ethylene levels to rise and ripening to accelerate.

Poached Eggs with Spinach and Walnuts

Serve protein-packed eggs over a side of spinach sautéed with mushrooms, walnuts, and Gruyère cheese.

Hands-on Time: 30 minutes   **Total Time:** 30 minutes   **Serves:** 4

1 tablespoon olive oil, divided

1 (10-ounce) package fresh baby spinach, chopped

3 garlic cloves, minced

3 vertically sliced shallots

1 tablespoon chopped fresh sage

¾ teaspoon chopped fresh thyme, divided

½ teaspoon freshly ground black pepper, divided

¼ teaspoon salt

1 (8-ounce) package cremini mushrooms, quartered

¾ cup toasted walnuts, chopped and divided

2 ounces Gruyère cheese, shredded (about ½ cup)

2 tablespoons red wine vinegar

8 cups water

2 tablespoons white vinegar

4 large eggs

1 Heat a large Dutch oven over medium-high heat. Add 1 teaspoon oil. Add spinach; sauté 2 minutes. Remove spinach from pan; drain, cool slightly, and squeeze out excess moisture. Add remaining oil to pan. Add garlic and shallots; sauté 3 minutes. Add sage, ½ teaspoon thyme, ¼ teaspoon pepper, salt, and mushrooms; sauté 7 minutes. Stir in spinach, ½ cup walnuts, cheese, and red wine vinegar; cook 30 seconds.

2 Combine 8 cups water and white vinegar in a large saucepan, and bring to a simmer. Break each egg gently into pan. Cook 3 minutes. Remove eggs using a slotted spoon. Spoon mushroom mixture onto 4 plates. Top each serving with 1 egg. Sprinkle with remaining thyme, pepper, and walnuts.

PER SERVING (serving size: ⅔ cup mushroom mixture, 1 egg, and 1 tablespoon walnuts):

Food Choices: 3 Nonstarchy Vegetables, 2 Medium-Fat Proteins, 3 Fats

Calories 350; **Fat** 24.3g (sat 5.5g, mono 7.5g, poly 10.2g, trans 0g); **Protein** 17g; **Carbohydrate** 18g; **Fiber** 5g; **Sugars** 4g; **Cholesterol** 196mg; **Iron** 4mg; **Sodium** 383mg; **Potassium** 896mg; **Phosphorus** 367mg; **Calcium** 257mg

Caprese Eggs Benedict

Pesto Hollandaise replaces the basil that's in a traditional Caprese salad. You will have extra hollandaise sauce left over; spoon it over grilled fish.

Hands-on Time: 11 minutes   **Total Time:** 11 minutes   **Serves:** 4

Cooking spray

4 large eggs

2 whole-wheat English muffins, split and toasted

4 (¼-inch-thick) slices tomato

4 (0.75-ounce) slices fresh mozzarella cheese

¼ cup Pesto Hollandaise

4 large basil leaves (optional)

1 Coat 4 (6-ounce) custard cups with cooking spray. Break 1 egg into each cup. Pierce yolk of each egg once with a wooden pick. Microwave at MEDIUM 1 minute and 15 seconds or to desired degree of doneness.

2 Place a muffin half, cut side up, on each of 4 plates. Top each with tomato, mozzarella, egg, Pesto Hollandaise, and a basil leaf, if desired.

PER SERVING (serving size: 1 muffin half, 1 tomato slice, 1 mozzarella slice, 1 egg, and 1 tablespoon Pesto Hollandaise):

Food Choices: 1 Starch, 2 Medium-Fat Proteins, 1 Fat

Calories 255; **Fat** 15.9g (sat 5.4g, mono 5.8g, poly 2.6g, trans 0g); **Protein** 13g; **Carbohydrate** 15g; **Fiber** 3g; **Sugars** 4g; **Cholesterol** 207mg; **Iron** 2mg; **Sodium** 270mg; **Potassium** 203mg; **Phosphorus** 272mg; **Calcium** 130mg

Pesto Hollandaise

Hands-on Time: 2 minutes   **Total Time:** 2 minutes, 45 seconds   **Serves:** 14

⅓ cup nonfat buttermilk

⅓ cup canola mayonnaise

2 tablespoons refrigerated pesto

1 tablespoon fresh lemon juice

1 teaspoon butter

1 Combine first 4 ingredients in a 1-cup glass measure, stirring with a whisk until blended. Microwave at MEDIUM 45 seconds or until warm. Add butter, stirring until melted. Keep warm.

PER SERVING (serving size: 1 tablespoon):

Food Choice: 1 Fat

Calories 54; **Fat** 5.5g (sat 0.7g, mono 2.4g, poly 1.2g, trans 0g); **Protein** 1g; **Carbohydrate** 1g; **Fiber** 0g; **Sugars** 0g; **Cholesterol** 3mg; **Iron** 0mg; **Sodium** 65mg; **Potassium** 15mg; **Phosphorus** 12mg; **Calcium** 13mg

Open-Faced Mexican Egg Sandwiches

Queso fresco, a Mexican cheese, has a crumbly and creamy texture and a delicious salty-sour flavor. You can substitute feta cheese for the queso fresco. The sodium content of storebought salsa verde can vary widely, so be sure to read the label and choose a brand with the least amount of sodium.

Hands-on Time: 8 minutes   **Total Time:** 15 minutes   **Serves:** 4

¼ **pound Mexican chorizo**

4 large egg whites, lightly beaten

2 large eggs, lightly beaten

2 tablespoons chopped fresh cilantro

2 whole-wheat English muffins, **split and toasted**

¼ **cup** salsa verde **(optional)**

1 ounce queso fresco, crumbled (about ¼ cup)

1 Remove casing from chorizo. Cook chorizo in a large nonstick skillet over medium-high heat 5 minutes or until browned; stir to crumble. Drain well; return chorizo to pan.

2 Combine egg whites, eggs, and cilantro in a medium bowl, stirring with a whisk.

3 Add egg mixture to chorizo; cook over medium heat 2 minutes. Do not stir until mixture begins to set on bottom. Draw a heat-resistant spatula through egg mixture to form large curds. Do not stir constantly. Egg mixture is done when thickened but still moist.

4 Place a muffin half, cut side up, on each of 4 plates. Spoon egg mixture onto English muffin halves; top each with 1 tablespoon salsa verde, if desired, and 1 tablespoon queso fresco.

PER SERVING (serving size: 1 sandwich):

Food Choices: 1 Starch, 2 Medium-Fat Proteins, ½ Fat

Calories 238; **Fat** 12.5g (sat 5.4g, mono 1.5g, poly 0.8g, trans 0g); **Protein** 16g; **Carbohydrate** 16g; **Fiber** 3g; **Sugars** 3g; **Cholesterol** 138mg; **Iron** 1mg; **Sodium** 443mg; **Potassium** 291mg; **Phosphorus** 220mg; **Calcium** 148mg

small change, big result

This open-faced egg sandwich uses a combination of egg whites and whole eggs—this small change saves 240 calories and 5 grams of fat.

Eggs Poached in Curried Tomato Sauce

Lessen the heat by removing some or all of the jalapeño's seeds.

Hands-on Time: 30 minutes   **Total Time:** 35 minutes   **Serves:** 4

1 teaspoon peanut oil

1½ cups chopped onion

1 tablespoon minced fresh garlic

1 tablespoon minced peeled fresh ginger

1 jalapeño pepper, minced

2 teaspoons curry powder

¼ teaspoon salt

¼ teaspoon freshly ground black pepper

1 (28-ounce) can unsalted diced tomatoes, undrained

½ cup light coconut milk

½ cup chopped fresh cilantro

4 large eggs

2 whole-wheat English muffins, split and toasted

¼ cup chopped green onions

Cilantro leaves (optional)

1 Heat a large skillet over medium-high heat. Add oil to pan; swirl to coat. Add onion, garlic, ginger, and jalapeño; sauté 5 minutes or until vegetables are tender, stirring occasionally. Add curry powder, salt, and black pepper; cook 2 minutes, stirring constantly. Drain tomatoes in a colander over a bowl; reserve liquid. Add tomatoes to pan; cook 5 minutes, stirring frequently. Add half of reserved tomato liquid; bring to a boil. Add coconut milk and chopped cilantro; return to a boil. Cover, reduce heat, and simmer 10 minutes. If sauce is too thick, add remaining reserved tomato liquid; maintain heat so that sauce bubbles gently.

2 Break each egg into a custard cup, and pour gently into pan over sauce. Cover and cook 5 minutes, just until whites are set and yolks have filmed over but are still runny. Place a muffin half, cut side up, on each of 4 plates. Carefully scoop egg and sauce onto muffin halves. Sprinkle with green onions; garnish with cilantro leaves, if desired.

PER SERVING (serving size: 1 muffin half, 1 egg, ½ cup sauce, and 1 tablespoon green onions):

Food Choices: 1½ Starches, 1 Nonstarchy Vegetable, 1 Medium-Fat Protein

Calories 247; **Fat** 8.3g (sat 3.3g, mono 2.6g, poly 1.6g, trans 0g); **Protein** 12g; **Carbohydrate** 32g; **Fiber** 6g; **Sugars** 12g; **Cholesterol** 186mg; **Iron** 4mg; **Sodium** 373mg; **Potassium** 699mg; **Phosphorus** 191mg; **Calcium** 175mg

Black Bean Omelet

This omelet is served with salsa, Monterey Jack cheese with jalapeño peppers, and black beans. Rinsing and draining the beans not only gets rid of excess sodium, it also makes a prettier omelet. Sprinkle with additional sliced green onions, if you'd like.

Hands-on Time: 14 minutes   **Total Time:** 14 minutes   **Serves:** 2

4 large egg whites

2 large eggs

¼ teaspoon freshly ground black pepper

⅛ teaspoon salt

Cooking spray

½ cup unsalted black beans, rinsed and drained

1 ounce preshredded Monterey Jack cheese with jalapeño peppers (about ¼ cup)

2 tablespoons sliced green onions

Tomato-Avocado Salsa

1 Combine first 4 ingredients in a medium bowl; stir with a whisk until blended.

2 Heat an 8-inch skillet over medium heat. Coat pan with cooking spray. Add egg mixture, and cook 3 minutes or until set (do not stir). Sprinkle with beans, cheese, and green onions. Loosen omelet with a spatula; fold in half. Cook 1 to 2 minutes or until cheese melts. Slide omelet onto a plate. Cut in half. Top each half with Tomato-Avocado Salsa.

PER SERVING (serving size: ½ omelet and ¼ cup salsa):

Food Choices: 1 Starch, 2 Lean Proteins, 2 Fats

Calories 252; **Fat** 12.9g (sat 4.6g, mono 5.3g, poly 1.2g, trans 0g); **Protein** 21g; **Carbohydrate** 14g; **Fiber** 5g; **Sugars** 2g; **Cholesterol** 227mg; **Iron** 2mg; **Sodium** 427mg; **Potassium** 512mg; **Phosphorus** 278mg; **Calc** 149mg

Tomato-Avocado Salsa

Hands-on Time: 3 minutes   **Total Time:** 3 minutes   **Serves:** 2

¼ cup chopped tomato

¼ cup chopped peeled avocado

1 tablespoon fresh lemon juice

⅛ teaspoon ground cumin

1 Combine all ingredients in a small bowl.

PER SERVING (serving size: ¼ cup):

Food Choices: 1 Nonstarchy Vegetable, ½ Fat

Calories 37; **Fat** 2.8g (sat 0.4g, mono 1.8g, poly 0.4g, trans 0g); **Protein** 1g; **Carbohydrate** 3g; **Fiber** 2g; **Sugars** 1g; **Cholesterol** 0mg; **Iron** 0mg; **Sodium** 3mg; **Potassium** 156mg; **Phosphorus** 16mg; **Calcium** 6mg

Mushroom and Spinach Frittata with Goat Cheese

This mushroom frittata with goat cheese is an impressive and sophisticated brunch dish that satisfies. Serve it with fresh prechopped fruit from the deli for a quick side.

Hands-on Time: 10 minutes **Total Time:** 48 minutes **Serves:** 6

2½ **cups refrigerated shredded hash brown potatoes**

1 **tablespoon olive oil, divided**

1 **teaspoon freshly ground black pepper, divided**

½ **teaspoon kosher salt, divided**

Cooking spray

4 **cups thinly sliced cremini or button mushrooms (about 8 ounces)**

1 **cup chopped onion**

4 **cups coarsely chopped fresh spinach (about 4 ounces)**

1 **tablespoon chopped fresh or 1 teaspoon dried thyme**

1 **garlic clove, minced**

1¾ **cups egg substitute**

2 **ounces crumbled goat cheese (about ½ cup)**

1 Preheat oven to 375°.

2 Combine potatoes, 2 teaspoons olive oil, ½ teaspoon freshly ground black pepper, and ¼ teaspoon salt in a medium bowl. Press potatoes into bottom and up sides of a 10-inch deep-dish pie plate coated with cooking spray. Bake at 375° for 10 minutes.

3 Heat a large skillet over medium-high heat. Coat pan with cooking spray. Add 1 teaspoon oil to pan; swirl to coat. Add mushrooms and onion to pan; sauté 6 minutes or until tender. Add ½ teaspoon pepper, ¼ teaspoon salt, spinach, thyme, and garlic; cook 3 minutes or until spinach wilts. Cool slightly; stir in egg substitute and cheese.

4 Pour mushroom mixture over potato mixture. Bake at 375° for 30 minutes or until set. Cool 5 minutes; cut into 6 wedges.

PER SERVING (serving size: 1 wedge):

Food Choices: 1 Starch, 1 Nonstarchy Vegetable, 1 Lean Protein

Calories 168; **Fat** 4.4g (sat 1.7g, mono 2.1g, poly 0.3g, trans 0g); **Protein** 12g; **Carbohydrate** 21g; **Fiber** 3g; **Sugars** 4g; **Cholesterol** 4mg; **Iron** 3mg; **Sodium** 412mg; **Potassium** 832mg; **Phosphorus** 178mg; **Calcium** 61mg

Frittata with Prosciutto

A topping combo of peppery arugula and tangy tomatoes gives this dish a burst of garden-fresh flavor; is low in calories; and adds vitamins A, C, and K.

Hands-on Time: 12 minutes   **Total Time:** 14 minutes   **Serves:** 8

Cooking spray
½ cup chopped onion
8 large eggs
¼ teaspoon freshly ground black pepper
⅛ teaspoon salt
2 ounces thinly sliced prosciutto, chopped
Arugula-Tomato Topping

1 Preheat broiler.

2 Heat a 10-inch ovenproof skillet over medium heat. Coat pan with cooking spray. Add onion; sauté 3 minutes or until onion is tender.

3 Combine eggs, pepper, and salt in a medium bowl; stir with a whisk until foamy. Stir in prosciutto. Pour egg mixture over onion in pan; cook 3 minutes or until almost set. Gently lift edge of egg mixture with a spatula, tilting pan to allow uncooked egg mixture to flow underneath. Broil frittata 2 minutes or until completely set in center.

4 While frittata cooks, prepare Arugula-Tomato Topping. Spoon topping over frittata, and cut into 8 wedges just before serving.

PER SERVING (serving size: 1 frittata wedge and about ⅓ cup topping):
Food Choices: 1 Medium-Fat Protein, ½ Fat
Calories 107; **Fat** 6.8g (sat 2g, mono 2.7g, poly 1.1g, trans 0g); **Protein** 9g; **Carbohydrate** 3g; **Fiber** 1g; **Sugars** 1g; **Cholesterol** 192mg; **Iron** 1mg; **Sodium** 336mg; **Potassium** 148mg; **Phosphorus** 105mg; **Calcium** 42mg

Arugula-Tomato Topping

Hands-on Time: 2 minutes   **Total Time:** 2 minutes   **Serves:** 8

2 cups arugula
1 cup grape tomatoes, halved
2 teaspoons olive oil
¼ teaspoon freshly ground black pepper
⅛ teaspoon salt

1 Combine all ingredients in a medium bowl, tossing gently. Serve immediately.

PER SERVING (serving size: about ⅓ cup):
Food Choice: Free
Calories 15; **Fat** 1.2g (sat 0.2g, mono 0.8g, poly 0.1g, trans 0g); **Protein** 0g; **Carbohydrate** 1g; **Fiber** 0g; **Sugars** 1g; **Cholesterol** 0mg; **Iron** 0mg; **Sodium** 39mg; **Potassium** 64mg; **Phosphorus** 5mg; **Calcium** 11mg

Spinach Frittata with Feta Cheese

All the egg's fat and cholesterol are contained in the yolk. By omitting some of the yolks and only using the whites, you cut down on these amounts without losing flavor.

Hands-on Time: 12 minutes **Total Time:** 12 minutes **Serves:** 6

2 teaspoons olive oil

¾ cup packed fresh baby spinach

2 green onions

6 large eggs

4 large egg whites

1.3 ounces crumbled reduced-fat feta cheese with basil and sun-dried tomatoes (about ⅓ cup)

2 teaspoons salt-free Greek seasoning (such as Cavender's)

¼ teaspoon salt

1 Preheat broiler.

2 Heat a 10-inch ovenproof skillet over medium heat. Add oil to pan; swirl to coat. While oil heats, coarsely chop spinach and finely chop onions. Combine eggs, egg whites, cheese, Greek seasoning, and salt in a large bowl; stir well with a whisk. Add spinach and onions, stirring well.

3 Add egg mixture to pan; cook until edges begin to set, about 2 minutes. Gently lift edge of egg mixture, tilting pan to allow uncooked egg mixture to flow underneath. Cook 2 minutes or until egg mixture is almost set.

4 Broil 2 to 3 minutes or until center is set. Cut frittata into 6 wedges.

PER SERVING (serving size: 1 wedge):

Food Choices: 1 Medium-Fat Protein, 1 Fat

Calories 115; **Fat** 7.4g (sat 2.3g, mono 3.0g, poly 1.1g, trans 0g); **Protein** 10g; **Carbohydrate** 1g; **Fiber** 0g; **Sugars** 1g; **Cholesterol** 188mg; **Iron** 1mg; **Sodium** 313mg; **Potassium** 153mg; **Phosphorus** 128mg; **Calcium** 57mg

ingredient pointer

Packaged fresh baby spinach, found in your grocer's produce section, is a time-saving ingredient. There's no need to rinse the spinach before using it or to trim the stems from the tender leaves.

Breakfast Grano Parfaits

Grano, which means "grains" in Italian, is the polished whole berries from durum semolina wheat. This type of grain has more protein than other types of wheat, giving it a chewier texture and making it a favorite for making pasta.

Hands-on Time: 26 minutes **Total Time:** 9 hours, 20 minutes **Serves:** 8

1 cup uncooked grano

12 cups water, divided

¼ teaspoon kosher salt

4 cups plain 2% reduced-fat Greek yogurt

2 cups fresh berries (such as blackberries, blueberries, or sliced strawberries)

1 Soak grano in 6 cups water overnight. Drain. Place grano in a medium saucepan with remaining 6 cups water over medium-high heat; bring to a boil. Reduce heat, and simmer 20 minutes or until grano is just tender. Drain well. Stir in salt. Cool to room temperature.

2 Spoon ¼ cup yogurt into each of 8 parfait glasses. Top yogurt with 3 tablespoons grano and 2 tablespoons berries. Repeat layers with remaining ingredients.

PER SERVING (serving size: 1 parfait):

Food Choices: 1 Starch, 1 Reduced-Fat Milk

Calories 196; **Fat** 3.1g (sat 2.1g, mono 0.1g, poly 0.2g, trans 0g); **Protein** 14g; **Carbohydrate** 30g; **Fiber** 5g; **Sugars** 9g; **Cholesterol** 7mg; **Iron** 1mg; **Sodium** 106mg; **Potassium** 99mg; **Phosphorus** 60mg; **Calcium** 129mg

Banana-Blueberry Smoothies

Whether you're enjoying the paper or stuck in rush hour, this smoothie is sure to keep you satisfied all morning. Be sure to use unsweetened blueberries to keep the carbohydrates in check.

Hands-on Time: 5 minutes   **Total Time:** 5 minutes   **Serves:** 3

1 cup fresh or frozen blueberries

½ cup soft silken tofu

2 tablespoons water

1 teaspoon vanilla extract

1 medium-sized ripe banana, broken into pieces

1 (5.3-ounce) carton plain fat-free Greek yogurt

1 Place all ingredients in a blender; process until smooth, scraping sides as necessary.

PER SERVING (serving size: 1 cup):

Food Choices: 1½ Fruits, 1 Lean Protein

Calories 133; **Fat** 2g (sat 0.3g, mono 0.4g, poly 1.1g, trans 0g); **Protein** 8g; **Carbohydrate** 22g; **Fiber** 3g; **Sugars** 13g; **Cholesterol** 0mg; **Iron** 1mg; **Sodium** 23mg; **Potassium** 374mg; **Phosphorus** 113mg; **Calcium** 57mg

ingredient pointer

Silken tofu blends smoothly and gives creamy beverages and desserts a luscious texture, eliminating the need for high-fat cream. Other types of tofu have a denser texture and aren't a good substitute for the silken variety.

Prosciutto-Melon Bites,
page 77

Party Nibbles

Looking for irresistible appetizers for your next gathering? Try these delicious dips, salsas, and mini bites that won't derail your meal plan.

Fresh Salsa

Tomato seeds can be bitter, so remove them. Seeding a tomato is easy: Cut it in half lengthwise, and use a spoon or your finger to quickly scrape out the seeds.

Hands-on Time: 13 minutes   **Total Time**: 13 minutes   **Serves**: 14

1⅔ cups chopped seeded tomato (1 large)

½ cup chopped onion

¼ cup chopped fresh cilantro

2 tablespoons fresh lime juice

¼ teaspoon salt

2 garlic cloves, minced

1 jalapeño pepper, seeded and minced

1 Combine all ingredients in a medium bowl.

PER SERVING (serving size: 2 tablespoons):

Food Choice: Free

Calories 8; **Fat** 0.1g (sat 0g, mono 0g, poly 0g, trans 0g); **Protein** 0g; **Carbohydrate** 2g; **Fiber** 0g; **Sugars** 1g; **Cholesterol** 0mg; **Iron** 0mg; **Sodium** 44mg; **Potassium** 53mg; **Phosphorus** 7mg; **Calcium** 5mg

Southwest Melon Salsa

Not only do naturally sweet cantaloupe and honeydew melon make this salsa refreshing, they also fortify it with vitamin C.

Hands-on Time: 10 minutes   **Total Time**: 10 minutes   **Serves**: 10

1½ cups diced cantaloupe

1½ cups diced honeydew melon

½ cup chopped green bell pepper

½ cup chopped purple onion

2 tablespoons chopped fresh cilantro

2 serrano chiles, seeded and chopped

1 garlic clove, minced

3 tablespoons fresh lime juice

1 tablespoon white wine vinegar

1 teaspoon canola oil

¼ teaspoon ground cumin

1 Combine first 7 ingredients in a large bowl; stir well.

2 Combine lime juice and remaining ingredients; stir with a wire whisk. Pour over melon mixture, and toss gently. Cover and store in refrigerator. Serve with baked tortilla chips, chicken, or fish.

PER SERVING (serving size: ¼ cup):

Food Choice: ½ Fruit

Calories 28; **Fat** 0.6g (sat 0.1g, mono 0.3g, poly 0.2g, trans 0g); **Protein** 1g; **Carbohydrate** 6g; **Fiber** 1g; **Sugars** 4g; **Cholesterol** 0mg; **Iron** 0mg; **Sodium** 9mg; **Potassium** 156mg; **Phosphorus** 12mg; **Calcium** 8mg

Fresh Salsa

Tomato-Avocado Dip

This dip's smooth texture also makes it an ideal sandwich spread or taco topping. Sprinkle with fresh cilantro leaves, if you like.

Hands-on Time: 5 minutes   **Total Time:** 5 minutes   **Serves:** 6

1 cup chopped tomato

1 tablespoon fresh lime **juice**

1½ teaspoons chopped fresh cilantro

¼ teaspoon salt

¼ teaspoon ground cumin

1 ripe peeled avocado, **coarsely mashed**

1 garlic clove, minced

36 baked tortilla chips

1 Combine first 7 ingredients in a medium bowl. Serve immediately with chips.

PER SERVING (serving size: ¼ cup dip and 6 tortilla chips):

Food Choices: ½ Starch, 1 Nonstarchy Vegetable, 1 Fat

Calories 103; **Fat** 5.4g (sat 0.7g, mono 3.3g, poly 0.6g, trans 0g); **Protein** 2g; **Carbohydrate** 14g; **Fiber** 3g; **Sugars** 1g; **Cholesterol** 0mg; **Iron** 0mg; **Sodium** 177mg; **Potassium** 239mg; **Phosphorus** 49mg; **Calcium** 24mg

Hot Fiesta Dip

Turn a corn salsa into a hot dip by heating it in the microwave, and then topping it with cheese.

Hands-on Time: 3 minutes   **Total Time:** 14 minutes   **Serves:** 10

1 (10-ounce) package frozen whole-kernel corn

1½ cups Fresh Salsa **(page 62)**

3 ounces preshredded reduced-fat 4-cheese Mexican-blend cheese (about ¾ cup)

2 tablespoons chopped green onions

1 Microwave frozen corn according to package directions. Drain.

2 Combine corn and salsa in a microwave-safe 9-inch pie plate. Cover with plastic wrap; vent. Microwave at HIGH 2 minutes or until bubbly.

3 Sprinkle cheese over corn mixture; cover and let stand 5 minutes or until cheese melts. Top with chopped onions.

PER SERVING (serving size: ¼ cup):

Food Choice: ½ Starch

Calories 63; **Fat** 1.9g (sat 1.4g, mono 0.1g, poly 0.1g, trans 0g); **Protein** 3g; **Carbohydrate** 8g; **Fiber** 1g; **Sugars** 3g; **Cholesterol** 5mg; **Iron** 0mg; **Sodium** 158mg; **Potassium** 206mg; **Phosphorus** 86mg; **Calcium** 99mg

Tomato-Avocado Dip

Artichoke, Spinach, and White Bean Dip

If you can't find baby artichoke hearts, use quartered artichoke hearts and chop them. Serve this warm dip with pita chips or your favorite multigrain crackers.

Hands-on Time: 15 minutes   **Total Time:** 35 minutes   **Serves:** 12

1 ounce fresh pecorino Romano cheese, grated (about ¼ cup)

¼ cup canola mayonnaise

1 teaspoon fresh lemon juice

¼ teaspoon salt

¼ teaspoon freshly ground black pepper

⅛ teaspoon ground red pepper

2 garlic cloves, minced

1 (15-ounce) can organic white beans, rinsed and drained

1 (14-ounce) can baby artichoke hearts, drained and quartered

1 (9-ounce) package frozen chopped spinach, thawed, drained, and squeezed dry

Cooking spray

2 ounces shredded part-skim mozzarella cheese (about ½ cup)

1 Preheat oven to 350°.

2 Place pecorino Romano cheese, ¼ cup mayonnaise, 1 teaspoon lemon juice, salt, black pepper, red pepper, minced garlic, and white beans in a food processor, and process until smooth. Spoon into a medium bowl. Stir in artichokes and spinach.

3 Spoon mixture into a 1-quart glass or ceramic baking dish coated with cooking spray. Sprinkle with ½ cup mozzarella. Bake at 350° for 20 minutes or until bubbly and brown.

PER SERVING (serving size: ¼ cup):

Food Choices: 1 Nonstarchy Vegetable, 1 Fat

Calories 87; **Fat** 5.4g (sat 1.4g, mono 2.3g, poly 1g, trans 0g); **Protein** 4g; **Carbohydrate** 5g; **Fiber** 1g; **Sugars** 0g; **Cholesterol** 6mg; **Iron** 1mg; **Sodium** 232mg; **Potassium** 186mg; **Phosphorus** 77mg; **Calcium** 91mg

small change, big result

Full-flavored pecorino Romano adds cheesy goodness while beans add body. Using part-skim mozzarella instead of the whole-milk variety saves about 50 calories and 7 grams of fat.

Texas Caviar

The name "Texas Caviar" originated in the 1940s when renowned food consultant Helen Corbitt served this dish at the Houston Country Club on New Year's Eve. Less fancy than real caviar, this recipe reflects casual Texas style.

Hands-on Time: 5 minutes **Total Time:** 5 minutes **Serves:** 20

- 2 **tablespoons chopped fresh cilantro**
- 3 **tablespoons red wine vinegar**
- 2 **tablespoons canola oil**
- 2 **tablespoons hot sauce**
- ½ **teaspoon salt**
- 1 **garlic clove, minced**
- 2 **(15.8-ounce) cans black-eyed peas, rinsed and drained**
- 1⅓ **cups diced red onion**
- 1 **cup diced seeded** tomato
- 1 **cup diced green bell pepper**

1 Combine first 6 ingredients in a large bowl; stir well with a whisk. Add peas and remaining ingredients; toss gently to coat.

PER SERVING (serving size: ¼ cup):

Food Choice: 1 Nonstarchy Vegetable

Calories 43; **Fat** 1.6g (sat 0.2g, mono 0.8g, poly 0.5g, trans 0g); **Protein** 2g; **Carbohydrate** 6g; **Fiber** 1g; **Sugars** 1g; **Cholesterol** 0mg; **Iron** 0mg; **Sodium** 150mg; **Potassium** 103mg; **Phosphorus** 27mg; **Calcium** 11mg

Low-Carb
Party Dippers

Snack chips and crackers can pile on the carbs when you're dunking into your favorite dip, but carrot and celery sticks can be boring. Surround your dip with a few of these low-carb veggies for dippers that are fresh and delicious:

- Bell pepper, fresh fennel, or jicama strips
- Regular cucumber slices or Kirby cucumber spears
- Broccoli and cauliflower florets
- Cherry or grape tomatoes
- Thinly sliced large round radishes or halved icicle radishes
- Snow peas or sugar snap peas (both can be eaten raw)

- Small white mushroom caps
- Baby zucchini or summer squash
- Cooked and chilled asparagus, green beans, or artichoke leaves
- Belgian endive leaves
- Inner leaves of hearts of romaine

Rosemary-Garlic White Bean Spread

Use this flavorful high-fiber spread as an accompaniment to toasted baguette slices or as a dip for pita bread, carrot sticks, or cucumber slices. It also makes a terrific spread for pita sandwiches. If you don't have a food processor, simply mash the bean mixture with a fork; the spread will have a slightly chunkier consistency.

Hands-on Time: 6 minutes **Total Time:** 6 minutes **Serves:** 8

2 tablespoons olive oil

4 garlic cloves, coarsely chopped

1 (15-ounce) can Great Northern beans, **rinsed and drained**

2 tablespoons fresh lemon **juice**

1 teaspoon finely chopped fresh rosemary

¼ teaspoon salt

Rosemary sprig (optional)

1 Heat a small skillet over medium heat. Add oil to pan; swirl to coat. Add garlic; sauté 1 minute. Place garlic mixture, beans, and next 3 ingredients (through salt) in a food processor; process until smooth. Serve immediately, or cover and chill until ready to serve. Garnish with rosemary sprig, if desired.

PER SERVING (serving size: 2 tablespoons):

Food Choices: ½ Starch, ½ Fat

Calories 70 **Fat** 3.5g (sat 0.5g, mono 2.5g, poly 0.4g, trans 0g); **Protein** 3g; **Carbohydrate** 8g; **Fiber** 2g; **Sugars** 0g; **Cholesterol** 0mg; **Iron** 0mg; **Sodium** 74mg; **Potassium** 123mg; **Phosphorus** 46mg; **Calcium** 13mg

small change, big result

Rinsing and draining the canned beans is an easy way to cut the sodium in the beans by 40%.

Parmesan-Rosemary Flatbread Crackers

These crackers can be stored in an airtight container for up to three days.

Hands-on Time: 45 minutes   **Total Time:** 50 minutes   **Serves:** 27

6.8 ounces all-purpose flour (about 1½ cups)

3 tablespoons finely ground flaxseed meal

1½ tablespoons chopped fresh rosemary

1 teaspoon baking powder

¼ teaspoon freshly ground black pepper

1.5 ounces Parmigiano-Reggiano cheese, grated (about ⅓ cup)

½ cup water

5 tablespoons butter, softened

1½ teaspoons kosher salt

1 Place a baking sheet on the middle rack in oven. Preheat oven to 425° (keep pan in oven as it preheats).

2 Weigh or lightly spoon flour into dry measuring cups; level with a knife. Combine flour and next 5 ingredients (through cheese) in a large bowl. Make a well in center of mixture; add ½ cup water and butter. Stir with a wooden spoon until dough pulls together in a shaggy mass. Turn dough out onto a lightly floured work surface; knead gently 6 to 8 times or until dough is smooth and soft.

3 Divide dough into 9 equal portions. Working with 1 portion at a time (keep remaining portions covered with a damp towel to prevent drying), divide into 3 equal pieces. Place 3 dough pieces 3 inches apart in the center of a baking sheet–sized piece of parchment paper. Top with another piece of parchment paper. Roll dough pieces into long oval shapes, about 6 x 3 inches. (Dough will be very thin.) Carefully remove the top piece of parchment. Sprinkle dough lightly with salt, pressing to adhere. Place parchment with rolled dough on preheated baking sheet. Bake at 425° for 5 minutes or until crackers are browned in spots. Remove parchment and crackers from oven, and place on a wire rack to cool.

PER SERVING (serving size: 1 cracker):

Food Choices: ½ Starch, ½ Fat

Calories 52; **Fat** 2.7g (sat 1.5g, mono 0.7g, poly 0.3g, trans 0g); **Protein** 1g; **Carbohydrate** 6g; **Fiber** 0g; **Sugars** 0g; **Cholesterol** 7mg; **Iron** 0mg; **Sodium** 180mg; **Potassium** 10mg; **Phosphorus** 19mg; **Calcium** 24mg

Can I Still Have a Cocktail or a Glass of Wine?

It's certainly possible. Just follow these simple guidelines:

• Check with your doctor first to determine if alcohol is safe for you to consume. Your medications, level of glucose control, and blood triglyceride levels may make alcohol off-limits.

• Drink only in moderation, which for women is no more than one drink per day and for men, two drinks per day. A drink is a 12-ounce beer, a 5-ounce glass of wine, or 1½ ounces of vodka, gin, whiskey, or other distilled spirits.

• Enjoy a drink along with food—never on an empty stomach.

• Don't replace food on your meal plan with alcohol. If you use the carb-counting method of meal planning, don't count alcohol as part of your carbs.

• Alcohol can cause your blood glucose level to drop, resulting in hypoglycemia. Or if you're having a sugary mixed drink, it can cause blood glucose to rise. Keep close check on your blood sugar after drinking, since hypoglycemia can occur shortly after you drink and up to 24 hours after. If you have a mixed drink, use a sugar-free mixer like diet soda, tonic water, club soda, seltzer, or plain water.

• Be wary of craft beers and some wines. They sometimes contain as much as twice the alcohol of regular beer.

SAY CHEERS TO LOW-CALORIE COCKTAILS

Alcohol doesn't just affect your blood sugar. It also has a lot of calories, which in excess can lead to weight gain. The next time you're at a party, try these ideas to lighten up happy hour:

• Enjoy a wine spritzer made with half sparkling water and half white wine.

• Choose translucent spirits like gin and vodka over darker varieties like rum. Clear liquors have fewer calories.

• Always order drinks made with diet soda or diet tonic water. Surprisingly, 6 ounces of regular tonic water has 18 grams of carbs—the same amount as 1½ tablespoons of sugar.

• Try sugar-free flavored syrups for flavoring your cocktails without adding calories or carbs. You can also add a splash of one of these to club soda or seltzer water for a nonalcoholic refresher. There are dozens of flavors available, from peach to peppermint.

• If you like cocktails made with fruit juice, lighten up on the calorie- and carb-laden juice. Order your liquor of choice with just a splash of orange or cranberry juice. Ask the bartender to fill the rest of the glass with water, sparkling water, or seltzer.

Calories in Common Drinks

Drink	Calories
Regular beer (12 ounces)	150
Light beer (12 ounces)	100
Craft beer (12 ounces)	150-450
Dry white wine (5 ounces)	120
Dry red wine (5 ounces)	125
Distilled spirits (1½ ounces of 80 proof vodka, gin, whiskey)	100
Cosmopolitan	145
Margarita	170
Mojito	145

Broccoli Pesto Bruschetta

Using broccoli to make pesto is a fresh way to add color and texture to the traditional spread and to pack vitamins A and C and fiber into each bite. The pine nuts and garlic balance the veggie's flavor, and the pecorino Romano topping gives it a sharp, salty finish.

Hands-on Time: 4 minutes   **Total Time:** 6 minutes   **Serves:** 12

12 (½-ounce) slices diagonally cut French bread baguette
Cooking spray
2 cups broccoli florets
1 garlic clove
1 ounce grated fresh Parmesan cheese (about ¼ cup)
2 tablespoons pine nuts
2 tablespoons olive oil
1½ ounces shaved pecorino Romano cheese (about ⅓ cup)
¼ teaspoon freshly ground black pepper

1 Preheat oven to 450°.

2 Lightly coat bread slices with cooking spray; place on a baking sheet. Bake at 450° for 5 minutes or until crisp.

3 While bread bakes, cook broccoli in boiling water 6 minutes or just until tender; drain.

4 Drop garlic through food chute with processor on; process until minced. Add broccoli, Parmesan cheese, pine nuts, and olive oil. Process until smooth.

5 Top toast slices with broccoli mixture and pecorino Romano cheese. Sprinkle with pepper. Serve immediately.

PER SERVING (serving size: 1 bruschetta):
Food Choices: ½ Starch, 1 Fat

Calories 79; **Fat** 4.4g (sat 1g, mono 1.9g, poly 0.8g, trans 0g); **Protein** 3g; **Carbohydrate** 8g; **Fiber** 1g; **Sugars** 0g; **Cholesterol** 3mg; **Iron** 1mg; **Sodium** 149mg; **Potassium** 53mg; **Phosphorus** 64mg; **Calcium** 52mg

ingredient pointer

Pine nuts are not nuts but seeds borne on the cones of certain pine trees and harvested throughout the Mediterranean and across much of Asia. Like nuts, they are high in the "good" fats. Keep them fresh by storing in the refrigerator for up to 1 month or freezer for up to 9 months.

Prosciutto-Melon Bites

Mini Pizza Margheritas

For your next casual party, prepare this appetizer inspired by the classic Neapolitan pizza, which showcases the colors of the Italian flag: red, white, and green.

Hands-on Time: 5 minutes   **Total Time:** 14 minutes   **Serves:** 18

9 mini pitas, cut in half horizontally (such as Toufayan Pitettes)

Olive oil–flavored cooking spray

3 ounces fresh mozzarella cheese, diced (about ¾ cup)

½ cup diced seeded plum tomato

¼ teaspoon kosher salt

3 tablespoons thinly sliced fresh basil

¼ teaspoon freshly ground black pepper

1 Preheat oven to 425°.

2 Place mini pita halves, cut sides up, on a baking sheet; lightly coat with cooking spray. Divide cheese among pita halves. Top with tomato, and sprinkle with salt.

3 Bake at 425° for 9 minutes or until cheese melts and bread is lightly browned. Sprinkle pita halves with basil and pepper.

PER SERVING (serving size: 1 mini pizza):

Food Choice: ½ Starch

Calories 50; **Fat** 1g (sat 0.7g, mono 0.3g, poly 0g, trans 0g); **Protein** 2g; **Carbohydrate** 8g; **Fiber** 1g; **Sugars** 0g; **Cholesterol** 4mg; **Iron** 1mg; **Sodium** 66mg; **Potassium** 45mg; **Phosphorus** 52mg; **Calcium** 38mg

Prosciutto-Melon Bites

Juicy fruit wrapped in thin slices of cured meat is the ultimate salty-sweet combination.

Hands-on Time: 15 minutes   **Total Time:** 15 minutes   **Serves:** 8

16 (1-inch) cubes cantaloupe

16 (1-inch) cubes honeydew melon

16 (¼-ounce) very thin slices prosciutto, cut in half lengthwise

1 tablespoon fresh lime juice

2 teaspoons extra-virgin olive oil

¼ teaspoon crushed red pepper

2 tablespoons thinly sliced fresh mint

1 Wrap each cantaloupe cube and each honeydew cube with ½ prosciutto slice. Thread 1 wrapped cantaloupe cube and 1 wrapped honeydew cube onto each of 16 (4-inch) skewers. Arrange skewers on a serving platter.

2 Combine juice, oil, and pepper, stirring with a whisk; drizzle over skewers. Sprinkle with mint.

PER SERVING (serving size: 2 skewers):

Food Choices: ½ Fruit, ½ Fat

Calories 55; **Fat** 2.5g (sat 0.6g; mono 1.5g; poly 0.4g, trans 0g); **Protein** 4g; **Carbohydrate** 5g; **Fiber** 1g; **Sugars** 4g; **Cholesterol** 8mg; **Iron** 0mg; **Sodium** 222mg; **Potassium** 191mg; **Phosphorus** 41mg; **Calcium** 7mg

Kale Salad with Apple and
Cheddar, page 107

Farm-Fresh Salads

Abundant with fruits, vegetables, and flavorful toppings, these salads are quick and easy, require minimal cooking, and are chock-full of antioxdants, vitamins, and minerals.

Chile-Spiced Fruit Salad with Queso Fresco

Watermelon develops more of the antioxidant lycopene when stored at room temperature. Serve this zesty salad as a side for roasted meats or as a sweet-spicy dessert.

Hands-on Time: 12 minutes   **Total Time:** 1 hour, 12 minutes   **Serves:** 5

¼ cup hot water

2 tablespoons granulated no-calorie sweetener (such as Splenda)

1 large jalapeño pepper, sliced in half lengthwise

2 cups cubed seedless watermelon

1 cup fresh blueberries

1 large peach, peeled and sliced

2 tablespoons fresh lime juice

7½ teaspoons crumbled queso fresco

1 Combine ¼ cup hot water and sweetener until sweetener dissolves. Add jalapeño pepper. Cover and let stand 1 hour or until cooled to room temperature. Strain sugar substitute mixture through a fine mesh sieve over a bowl; discard solids.

2 Combine watermelon, blueberries, and peach in a large bowl. Stir in sugar substitute mixture and juice, tossing gently to coat. Sprinkle each serving with cheese.

PER SERVING (serving size: about ⅔ cup salad and 1½ teaspoons cheese):

Food Choice: 1 Fruit

Calories 69 **Fat** 0.9g (sat 0.4g, mono 0.3g, poly 0.1g, trans 0g); **Protein** 2g; **Carbohydrate** 15g; **Fiber** 2g; **Sugars** 11g; **Cholesterol** 2mg; **Iron** 0mg; **Sodium** 12mg; **Potassium** 201mg; **Phosphorus** 36mg; **Calcium** 32mg

ingredient pointer

Look for plump blueberries that are dark blue with a silvery bloom on their surface. Do not wash them before storing. Place them in a plastic or perforated produce bag in the vegetable bin of your refrigerator for 7 to 10 days.

Minty Cucumber and Honeydew Salad

Fresh mint, lime juice, and sweet honeydew are a refreshing combination in this side. There's no need to peel thin-skinned English cucumbers, but you'll want to if you substitute another variety.

Hands-on Time: 15 minutes   **Total Time:** 30 minutes   **Serves:** 4

- **2 cups cubed** honeydew melon
- **2 cups chopped English cucumber**
- **2 tablespoons chopped fresh mint**
- **2 tablespoons fresh** lime **juice**
- **2 tablespoons finely chopped red onion**
- **⅛ teaspoon salt**
- **Mint sprigs (optional)**

1 Combine first 6 ingredients in a large bowl; toss gently to coat. Cover and chill 15 minutes or until ready to serve. Garnish with mint sprigs, if desired.

PER SERVING (serving size: 1 cup):

Food Choices: 1 Nonstarchy Vegetable, ½ Fat

Calories 42; **Fat** 0.2g (sat 0.1g, mono 0g, poly 0.1g, trans 0g); **Protein** 1g; **Carbohydrate** 11g; **Fiber** 1g; **Sugars** 8g; **Cholesterol** 0mg; **Iron** 0mg; **Sodium** 89mg; **Potassium** 313mg; **Phosphorus** 27mg; **Calcium** 18mg

Tomato-and-Mango Salad with Curry-Orange Vinaigrette

This recipe is also delicious with peaches or nectarines in place of the mangoes.

Hands-on Time: 15 minutes   **Total Time:** 25 minutes   **Serves:** 8

2 cups fresh orange juice (about 6 oranges)

1 tablespoon canola oil

1 teaspoon curry powder

⅛ teaspoon salt

3 medium tomatoes (about 1½ pounds), cored and cut into ¾-inch-thick wedges

2 medium mangoes (about 2 pounds), peeled, pitted, and cut into ½-inch-thick strips

1 tablespoon thinly sliced mint leaves

1 Bring orange juice to a boil in a medium saucepan. Reduce heat to medium, and cook until reduced to ½ cup (about 25 minutes). Remove from heat. Stir in oil, curry powder, and salt. Cool to room temperature.

2 Divide tomato wedges and mango strips among 8 plates. Drizzle with dressing; sprinkle with mint.

PER SERVING (serving size: about ¾ cup):

Food Choices: 1½ Fruits, 1 Nonstarchy Vegetable, ½ Fat

Calories 136; **Fat** 2.4g (sat 0.3g, mono 0.5g, poly 1g, trans 0g); **Protein** 2g; **Carbohydrate** 30g; **Fiber** 3g; **Sugars** 19g; **Cholesterol** 0mg; **Iron** 1mg; **Sodium** 46mg; **Potassium** 471mg; **Phosphorus** 44mg; **Calcium** 23mg

Gazpacho Salad
with Tomato Vinaigrette

Tomatoes bring a wealth of nutrients like iron and vitamin E to the table. Squeezing your own tomatoes to make juice is best, but if you buy a bottled variety be sure to check the label for added salt and sugar.

Hands-on Time: 10 minutes   **Total Time:** 10 minutes   **Serves:** 5

Vinaigrette:

3 tablespoons tomato juice

2 tablespoons red wine vinegar

1 tablespoon extra-virgin olive oil

1 teaspoon Worcestershire sauce

¼ teaspoon salt

¼ to ½ teaspoon hot sauce

⅛ teaspoon freshly ground black pepper

Salad:

2 cups (½-inch) diced tomato (about 1 pound)

1½ cups (½-inch) diced cucumber

½ cup (¼-inch) diced green bell pepper

2 tablespoons minced shallots

2 tablespoons coarsely chopped fresh basil

1 To prepare vinaigrette, combine first 7 ingredients, stirring with a whisk.

2 To prepare salad, combine tomato, cucumber, bell pepper, shallots, and basil in a large bowl. Add vinaigrette; toss gently to coat.

PER SERVING (serving size: ¾ cup):

Food Choices: 1 Nonstarchy Vegetable, ½ Fat

Calories 57; **Fat** 3.1g (sat 0.4g, mono 2g, poly 0.4g, trans 0g); **Protein** 1g; **Carbohydrate** 8g; **Fiber** 2g; **Sugars** 5g; **Cholesterol** 0mg; **Iron** 1mg; **Sodium** 171mg; **Potassium** 415mg; **Phosphorus** 48mg; **Calcium** 20mg

Chickpea, Feta, and Orzo Salad

This Mediterranean-style salad combines the chewy texture of chickpeas with the tangy flavor of feta. Chopped tomato adds a pop of color.

Hands-on Time: 9 minutes   **Total Time:** 15 minutes   **Serves:** 6

1 cup uncooked orzo (rice-shaped pasta)

Cucumber-Thyme Relish

1 cup refrigerated prechopped tomato

1 (16-ounce) can unsalted chickpeas (garbanzo beans), rinsed and drained

¼ teaspoon salt

1.3 ounces crumbled feta cheese with basil and sun-dried tomatoes (about ⅓ cup)

1 Cook pasta according to package directions; drain and rinse under cold water. Drain well. While pasta cooks, prepare Cucumber-Thyme Relish.

2 Combine tomato and chickpeas in a large bowl, tossing gently; stir in pasta, salt, and Cucumber-Thyme Relish. Add feta cheese; toss gently.

PER SERVING (serving size: 1 cup):

Food Choices: 2 Starches, 1 Nonstarchy Vegetable

Calories 199; **Fat** 4.6g (sat 1.1g, mono 2.4g, poly 0.9g, trans 0g); **Protein** 8g; **Carbohydrate** 32g; **Fiber** 4g; **Sugars** 3g; **Cholesterol** 5mg; **Iron** 1mg; **Sodium** 249mg; **Potassium** 246mg; **Phosphorus** 166mg; **Calcium** 52mg

Cucumber-Thyme Relish

Hands-on Time: 4 minutes   **Total Time:** 4 minutes   **Makes:** ⅔ cup

1½ tablespoons fresh lemon juice

1 tablespoon extra-virgin olive oil

½ cup chopped English cucumber

2 tablespoons finely chopped red onion

1 tablespoon thyme leaves

¼ teaspoon salt

¼ teaspoon freshly ground black pepper

1 Combine lemon juice and olive oil in a medium bowl, stirring with a whisk. Stir in cucumber and remaining ingredients.

PER SERVING (serving size: about 3 tablespoons):

Food Choice: 1 Fat

Calories 37; **Fat** 3.5g (sat 0.5g, mono 2.5g, poly 0.5g, trans 0g); **Protein** 0g; **Carbohydrate** 2g; **Fiber** 0g; **Sugars** 1g; **Cholesterol** 0mg; **Iron** 0mg; **Sodium** 146mg; **Potassium** 39mg; **Phosphorus** 6mg; **Calcium** 7mg

Edamame Salad

Double the portion for an easy, quick lunch entrée. Take along a piece of fresh fruit, and it's a portable lunch.

Hands-on Time: 8 minutes   **Total Time:** 8 minutes   **Serves:** 4

- 1 (10-ounce) package fully cooked refrigerated shelled edamame (green soybeans)
- 1 large navel orange, peeled and sectioned
- ¼ cup minced red onion
- 1 tablespoon chopped fresh mint
- 1 teaspoon granulated no-calorie sweetener (such as Splenda)
- 2 teaspoons fresh orange juice
- 1 teaspoon seasoned rice vinegar
- 1 teaspoon extra-virgin olive oil
- ¼ teaspoon salt
- ¼ teaspoon freshly ground black pepper
- Mint leaves (optional)

1 Combine first 4 ingredients in a large bowl.

2 Combine sweetener and next 5 ingredients (through pepper). Pour over edamame mixture; toss gently to coat. Garnish with mint leaves, if desired.

PER SERVING (serving size: about ½ cup):

Food Choices: 1 Starch, 1 Lean Protein

Calories 129; **Fat** 4.1g (sat 0.2g, mono 1.9g, poly 1.8g, trans 0g); **Protein** 8g; **Carbohydrate** 15g; **Fiber** 5g; **Sugars** 5g; **Cholesterol** 0mg; **Iron** 2mg; **Sodium** 194mg; **Potassium** 498mg; **Phosphorus** 150mg; **Calcium** 66mg

Barley Salad with Asparagus and Arugula

Check out this high-fiber barley-vegetable mix; it's a great side for grilled seafood or chicken. Increase the serving size to 1½ cups for an excellent meatless main-dish salad.

Hands-on Time: 16 minutes   **Total Time:** 22 minutes   **Serves:** 6

½ **pound thin** asparagus

2 **cups water**

1 **cup uncooked quick-cooking** barley

2 **tablespoons olive oil**

2 **tablespoons red wine vinegar**

2 **tablespoons fresh** lemon **juice**

1 **teaspoon freshly ground black pepper**

2 **teaspoons Dijon mustard**

½ **teaspoon salt**

1½ **cups trimmed** arugula **or** spinach

1½ **cups halved grape** tomatoes

½ **cup chopped red onion**

2¼ **ounces small diced smoked part-skim mozzarella cheese (about ⅓ cup)**

1 Snap off tough ends of asparagus; discard. Cut asparagus into 2-inch pieces.

2 Bring 2 cups water to a boil in a large saucepan. Add asparagus; cook 1 minute or until bright green and crisp-tender. Drain and plunge into ice water; drain.

3 Cook barley according to package directions, omitting salt and fat.

4 While barley cooks, combine olive oil and next 5 ingredients (through salt) in a small bowl; stir well with a whisk.

5 Drain barley. Rinse under cold water; drain. Combine asparagus, barley, arugula or spinach, and next 3 ingredients (through cheese) in a large bowl. Add dressing; toss gently to coat. Serve at room temperature or chilled.

PER SERVING (serving size: 1 cup):

Food Choices: ½ Starch, 2 Nonstarchy Vegetables, 1 Fat

Calories 149; **Fat** 5.2g (sat 1.6g, mono 1g, poly 1.8g, trans 0g); **Protein** 6g; **Carbohydrate** 15g; **Fiber** 5g; **Sugars** 2g; **Cholesterol** 0mg; **Iron** 1mg; **Sodium** 85mg; **Potassium** 240mg; **Phosphorus** 107mg; **Calcium** 81mg

Couscous, Sweet Potato, and Black Soybean Salad

Choose this lime-and-basil–infused salad, including chunks of beta-carotene–laced sweet potatoes and tender, high-fiber, protein-rich black soybeans, for a healthy meatless main dish you can have on the table in 15 minutes.

Hands-on Time: 5 minutes   **Total Time:** 15 minutes   **Serves:** 8

¾ cup water

⅔ cup uncooked whole-wheat couscous

1 (16-ounce) package refrigerated cubed peeled sweet potato

¼ cup fat-free lime-basil vinaigrette

½ teaspoon freshly ground black pepper

¼ teaspoon salt

2 cups fresh baby spinach

1 (15-ounce) can unsalted black soybeans, rinsed and drained

5 tablespoons and 1 teaspoon crumbled reduced-fat feta cheese

3 green onions, chopped

1 Bring ¾ cup water to a boil in a medium saucepan; gradually stir in couscous. Remove from heat; cover and let stand 5 minutes. Fluff with a fork.

2 While couscous stands, place sweet potato on a microwave-safe plate. Microwave at HIGH 5 minutes or until tender.

3 Combine vinaigrette, pepper, and salt in a large bowl; stir well with a whisk. Add couscous, sweet potato, spinach, and soybeans; toss gently to coat. Top each serving with cheese; sprinkle with onions.

PER SERVING (serving size: about ¾ cup couscous salad, 2 teaspoons cheese, and about 2 teaspoons green onions):

Food Choices: 1½ Starches, ½ Fat

Calories 142; **Fat** 2.5g (sat 0.7g, mono 0.4g, poly 1.1g, trans 0g); **Protein** 7g; **Carbohydrate** 25g; **Fiber** 5g; **Sugars** 5g; **Cholesterol** 2mg; **Iron** 2mg; **Sodium** 180mg; **Potassium** 379mg; **Phosphorus** 119mg; **Calcium** 64mg

ingredient pointer

Black soybeans are a great substitute for other bean varieties in recipes. The canned variety is more readily available than the dried beans and can be purchased in most supermarkets.

Curried Quinoa Salad with Cucumber-Mint Raita

This Indian-inspired dish features quinoa, a high-protein grain that cooks relatively quickly. We like the heat that Madras curry powder brings, but use regular curry powder, if you prefer.

Hands-on Time: 10 minutes   **Total Time:** 40 minutes   **Serves:** 6

1 teaspoon olive oil

2 teaspoons Madras curry powder

1 garlic clove, crushed

1 cup uncooked quinoa, rinsed and drained

2 cups water

¾ teaspoon kosher salt

1 diced peeled ripe mango

½ cup diced celery

¼ cup thinly sliced green onions

3 tablespoons chopped fresh cilantro

3 tablespoons currants

¼ cup finely diced peeled English cucumber

2 teaspoons chopped fresh mint

1 (6-ounce) carton plain fat-free yogurt

1 (6-ounce) package fresh baby spinach

Freshly ground black pepper (optional)

1 Heat a medium saucepan over medium-high heat. Add oil to pan; swirl to coat. Add curry powder and garlic to pan; cook 1 minute, stirring constantly. Add quinoa and 2 cups water; bring to a boil. Cover, reduce heat, and simmer 16 minutes or until tender. Remove from heat; stir in salt. Cool completely.

2 Add mango and next 4 ingredients (through currants) to cooled quinoa; toss gently.

3 Combine ¼ cup cucumber, 2 teaspoons mint, and yogurt in a small bowl; stir well. Divide spinach among 6 plates, and top each serving with about ¾ cup quinoa mixture and about 2 tablespoons raita. Sprinkle with black pepper, if desired.

PER SERVING (serving size: about 1 cup):

Food Choices: 1 Starch, ½ Fruit, 1 Nonstarchy Vegetable, ½ Fat

Calories 136; **Fat** 2.2g (sat 0.3g, mono 0.9g, poly 0.9g, trans 0g); **Protein** 5g; **Carbohydrate** 26g; **Fiber** 3g; **Sugars** 10g; **Cholesterol** 0mg; **Iron** 2mg; **Sodium** 182mg; **Potassium** 397mg; **Phosphorus** 145mg; **Calcium** 71mg

Spicy Bean and Quinoa Salad with "Mole" Vinaigrette

To make ahead, leave out the spinach and keep the quinoa mixture covered in the refrigerator for up to 2 days. Add the spinach just before serving. To tame the heat, seed the chile or substitute chopped red bell pepper.

Hands-on Time: 15 minutes   **Total Time:** 15 minutes   **Serves:** 8

1 teaspoon grated orange rind

2 tablespoons fresh orange juice

1½ tablespoons red wine vinegar

1 tablespoon adobo sauce from canned chipotle chiles in adobo sauce

¾ teaspoon unsweetened cocoa

½ teaspoon ground cumin

½ teaspoon ground cinnamon

2 tablespoons olive oil

3 cups cooked quinoa, at room temperature

½ cup unsalted pumpkinseed kernels (pepitas), toasted

¼ cup chopped fresh cilantro

¼ teaspoon kosher salt

2 green onions, thinly sliced

1 Fresno chile or jalapeño pepper, very thinly sliced

1 (15-ounce) can black beans, rinsed and drained

4 cups fresh baby spinach

1 Combine first 7 ingredients in a small bowl; gradually add oil, stirring well with a whisk.

2 Combine quinoa and next 6 ingredients (through beans) in a large bowl. Add vinaigrette; toss to coat. Add spinach; toss to combine.

PER SERVING (serving size: 1¼ cups):

Food Choices: 1 Starch, 1 Nonstarchy Vegetable, 1½ Fats

Calories 194; **Fat** 8.7g (sat 1.1g, mono 3.9g, poly 1.8g, trans 0g); **Protein** 7g; **Carbohydrate** 24g; **Fiber** 5g; **Sugars** 1g; **Cholesterol** 0mg; **Iron** 3mg; **Sodium** 223mg; **Potassium** 421mg; **Phosphorus** 240mg; **Calcium** 41mg

small change, big result

Incorporating fresh veggies into grain salads not only adds bulk but also pumps up the flavor, texture, and nutrient content of the salads.

Baby Arugula, Pear, and Gorgonzola Salad

To toast the walnuts, place them in a dry skillet over medium heat. Cook 2 to 3 minutes or until golden and fragrant.

Hands-on Time: 10 minutes   **Total Time:** 10 minutes   **Serves:** 8

2 **Bartlett pears, cored and sliced**

1 **(5-ounce) package baby** arugula

½ **cup refrigerated fat-free raspberry vinaigrette**

1 **ounce crumbled Gorgonzola cheese (about ¼ cup)**

2 **tablespoons chopped** walnuts, **toasted**

½ **teaspoon freshly ground black pepper**

1 Combine all ingredients in a large bowl; toss gently to coat. Serve immediately.

PER SERVING (serving size: 1½ cups):

Food Choices: ½ Fruit, 1 Nonstarchy Vegetable, ½ Fat

Calories 68; **Fat** 2.4g (sat 0.9g, mono 0.2g, poly 0.9g, trans 0g); **Protein** 2g; **Carbohydrate** 12g; **Fiber** 2g; **Sugars** 12g; **Cholesterol** 3mg; **Iron** 0mg; **Sodium** 138mg; **Potassium** 180mg; **Phosphorus** 45mg; **Calcium** 53mg

Orange Salad with Arugula and Oil-Cured Olives

The dressing can be prepared several hours or even a day ahead; just bring to room temperature before tossing with the arugula.

Hands-on Time: 15 minutes **Total Time:** 15 minutes **Serves:** 10

Dressing:

⅓ cup thinly sliced shallots

¼ cup fresh lemon juice

2 tablespoons finely chopped mint leaves

1 teaspoon granulated no-calorie sweetener (such as Splenda)

2 teaspoons Dijon mustard

¼ teaspoon kosher salt

⅛ teaspoon freshly ground black pepper

2 tablespoons extra-virgin olive oil

Salad:

1 (5-ounce) package arugula

5 oranges, peeled and thinly sliced

30 oil-cured black olives

Freshly ground black pepper (optional)

1 To prepare dressing, combine first 7 ingredients in a medium bowl, stirring with a whisk. Gradually add oil, stirring constantly with a whisk.

2 To prepare salad, combine arugula and three-fourths of dressing in a large bowl; toss gently to coat. Arrange about ½ cup arugula mixture on each of 10 salad plates; arrange orange slices evenly over salads. Drizzle remaining one-fourth of dressing evenly over salads; top each salad with 3 olives. Sprinkle evenly with additional black pepper, if desired. Serve immediately.

PER SERVING (serving size: about 1 cup):

Food Choices: ½ Fruit, 1 Nonstarchy Vegetable, ½ Fat

Calories 78; **Fat** 4.2g (sat 0.4g, mono 2.2g, poly 0.3g, trans 0g); **Protein** 1g; **Carbohydrate** 10g; **Fiber** 2g; **Sugars** 7g; **Cholesterol** 0mg; **Iron** 1mg; **Sodium** 221mg; **Potassium** 197mg; **Phosphorus** 142mg; **Calcium** 63mg

ingredient pointer

To quickly peel an orange, cut the bottom portion from the fruit to create a stable cutting surface. Next, stand the fruit upright, and then use a paring knife to slice downward in a long, slow curve to remove the rind and the white pith.

Raspberry and Blue Cheese Salad

Fresh raspberries shine in this tasty salad and add a healthy dose of vitamin C and fiber.

Hands-on Time: 7 minutes   **Total Time:** 7 minutes   **Serves:** 4

2 teaspoons olive oil

2 teaspoons red wine vinegar

¼ teaspoon Dijon mustard

⅛ teaspoon salt

⅛ teaspoon freshly ground
  black pepper

5 cups mixed baby greens

½ cup fresh raspberries

¼ cup chopped toasted pecans

1 ounce blue cheese, crumbled
  (about ¼ cup)

1 Combine olive oil, vinegar, Dijon mustard, salt, and pepper in a large bowl, stirring well with a whisk. Add mixed baby greens; toss. Top with raspberries, pecans, and blue cheese.

PER SERVING (serving size: about 1½ cups):

Food Choices: 1 Nonstarchy Vegetable, 2 Fats

Calories 108; **Fat** 9.4g (sat 2.1g mono 5g, poly 1.9g, trans 0g); **Protein** 3g; **Carbohydrate** 4g; **Fiber** 2g; **Sugars** 1g; **Cholesterol** 5mg; **Iron** 1mg; **Sodium** 193mg; **Potassium** 158mg; **Phosphorus** 64mg; **Calcium** 62mg

small change, big result

Mixing and matching a combination of fruits, nuts, and other well-chosen ingredients for salads offers flavor, texture, variety, and, more importantly, satisfaction. Just limit high-calorie add-ins like nuts and cheese to 1 tablespoon per serving to keep your portions in check.

Spinach-Strawberry Salad

Use organic locally grown strawberries in the spring when you can find them. Their intensely sweet flavor combined with the homemade dressing makes this salad sublime.

Hands-on Time: 12 minutes   **Total Time:** 12 minutes   **Serves:** 6

- 2 tablespoons granulated no-calorie sweetener (such as Splenda)
- 2 tablespoons sherry or white wine vinegar
- 2 teaspoons minced red onion
- 1½ teaspoons sesame seeds, toasted
- 1½ teaspoons olive oil
- ¾ teaspoon poppy seeds
- ¼ teaspoon Hungarian sweet paprika
- ⅛ teaspoon salt
- 6 cups torn spinach (about 1 pound)
- 2 cups halved fresh strawberries
- 2 tablespoons slivered almonds, toasted

1 Combine first 8 ingredients in a jar; cover dressing tightly, and shake vigorously.

2 Combine spinach and strawberry halves in a large bowl, and toss gently. Pour dressing over spinach mixture, tossing gently to coat. Spoon salad onto plates; sprinkle with toasted almonds.

PER SERVING (serving size: 1 cup salad and 1 teaspoon almonds):

Food Choices: 1 Nonstarchy Vegetable, ½ Fat

Calories 57; **Fat** 3.1g (sat 0.3g, mono 1.5g, poly 0.5g, trans 0g); **Protein** 2g; **Carbohydrate** 6g; **Fiber** 2g; **Sugars** 3g; **Cholesterol** 0mg; **Iron** 2mg; **Sodium** 185mg; **Potassium** 150mg; **Phosphorus** 102mg; **Calcium** 50mg

ingredient pointer

Look for bright red, firm strawberries that have vibrant green caps and are free from mushy spots. Leave the caps on until you are ready to eat the berries to preserve their quality. Refrigerate unwashed berries and store them in a produce bag to prevent drying.

Asparagus and Spring Greens Salad with Gorgonzola Vinaigrette

Serve this savory salad alongside a juicy steak or a piece of flavorful fish, such as tuna or salmon.

Hands-on Time: 10 minutes   **Total Time:** 10 minutes   **Serves:** 8

- **1 pound green and white asparagus, trimmed and cut into 2-inch pieces**
- **2¼ teaspoons salt, divided**
- **2 tablespoons minced shallots**
- **2 tablespoons white balsamic vinegar**
- **1 tablespoon extra-virgin olive oil**
- **½ teaspoon grated lemon rind**
- **¼ teaspoon freshly ground black pepper**
- **2 ounces crumbled Gorgonzola cheese (about ½ cup), divided**
- **1 (5-ounce) package mixed salad greens**

1 Cook asparagus and 2 teaspoons salt in boiling water 2 minutes or until crisp-tender. Drain and rinse asparagus under cold water; drain.

2 Combine ¼ teaspoon salt, shallots, and next 4 ingredients (through pepper) in a small bowl, stirring with a whisk. Stir in ¼ cup cheese.

3 Combine asparagus and greens in a large bowl. Drizzle with dressing; toss gently to coat. Sprinkle with ¼ cup cheese.

PER SERVING (serving size: about 1 cup salad):

Food Choices: 1 Nonstarchy Vegetable, ½ Fat

Calories 60; **Fat** 3.8g (sat 1.6g, mono 1.8g, poly 0.3g, trans 0g); **Protein** 3g; **Carbohydrate** 4g; **Fiber** 1g; **Sugars** 2g; **Cholesterol** 5mg; **Iron** 1mg; **Sodium** 239mg; **Potassium** 240mg; **Phosphorus** 72mg; **Calcium** 62mg

Kale Salad with Roasted Garlic–Bacon Dressing and Beets

Kale is packed with antioxidants and anti-inflammatory benefits that help fight cancer and guard the heart.

Hands-on Time: 20 minutes   **Total Time:** 1 hour, 30 minutes   **Serves:** 6

1 whole garlic head
6 ounces baby yellow beets
6 ounces baby red beets
6 ounces baby striped beets (such as Chioggia)
3 tablespoons extra-virgin olive oil
1 tablespoon water
1 tablespoon heavy cream
1½ teaspoons fresh lemon juice
1 teaspoon red wine vinegar
¼ teaspoon kosher salt
¼ teaspoon freshly ground black pepper
8 cups Lacinato kale, torn
1 thick applewood-smoked bacon slice, chopped

1 Preheat oven to 350°.

2 Remove white papery skin from garlic head (do not peel or separate cloves). Wrap head in foil. Arrange yellow beets on a large sheet of foil; wrap tightly. Repeat procedure with red and striped beets. Bake garlic and beets at 350° for 1 hour or until beets are tender; cool 10 minutes. Separate garlic cloves; squeeze to extract garlic pulp. Discard skins. Combine garlic pulp, oil, and next 6 ingredients (through pepper) in a small bowl, stirring with a whisk. Place kale in a large bowl.

3 Heat a medium skillet over medium heat, and add bacon. Cook 5 minutes or until crisp, stirring occasionally. Increase heat to high. Stir in garlic mixture; remove from heat. Pour hot bacon mixture over kale, tossing to coat.

4 Peel beets; discard skins. Cut beets in half. Arrange over kale mixture.

PER SERVING (serving size: 1 cup):

Food Choices: 3 Nonstarchy Vegetables, 2 Fats

Calories 149; **Fat** 9.2g (sat 1.9g, mono 5.3g, poly 1.1g, trans 0g); **Protein** 5g; **Carbohydrate** 15g; **Fiber** 3g; **Sugars** 3g; **Cholesterol** 5mg; **Iron** 2mg; **Sodium** 189mg; **Potassium** 565mg; **Phosphorus** 81mg; **Calcium** 140mg

Kale and Beet Salad with Blue Cheese and Walnuts

A bag of baby kale leaves saves the time of washing, stemming, and chopping larger leaves. Treat these small, tender leaves like baby spinach and use them as the base for salads or stir into soups and stews at the end.

Hands-on Time: 14 minutes **Total Time:** 14 minutes **Serves:** 6

1 cup torn mint leaves

⅓ cup thinly vertically sliced red onion

1 (5-ounce) package baby kale

¼ cup plain 2% reduced-fat Greek yogurt

2 tablespoons nonfat buttermilk

2 teaspoons white wine vinegar

1½ teaspoons extra-virgin olive oil

¼ teaspoon freshly ground black pepper

⅛ teaspoon kosher salt

4 hard-cooked large eggs, quartered lengthwise

1 (8-ounce) package peeled and steamed baby beets, quartered

½ cup coarsely chopped walnuts

2 ounces blue cheese, crumbled (about ½ cup)

1 Combine mint, onion, and kale in a large bowl. Combine yogurt, buttermilk, vinegar, oil, pepper, and salt in a bowl, stirring with a whisk. Drizzle yogurt mixture over kale mixture; toss gently to coat. Arrange eggs and beets over salad; sprinkle with nuts and cheese.

PER SERVING (serving size: 1½ cups):

Food Choices: 2 Nonstarchy Vegetables, 1 Medium-Fat Protein, 2 Fats

Calories 202; **Fat** 14.2g (sat 3.8g, mono 3.8g, poly 5.4g, trans 0g); **Protein** 10g; **Carbohydrate** 11g; **Fiber** 2g; **Sugars** 5g; **Cholesterol** 132mg; **Iron** 1mg; **Sodium** 246mg; **Potassium** 389mg; **Phosphorus** 166mg; **Calcium** 139mg

small change, big result

Versatile Greek yogurt is the perfect ingredient for adding creaminess (without the cream) to salad dressings. Using 2% reduced-fat Greek yogurt instead of heavy whipping cream cuts 150 calories and 19 grams of fat.

Kale Salad with Apple and Cheddar

Sweet apples and extra-sharp white cheddar cheese are a delightful combination, and together they boost the flavor of the kale.

Hands-on Time: 10 minutes   **Total Time:** 10 minutes   **Serves:** 6

1 tablespoon cider vinegar

1 tablespoon olive oil

1 teaspoon Dijon mustard

¼ teaspoon granulated no-calorie sweetener (such as Splenda)

¼ teaspoon freshly ground black pepper

⅛ teaspoon salt

6 cups chopped stemmed Lacinato kale

1 small sweet apple, thinly sliced

1 ounce shredded extra-sharp white cheddar cheese (about ¼ cup)

1 Combine first 6 ingredients in a large bowl, stirring with a whisk. Add kale and apple; toss. Top with white cheddar cheese.

PER SERVING (serving size: 1 cup):

Food Choices: 2 Nonstarchy Vegetables, 1 Fat

Calories 84; **Fat** 4.3g (sat 1.4g, mono 1.7g, poly 0.5g, trans 0g); **Protein** 3g; **Carbohydrate** 10g; **Fiber** 2g; **Sugars** 2g; **Cholesterol** 5mg; **Iron** 1mg; **Sodium** 129mg; **Potassium** 326mg; **Phosphorus** 63mg; **Calcium** 126mg

Crunchy Noodles and Greens Salad

This makes an easy, portable lunch; simply pack the noodles, greens, and dressing in separate containers and toss together just before eating. Just add a protein food and a few whole-grain crackers to make it a complete meal.

Hands-on Time: 5 minutes   **Total Time:** 15 minutes   **Serves:** 8

- 1 (3-ounce) package ramen noodles
- ½ cup chopped pecans
- 1 (5-ounce) package gourmet salad greens
- 2 cups quartered fresh strawberries
- 1 cup fresh blueberries
- ¾ cup thinly sliced red onion
- ⅓ cup white balsamic vinegar
- 2 tablespoons granulated no-calorie sweetener (such as Splenda)
- 1 tablespoon sesame oil
- ¾ teaspoon curry powder
- ¼ teaspoon salt
- ⅛ teaspoon crushed red pepper
- Freshly ground black pepper (optional)

1 Heat a large nonstick skillet over medium heat. Add ramen noodles and pecans; cook 10 minutes or until lightly browned. Remove from heat, and cool to room temperature.

2 Combine ramen noodles, pecans, salad greens, and next 3 ingredients (through onion) in a large bowl.

3 Combine balsamic vinegar and next 5 ingredients (through red pepper) in a small bowl, stirring well with a whisk. Pour dressing over salad mixture; toss well. Sprinkle with black pepper, if desired.

PER SERVING (serving size: 1 cup):

Food Choices: 1 Fruit, 1 Nonstarchy Vegetable, 1 Fat

Calories 137; **Fat** 6.5g (sat 0.7g, mono 3.2g, poly 2.1g, trans 0g); **Protein** 3g; **Carbohydrate** 18g; **Fiber** 3g; **Sugars** 8g; **Cholesterol** 0mg; **Iron** 1mg; **Sodium** 195mg; **Potassium** 264mg; **Phosphorus** 48mg; **Calcium** 29mg

ingredient pointer

Unlike traditional balsamic vinegar, which is made from only grape pressings, white balsamic vinegar is made from grape pressings plus white wine vinegar. The high pressure at which white balsamic vinegar is cooked keeps it from caramelizing and losing its classic golden color.

Southeast Asian Grilled Beef Salad

This bold, flavorful salad is great for company because you can prep all the ingredients and marinate the beef ahead of time.

Hands-on Time: 15 minutes **Total Time:** 50 minutes **Serves:** 6

Steak:

1 tablespoon freshly ground black pepper

1 tablespoon thinly sliced green onions

2 tablespoons lower-sodium soy sauce

2 tablespoons minced peeled fresh ginger

½ teaspoon kosher salt

6 garlic cloves, minced

1 (1-pound) flank steak, trimmed

Cooking spray

Dressing:

¼ cup fresh lime juice

2 tablespoons finely chopped fresh basil

2 tablespoons finely chopped fresh cilantro

1 tablespoon lower-sodium soy sauce

1 teaspoon granulated no-calorie sweetener (such as Splenda)

1 teaspoon dark sesame oil

Salad:

12 cups mixed salad greens

2 cups grape or cherry tomatoes, halved

1 cup thinly sliced red bell pepper

½ cup thinly sliced red onion

1 To prepare steak, combine first 6 ingredients. Rub over steak; cover and refrigerate 30 minutes.

2 Preheat grill to medium-high heat.

3 Place steak on grill rack coated with cooking spray; grill 8 minutes on each side or until desired degree of doneness. Cut steak diagonally across grain into thin slices.

4 To prepare dressing, combine juice and next 5 ingredients (through oil), stirring well with a whisk.

5 To prepare salad, combine greens and next 3 ingredients (through onion) in a large bowl. Drizzle dressing over salad; toss gently to coat. Divide salad among 6 plates; top each serving with steak.

PER SERVING (serving size: about 3 cups salad and 3 ounces steak):

Food Choices: 4 Nonstarchy Vegetables, 3 Lean Proteins

Calories 261; **Fat** 8.1g (sat 3g, mono 3.1g, poly 0.8g, trans 0g); **Protein** 28g; **Carbohydrate** 19g; **Fiber** 4g; **Sugars** 11g; **Cholesterol** 65mg; **Iron** 3mg; **Sodium** 484mg; **Potassium** 1,039mg; **Phosphorus** 28mg; **Calcium** 91mg

Steak Taco Salad
with Black Bean–Corn Relish

A squeeze of lime at the end adds wonderful bright flavor.

Hands-on Time: 19 minutes   **Total Time:** 19 minutes   **Serves:** 4

Cooking spray

1 (12-ounce) skirt steak, trimmed

2 teaspoons salt-free fiesta-lime seasoning

Black Bean–Corn Relish

6 cups chopped romaine lettuce, refrigerated

4 lime wedges

1 Heat a grill pan over medium-high heat. Coat pan with cooking spray. Sprinkle steak with fiesta-lime seasoning. Cook steak 3 minutes on each side or to desired degree of doneness. Remove from heat; let stand 5 minutes.

2 While steak stands, prepare Black Bean–Corn Relish.

3 Cut steak diagonally across grain into thin slices. Divide lettuce among 4 plates; top with Black Bean–Corn Relish and steak. Serve with lime wedges.

PER SERVING (serving size: 1½ cups lettuce, about ⅔ cup Black Bean–Corn Relish, and 3 ounces steak):

Food Choices: 1½ Starches, 3 Lean Proteins

Calories 258; **Fat** 7.5g (sat 2.8g, mono 3.8g, poly 0.5g, trans 0g); **Protein** 24g; **Carbohydrate** 25g; **Fiber** 5g; **Sugars** 7g; **Cholesterol** 55mg; **Iron** 4mg; **Sodium** 309mg; **Potassium** 747mg; **Phosphorus** 278mg; **Calcium** 63mg

Black Bean–Corn Relish

Hands-on Time: 3 minutes   **Total Time:** 6 minutes   **Serves:** 4

Cooking spray

1 cup fresh corn kernels (about 2 ears)

¾ cup pico de gallo

1 tablespoon chopped fresh cilantro

¼ teaspoon ground cumin

1 (15-ounce) can unsalted black beans, rinsed and drained

1 Heat a medium skillet over medium-high heat. Coat pan with cooking spray. Add corn to pan. Sauté 3 minutes or until corn begins to brown. Transfer corn to a medium bowl; stir in remaining ingredients.

PER SERVING (serving size: about ⅔ cup):

Food Choices: 1½ Starches

Calories 103; **Fat** 0.8g (sat 0.1g, mono 0.2g, poly 0.2g, trans 0g); **Protein** 5g; **Carbohydrate** 22g; **Fiber** 4g; **Sugars** 3g; **Cholesterol** 0mg; **Iron** 1mg; **Sodium** 242mg; **Potassium** 448mg; **Phosphorus** 110mg; **Calcium** 24mg

Roast Beef, Beet, and Arugula Salad with Orange Vinaigrette

To keep the beets from bleeding as they cook, leave the roots and an inch of the stems intact until the beets are ready to be removed from the water. Then trim the roots and stems before you peel and slice.

Hands-on Time: 8 minutes   **Total Time:** 14 minutes   **Serves:** 4

3 small beets

8 cups loosely packed arugula

Orange Vinaigrette

1 (4-ounce) slice low-sodium deli roast beef (about ¼ inch thick), cut into strips

2 tablespoons pine nuts, toasted

1 Place beets in a microwave-safe bowl; add enough water to come halfway up sides of bowl. Cover with plastic wrap; vent. Microwave at HIGH 8 minutes or until tender; drain and cool. Remove roots and stems. Peel and slice into wedges.

2 While beets cook, combine arugula and Orange Vinaigrette, tossing gently to coat. Arrange arugula mixture on each of 4 plates. Top each serving with beef, beet wedges, and nuts.

PER SERVING (serving size: about 1½ cups arugula salad, 1 ounce beef, 3 beet wedges, and ½ tablespoon nuts):

Food Choices: 2 Nonstarchy Vegetables, 1 Lean Protein, 2 Fats

Calories 187; **Fat** 11g (sat 2.1g, mono 6g, poly 2.3g, trans 0g); **Protein** 10g; **Carbohydrate** 10g; **Fiber** 3g; **Sugars** 6g; **Cholesterol** 19mg; **Iron** 2mg; **Sodium** 182mg; **Potassium** 524mg; **Phosphorus** 140mg; **Calcium** 100mg

Orange Vinaigrette

Hands-on Time: 8 minutes   **Total Time:** 8 minutes   **Makes:** ⅓ cup

1 orange

2 tablespoons white wine vinegar

1 tablespoon minced shallots

2 teaspoons Dijon mustard

¼ teaspoon granulated no-calorie sweetener (such as Splenda)

2 tablespoons olive oil

1 Grate 1 teaspoon orange rind; squeeze 2 tablespoons juice from orange over a bowl.

2 Combine orange rind and juice, white wine vinegar, and next 3 ingredients (through sweetener) in a small bowl, stirring well with a whisk. Slowly add oil, stirring well with a whisk.

PER SERVING (serving size: about 1 tablespoon):

Food Choice: 1 Fat

Calories 52; **Fat** 5g (sat 0.7g, mono 3.7g, poly 0.5g, trans 0g); **Protein** 0g; **Carbohydrate** 1g; **Fiber** 0g; **Sugars** 1g; **Cholesterol** 0mg; **Iron** 0mg; **Sodium** 46mg; **Potassium** 21mg; **Phosphorus** 2mg; **Calcium** 2mg

Coriander-Crusted Beef Salad with Black Bean Salsa

This Southwestern beef has a spicy crust made with coriander, cumin, and black pepper. You can also serve it on chopped romaine.

Hands-on Time: 15 minutes   **Total Time:** 20 minutes   **Serves:** 4

1 tablespoon ground coriander

1 teaspoon ground cumin

¾ teaspoon kosher salt, divided

¼ teaspoon freshly ground black pepper

4 (3-ounce) beef tenderloin steaks, trimmed

1 teaspoon olive oil

1 cup diced plum tomato (about 3 tomatoes)

½ cup chopped yellow bell pepper

¼ cup sliced green onions

3 tablespoons chopped fresh cilantro

2 tablespoons fresh lime juice

1 (15-ounce) can unsalted black beans, rinsed and drained

4 cups mixed salad greens

1 Combine coriander, cumin, ½ teaspoon salt, and black pepper in a small bowl. Rub spice mixture over both sides of steak.

2 Heat a large nonstick skillet over medium-high heat. Add oil to pan; swirl to coat. Add beef to pan; cook 4 minutes on each side or until desired degree of doneness. Remove from heat. Let stand 5 minutes. Cut tenderloin into slices.

3 While beef cooks, combine tomato and next 5 ingredients (through beans) in a medium bowl. Stir in ¼ teaspoon salt, and toss well.

4 Divide greens among 4 plates. Top each with tenderloin and salsa.

PER SERVING (serving size: 1 cup greens, 1 tenderloin, and about ¾ cup salsa):

Food Choices: ½ Starch, 1 Nonstarchy Vegetable, 3 Lean Proteins

Calories 213; **Fat** 6.7g (sat 2.1g, mono 2.9g, poly 0.4g, trans 0g); **Protein** 23g; **Carbohydrate** 15g; **Fiber** 6g; **Sugars** 3g; **Cholesterol** 51mg; **Iron** 3mg; **Sodium** 362mg; **Potassium** 745mg; **Phosphorus** 251mg; **Calcium** 88mg

Thai Chicken Salad

Thanks to quick-cooking chicken tenders, you can have a light weeknight dinner on the table in a flash. The marinade in this dish doubles as a piquant vinaigrette for the salad.

Hands-on Time: 15 minutes **Total Time:** 15 minutes **Serves:** 4

¼ cup unsalted chicken stock (such as Swanson)

2 tablespoons rice wine vinegar

1 tablespoon lower-sodium soy sauce

1 garlic clove, minced

1½ teaspoons granulated no-calorie sweetener (such as Splenda)

1½ teaspoons Thai fish sauce

1 pound skinless, boneless chicken breast tenders

1 tablespoon peanut oil

4 cups mixed salad greens

¼ cup chopped fresh basil

½ cup thinly sliced red onion

2 tablespoons finely chopped unsalted, dry-roasted peanuts

Lime wedges (optional)

1 Combine first 6 ingredients in a medium bowl. Add chicken to broth mixture, stirring to coat. Let stand 3 minutes.

2 Heat a large nonstick skillet over medium-high heat. Add oil to pan; swirl to coat. Drain chicken, reserving marinade. Add chicken to pan; cook 4 minutes or until done, stirring frequently. Stir in reserved marinade. Reduce heat; cook 1 minute or until slightly thick. Remove pan from heat.

3 Combine greens and basil in a large bowl. Add chicken mixture, tossing to coat. Divide salad mixture among 4 plates. Top each serving with onion and peanuts. Serve immediately. Serve with lime wedges, if desired.

PER SERVING (serving size: 1¼ cups salad mixture, 2 tablespoons onion, and 1½ teaspoons peanuts):

Food Choices: 1 Nonstarchy Vegetable, 3 Lean Proteins, 1 Fat

Calories 212; **Fat** 8.6g (sat 1.5g, mono 3.5g, poly 2.3g, trans 0g); **Protein** 27g; **Carbohydrate** 7g; **Fiber** 2g; **Sugars** 2g; **Cholesterol** 73mg; **Iron** 1mg; **Sodium** 471mg; **Potassium** 787mg; **Phosphorus** 305mg; **Calcium** 23mg

small change, big result

There's one good way to reduce the sodium content in Asian-inspired dishes—use plenty of herbs, garlic, and onion. Just a dash of potent, high-sodium ingredients like fish sauce or soy sauce is needed to achieve authentic flavor.

Pack and Go

Do something really healthy for yourself—pack a lunch! Our super-simple brown-bag ideas take just a few minutes to assemble and taste better—and are better for you—than anything from a drive thru.

SAVORY YOGURT BOWL

Pack plain fat-free Greek yogurt in a plastic container. In a separate container, combine ½ cup canned chickpeas with halved cherry tomatoes, sliced cucumber, diced red onion, a splash of fresh lemon juice, and a couple teaspoons olive oil. At lunchtime, top the yogurt with the bean mixture. Enjoy with half a small whole-grain pita bread.

BEAN AND AVOCADO WRAP

Combine ¼ cup canned black beans, ¼ cup diced avocado, and ¼ cup salsa in a plastic container. At lunchtime, layer a small whole-wheat tortilla with Bibb lettuce, top with the black bean mixture, and roll up.

EASY BEAN AND FETA SALAD

Toss ½ cup canned white beans with diced vegetables such as cucumber, bell pepper, tomato, and onion. Stir in 2 tablespoons crumbled feta cheese, a few teaspoons of olive oil, and a splash of white wine vinegar.

LEFTOVERS FOR LUNCH

Combine your favorite salad greens in a plastic container. Top with veggies such as shredded carrots, sliced cucumbers, chopped red bell peppers, or broccoli. Add leftovers from last night's dinner: 3 ounces chicken breast, lean beef, shrimp, or salmon. When it's time for your midday meal, drizzle with 2 tablespoons reduced-fat salad dressing.

TAKE-ALONG SOUP

Whether you've frozen a homemade version in individual containers or have your own favorite low-sodium canned brand, soup is a healthy, filling option for lunch. Include a whole-wheat roll or a few whole-grain crackers and a piece of fruit for dessert.

TUNA AND PASTA SALAD

Combine 3 ounces water-packed canned tuna, ½ cup cooked whole-wheat pasta, and 2 tablespoons reduced-fat vinaigrette dressing. Stir in chopped green onions, bell peppers, or celery, halved cherry tomatoes, or thinly sliced fresh fennel.

VEGGIE-PACKED TURKEY PITA

Fill a small whole-grain pita bread with 3 ounces of sliced turkey breast, and then add sliced roasted red bell peppers, thinly sliced cucumbers, and baby spinach. Drizzle with 1 tablespoon reduced-fat salad dressing. Pack the sandwich fillings and dressing separately, and assemble just before eating.

HUMMUS AND AVOCADO SANDWICH

Spread thin-sliced whole-wheat bread with hummus, and top with baby arugula and sliced avocado.

Chicken and Strawberries over Mixed Greens

If you already have leftover cooked chicken on hand, this dish is a snap to throw together for lunch. Serve with focaccia topped with coarse salt and rosemary to complement the sweet strawberries and raisins in the salad.

Hands-on Time: 15 minutes   **Total Time:** 1 hour, 15 minutes   **Serves:** 4

- **2 cups chopped roasted skinless, boneless chicken breast (about 2 breasts)**
- **2 cups quartered small fresh strawberries (about 1 pint)**
- **⅓ cup finely chopped celery**
- **⅓ cup finely chopped red onion**
- **2 tablespoons golden raisins**
- **1 tablespoon sesame seeds, toasted**
- **1 tablespoon chopped fresh or 1 teaspoon dried tarragon**
- **1 tablespoon extra-virgin olive oil**
- **1 tablespoon balsamic vinegar**
- **½ teaspoon paprika**
- **⅛ teaspoon salt**
- **⅛ teaspoon freshly ground black pepper**
- **4 cups gourmet salad greens**

1 Combine first 5 ingredients in a large bowl. Combine sesame seeds and next 6 ingredients (through pepper) in a small bowl, stirring well with a whisk. Pour over chicken mixture; toss well to coat. Cover and chill 1 hour. Serve over salad greens.

PER SERVING (serving size: 1 cup greens and 1¼ cups chicken mixture):

Food Choices: ½ Fruit, 1 Nonstarchy Vegetable, 2 Lean Proteins

Calories 164; **Fat** 6.3g (sat 1.2g, mono 3.4g, poly 1.3g, trans 0g); **Protein** 15g; **Carbohydrate** 13g; **Fiber** 4g; **Sugars** 9g; **Cholesterol** 35mg; **Iron** 2mg; **Sodium** 376mg; **Potassium** 485mg; **Phosphorus** 198mg; **Calcium** 78mg

ingredient pointer

Rotisserie chicken is a convenient and healthy choice when the skin is removed. Most of the salt and fat will be discarded with the skin.

Creamy Blueberry-Chicken Salad

Besides adding a touch of sweetness to this savory salad, blueberries may also boost the body's insulin sensitivity, helping it regulate blood sugar.

Hands-on Time: 15 minutes   **Total Time:** 15 minutes   **Serves:** 6

12 ounces shredded skinless, boneless rotisserie chicken (about 3 cups)

½ cup thinly vertically sliced red onion

⅓ cup diced celery

¼ cup torn fresh basil

½ teaspoon kosher salt, divided

½ cup plain fat-free Greek yogurt

2½ tablespoons fresh lemon juice, divided

1 teaspoon granulated no-calorie sweetener (such as Splenda)

2 cups fresh blueberries

1 (5-ounce) package baby arugula

2 teaspoons extra-virgin olive oil

¼ teaspoon freshly ground black pepper

1 Combine first 4 ingredients in a medium bowl; sprinkle with ¼ teaspoon salt. Combine yogurt, 1 tablespoon lemon juice, and sweetener in a small bowl, stirring with a whisk. Add yogurt mixture to chicken mixture; toss to coat. Gently stir in blueberries.

2 Place arugula, 1½ tablespoons lemon juice, oil, ¼ teaspoon salt, and pepper in a bowl; toss to coat. Divide arugula mixture among 6 plates; top each serving with chicken mixture.

PER SERVING (serving size: about ⅔ cup arugula mixture and about ¾ cup chicken mixture):

Food Choices: ½ Fruit, 1 Nonstarchy Vegetable, 2 Lean Proteins

Calories 188; **Fat** 8.5g (sat 1.9g, mono 2.9g, poly 1.3g, trans 0g); **Protein** 16g; **Carbohydrate** 10g; **Fiber** 2g; **Sugars** 7g; **Cholesterol** 74mg; **Iron** 1mg; **Sodium** 369mg; **Potassium** 339mg; **Phosphorus** 170mg; **Calcium** 65mg

Chicken, Edamame, and Rice Salad

The distinct and powerful taste combination of fresh ginger and mint lends a burst of flavor to this main-dish salad. The edamame adds texture and fiber.

Hands-on Time: 13 minutes   **Total Time:** 13 minutes   **Serves:** 6

1 (8.8-ounce) pouch microwaveable cooked long-grain rice

1¼ cups frozen shelled edamame (green soybeans)

3 tablespoons water

1 cup diced cooked chicken breast

2 tablespoons chopped fresh mint

1 tablespoon grated peeled fresh ginger

2 tablespoons rice vinegar

1 teaspoon canola oil

⅛ teaspoon salt

6 radicchio leaves

1 Microwave rice according to package directions. Set aside; keep warm.

2 Combine edamame and 3 tablespoons water in a small bowl. Cover with plastic wrap. Microwave at HIGH 3 minutes. Let stand 2 minutes; drain.

3 Combine rice, edamame, chicken, and next 5 ingredients (through salt) in a large bowl; toss to coat. Serve over radicchio.

PER SERVING (serving size: 1 radicchio leaf and about ½ cup salad):

Food Choices: 1 Starch, 1 Lean Protein, ½ Fat

Calories 155; **Fat** 3.8g (sat 0.3g, mono 0.8g, poly 0.4g, trans 0g); **Protein** 13g; **Carbohydrate** 17g; **Fiber** 2g; **Sugars** 3g; **Cholesterol** 20mg; **Iron** 2mg; **Sodium** 152mg; **Potassium** 238mg; **Phosphorus** 124mg; **Calcium** 40mg

Mediterranean Tuna Salad

Featuring flavors from the Mediterranean, this salad spotlights albacore tuna—a fish that is rich in omega-3 fatty acids. It's delicious served over sliced summer tomatoes, stuffed in a pita with shredded lettuce, or served with pita chips for lunch on the go.

Hands-on Time: 11 minutes   **Total Time:** 11 minutes   **Serves:** 3

1 (12-ounce) can albacore tuna in water, drained and flaked into large chunks

½ cup thinly sliced red onion

2 tablespoons coarsely chopped pitted kalamata olives

2 celery stalks, thinly sliced

2½ tablespoons fresh lemon juice

1 tablespoon olive oil

¼ teaspoon freshly ground black pepper

1⁄16 teaspoon kosher salt

2 large tomatoes, each cut into 3 slices

1 Combine first 4 ingredients in a medium bowl. Add lemon juice and next 3 ingredients (through salt); toss gently to combine. Serve salad over sliced tomatoes.

PER SERVING (serving size: 2 tomato slices and 1 cup tuna salad):

Food Choices: 2 Nonstarchy Vegetables, 3 Lean Proteins

Calories 203; **Fat** 8g (sat 1g, mono 4.6g, poly 1g, trans 0g); **Protein** 25g; **Carbohydrate** 9g; **Fiber** 2g; **Sugars** 4g; **Cholesterol** 39mg; **Iron** 1mg; **Sodium** 443mg; **Potassium** 543mg; **Phosphorus** 240mg; **Calcium** 31mg

ingredient pointer

Albacore tuna is a great source of heart-healthy omega-3 fatty acids, and buying the canned variety is an easy way to incorporate it into your diet. Choose tuna canned in water, not oil, to cut calories and excess fat.

Grilled Salmon and Spinach Salad

Perfect for a summer meal, this salad is an attractive dish to serve guests. Make the sweet citrus vinaigrette earlier in the day, and store it in an airtight container in the refrigerator.

Hands-on Time: 15 minutes   **Total Time:** 15 minutes   **Serves:** 4

Vinaigrette:

¼ cup fresh orange juice

2 tablespoons olive oil

2 tablespoons balsamic blend seasoned rice vinegar

½ teaspoon whole-grain honey mustard

½ teaspoon freshly ground black pepper

1 garlic clove, minced

Salad:

2 tablespoons fresh lemon juice

4 (4-ounce) salmon fillets

2 teaspoons freshly ground black pepper

Cooking spray

1 (6-ounce) package fresh spinach

4 oranges, each peeled and cut into 6 slices

1 Preheat grill to medium-high heat.

2 To prepare vinaigrette, combine first 6 ingredients in a large bowl; stir well with a whisk.

3 To prepare salad, drizzle lemon juice over fillets; sprinkle with 2 teaspoons pepper. Place fillets, skin sides up, on grill rack coated with cooking spray; grill 5 minutes on each side or until desired degree of doneness. Remove skin from fillets; discard.

4 Add spinach to vinaigrette in bowl; toss well. Divide spinach mixture among 4 plates; arrange orange slices and fillets on top of greens.

PER SERVING (serving size: 2 cups spinach mixture, 6 orange slices, and 1 fillet):

Food Choices: 1 Fruit, 2 Nonstarchy Vegetables, 3 Lean Proteins, 3 Fats

Calories 370; **Fat** 19g (sat 3.9g, mono 6.8g, poly 4.9g, trans 0g); **Protein** 25g; **Carbohydrate** 28g; **Fiber** 8g; **Sugars** 18g; **Cholesterol** 62mg; **Iron** 2mg; **Sodium** 225mg; **Potassium** 935mg; **Phosphorus** 315mg; **Calcium** 115mg

White Bean Salad with Shrimp and Asparagus

Warm bacon vinaigrette wilts the fresh spinach, so it's best to eat the salad immediately after tossing.

Hands-on Time: 12 minutes   **Total Time:** 15 minutes   **Serves:** 4

2 cups (1-inch) sliced asparagus (about ½ pound)

¾ pound peeled and deveined medium shrimp

½ teaspoon freshly ground black pepper, divided

1 teaspoon canola oil

2 cups torn spinach

1 (19-ounce) can cannellini beans, rinsed and drained

3 bacon slices

½ cup chopped green onions

1 garlic clove, minced

¼ cup fat-free, lower-sodium chicken broth

1 tablespoon chopped fresh parsley

2 tablespoons fresh lemon juice

1 tablespoon cider vinegar

1 Steam asparagus, covered, 3 minutes. Drain and rinse with cold water.

2 Sprinkle shrimp with ⅛ teaspoon pepper. Heat a medium nonstick skillet over medium-high heat. Add oil to pan; swirl to coat. Add shrimp; sauté 4 minutes. Remove from pan; place in a large bowl. Add asparagus, spinach, and beans to shrimp; toss well.

3 Add bacon to pan; cook over medium heat until crisp. Remove bacon from pan; crumble. Reserve 2 teaspoons drippings in pan. Add onions and garlic; cook 3 minutes or until soft, stirring frequently. Remove from heat; add ⅜ teaspoon pepper, bacon, broth, and remaining ingredients. Drizzle dressing over salad; toss to coat. Serve immediately.

PER SERVING (serving size: 1¾ cups):

Food Choices: 1 Starch, 1 Nonstarchy Vegetable, 2 Lean Proteins, ½ Fat

Calories 219; **Fat** 4.5g (sat 0.9g, mono 1.7g, poly 0.7g, trans 0g); **Protein** 20g; **Carbohydrate** 21g; **Fiber** 7g; **Sugars** 2g; **Cholesterol** 112mg; **Iron** 4mg; **Sodium** 382mg; **Potassium** 616mg; **Phosphorus** 357mg; **Calcium** 163mg

Curry Chicken Wraps with
Nectarine Chutney, page 163

Simple Soups and Sandwiches

From quick-fix dishes for on-the-go to easy slow-cooked comfort food, these yummy recipes will fit the bill for lunch or dinner.

Chunky Tomato-Fruit Gazpacho

Mangoes, melons, and nectarines, along with the cucumber, give this gazpacho a sweet spin and load it with nutrients like vitamin C, beta carotene, and potassium.

Hands-on Time: 20 minutes   **Total Time:** 2 hours, 20 minutes   **Serves:** 7

2 cups finely chopped tomato (about ¾ pound)

2 cups finely diced honeydew melon (about ¾ pound)

2 cups finely diced cantaloupe (about ¾ pound)

1 cup finely diced mango (about 1 medium)

1 cup finely diced seeded peeled cucumber (about 1 medium)

1 cup finely diced nectarines (about 3 medium)

1 cup fresh orange **juice (about 4 oranges)**

½ cup finely chopped Vidalia or other sweet onion

¼ cup chopped fresh basil

3 tablespoons chopped fresh mint

3 tablespoons fresh lemon **juice**

¼ teaspoon salt

1 jalapeño pepper, seeded and finely chopped

2 ounces crumbed feta cheese (about ½ cup)

1 Combine all ingredients except feta cheese in a large bowl. Cover and chill at least 2 hours. Sprinkle cheese on top just before serving.

PER SERVING (serving size: 1 cup):

Food Choices: 1 Fruit, 1 Nonstarchy Vegetable, ½ Fat

Calories 113; **Fat** 2.3g (sat 1.3g, mono 0.5g, poly 0.2g, trans 0g); **Protein** 3g; **Carbohydrate** 22g; **Fiber** 3g; **Sugars** 18g; **Cholesterol** 7mg; **Iron** 1mg; **Sodium** 195mg; **Potassium** 578mg; **Phosphorus** 77mg; **Calcium** 73mg

ingredient pointer

Chile peppers—like jalapeños— can add depth to a recipe, but they also add some heat. By removing as many or as few of the seeds as you'd like, you control the heat. Since capsaicin, the compound that gives peppers their kick, can stick to your hands, you should wear gloves when handling them.

Poblano-Tomato Soup

Pair this spicy soup with your favorite grilled cheese sandwich for a filling meal.

Hands-on Time: 14 minutes   **Total Time:** 14 minutes   **Serves:** 4

2 **pounds** tomatoes, **halved**

6 **garlic cloves**

3 **shallots, halved**

1 red bell pepper, **halved and seeded**

1 **poblano pepper, halved and seeded**

1 **tablespoon canola oil**

1 **cup unsalted chicken stock (such as Swanson)**

¼ **teaspoon salt**

¼ **teaspoon ground cumin**

⅛ **teaspoon ground coriander**

¼ **cup cilantro leaves**

4 lime **wedges**

1 Place a jelly-roll pan in oven. Preheat broiler.

2 Combine tomatoes, garlic, shallots, red bell pepper, and poblano pepper in a bowl. Add canola oil; toss. Carefully arrange vegetables on preheated pan; broil 10 minutes or until blackened.

3 Place roasted vegetables in a blender. Remove center piece of blender lid (to allow steam to escape); secure lid on blender. Place a clean towel over opening in lid (to avoid splatters). Blend until smooth. Stir in chicken stock, salt, cumin, and coriander. Top with cilantro leaves; serve with lime wedges.

PER SERVING (serving size: 1¼ cups soup and 1 lime wedge):
Food Choices: 3 Nonstarchy Vegetables, ½ Fat

Calories 102; **Fat** 4.2g (sat 0.3g, mono 2.3, poly 1.2, trans 0g); **Protein** 5g; **Carbohydrate** 17g; **Fiber** 4g; **Sugars** 9g; **Cholesterol** 0mg; **Iron** 1mg; **Sodium** 196mg; **Potassium** 667mg; **Phosphorus** 80mg; **Calcium** 50mg

Black Bean Soup

Make the soup the night before, and pack it in a microwave-safe container to heat up at work.

Hands-on Time: 5 minutes **Total Time:** 15 minutes **Serves:** 4

2 (15-ounce) cans unsalted **black beans, rinsed and drained**

1½ **cups organic vegetable broth**

½ **cup** fresh salsa

1 **tablespoon fresh** lime **juice**

1 **teaspoon chopped chipotle chile, canned in adobo sauce**

½ **teaspoon ground cumin**

2 **tablespoons chopped fresh cilantro**

⅓ **cup queso fresco, crumbled**

4 lime **wedges**

1 Place beans in a medium saucepan. Mash beans slightly with a potato masher.

2 Stir in broth and next 4 ingredients (through cumin). Bring to a boil; reduce heat, and simmer, uncovered, 5 minutes or until thoroughly heated. Remove from heat; stir in cilantro. Ladle soup into bowls; sprinkle with cheese. Serve with lime wedges.

PER SERVING (serving size: 1 cup soup, about 1 tablespoon cheese, and 1 lime wedge):

Food Choices: 1½ Starches, 1 Lean Protein

Calories 163; **Fat** 1.8g (sat 1.1g, mono 0.5g, poly 0.1g, trans 0g); **Protein** 10g; **Carbohydrate** 25g; **Fiber** 7g; **Sugars** 2g; **Cholesterol** 7mg; **Iron** 2mg; **Sodium** 339mg; **Potassium** 460mg; **Phosphorus** 168mg; **Calcium** 129mg

Chipotle Chicken Tortilla Soup

If you like food with a little kick, then this spicy, smoky soup is for you. Round out the meal with a salad and mini corn muffins.

Hands-on Time: 7 minutes   **Total Time:** 12 minutes   **Serves:** 4

- **1 tablespoon canola oil**
- **¾ pound chicken breast tenders, cut into bite-sized pieces**
- **1 garlic clove, minced**
- **1 teaspoon chipotle chile powder**
- **1 teaspoon ground cumin**
- **2 cups unsalted chicken stock (such as Swanson)**
- **1 cup water**
- **⅛ teaspoon salt**
- **1 (14.5-ounce) can unsalted stewed tomatoes, undrained**
- **1 cup crushed baked tortilla chips**
- **¼ cup chopped fresh cilantro**
- **1 lime, cut into 4 wedges**

1 Heat a large saucepan over medium-high heat. Add oil to pan; swirl to coat. Add chicken and minced garlic; sauté 2 minutes.

2 Add chile powder and cumin; stir well. Add stock, 1 cup water, salt, and tomatoes; bring to a boil. Cover, reduce heat, and simmer 5 minutes. Top with tortilla chips and cilantro, and serve with lime wedges.

PER SERVING (serving size: 1¼ cups soup, ¼ cup chips, 1 tablespoon cilantro, and 1 lime wedge):

Food Choices: 1 Starch, 1 Nonstarchy Vegetable, 2 Lean Proteins

Calories 213; **Fat** 4.2g (sat 0.6g, mono 1.4g, poly 0.7g, trans 0g); **Protein** 23g; **Carbohydrate** 21g; **Fiber** 3g; **Sugars** 3g; **Cholesterol** 54mg; **Iron** 1mg; **Sodium** 366mg; **Potassium** 564mg; **Phosphorus** 247mg; **Calcium** 56mg

Sweet Potato, Sausage, and Kale Soup

This recipe makes a large yield and will freeze well. For future single-serving meals, put leftovers in individual portion-sized containers and store in your freezer.

Hands-on Time: 18 minutes   **Total Time:** 52 minutes   **Serves:** 14

2 tablespoons olive oil

4 cups chopped onion (about 2 large)

½ teaspoon crushed red pepper

¼ teaspoon salt

6 garlic cloves, thinly sliced

1 pound sweet turkey Italian sausage

8 cups coarsely chopped peeled sweet potato (about 2¼ pounds)

5 cups water

4 cups unsalted chicken stock (such as Swanson)

1 (16-ounce) package prewashed torn kale

1 (16-ounce) can unsalted cannellini beans or other white beans, rinsed and drained

1 Heat a large Dutch oven over medium-high heat. Add oil to pan; swirl to coat. Add onion; sauté 5 minutes. Add pepper, ¼ teaspoon salt, and garlic; sauté 1 minute. Remove casings from sausage; add sausage to pan. Cook 5 minutes or until sausage is lightly browned, stirring to crumble.

2 Add potato, 5 cups water, and stock; bring to a boil. Reduce heat, and simmer 8 minutes. Gradually add kale; cook 10 minutes or until tender. Stir in beans; cook 5 minutes or until thoroughly heated.

PER SERVING (serving size: about 1¼ cups):

Food Choices: 1½ Starches, 1 Nonstarchy Vegetable, 1 Medium-Fat Protein

Calories 194; **Fat** 5.9g (sat 0.3g, mono 2.2g, poly 0.8g, trans 0g); **Protein** 11g; **Carbohydrate** 26g; **Fiber** 4g; **Sugars** 6g; **Cholesterol** 19mg; **Iron** 2mg; **Sodium** 254mg; **Potassium** 566mg; **Phosphorus** 143mg; **Calcium** 92mg

Pork, Bean, and Escarole Soup

Escarole is less bitter than other members of the endive family, with hearty leaves similar to kale or chard, which you can sub here. Use just the leaves for this soup.

Hands-on Time: 25 minutes   **Total Time:** 25 minutes   **Serves:** 6

- 1 (1-pound) pork tenderloin, trimmed and cut into bite-sized pieces
- 1 tablespoon minced fresh rosemary
- ½ teaspoon freshly ground black pepper
- ¼ teaspoon kosher salt
- ¼ teaspoon smoked paprika
- ¼ teaspoon ground red pepper
- 2 tablespoons extra-virgin olive oil
- 1 cup chopped onion
- 2 garlic cloves, minced
- 6 cups unsalted chicken stock (such as Swanson)
- 2 tablespoons tomato paste
- 2 (15-ounce) cans unsalted cannellini beans, rinsed and drained
- 8 cups chopped escarole leaves (1 large head)
- 1.5 ounces grated fresh Parmesan cheese (about 6 tablespoons)

1 Combine pork, rosemary, black pepper, salt, paprika, and red pepper in a bowl.

2 Heat a large Dutch oven over medium-high heat. Add oil to pan; swirl to coat. Add pork mixture; sauté 2 minutes. Add onion and garlic; sauté 4 minutes. Add stock, tomato paste, and beans; bring to a boil. Reduce heat and cook, partially covered, 10 minutes. Mash half of beans in pan with a potato masher. Stir in escarole; cook 2 minutes or until wilted. Ladle soup into bowls; top with cheese.

PER SERVING (serving size: 1¾ cups soup and 1 tablespoon cheese):

Food Choices: ½ Starch, 2 Nonstarchy Vegetables, 3 Lean Proteins, 1 Fat

Calories 265; **Fat** 9g (sat 2.4g, mono 4.5g, poly 0.9g, trans 0g); **Protein** 28g; **Carbohydrate** 17g; **Fiber** 6g; **Sugars** 3g; **Cholesterol** 55mg; **Iron** 3mg; **Sodium** 441mg; **Potassium** 768mg; **Phosphorus** 330mg; **Calcium** 172mg

White Turkey Chili

This white turkey chili is a tasty alternative to traditional red chili and pairs well with tortilla chips or a green salad. Ground turkey breast makes a good sub for the chopped cooked variety—just cook it after melting the butter.

Hands-on Time: 10 minutes   **Total Time:** 45 minutes   **Serves:** 11

2 teaspoons butter

1½ cups chopped onion

½ cup chopped celery

½ cup chopped red bell pepper

1 tablespoon minced seeded jalapeño pepper

1 garlic clove, minced

4 cups unsalted chicken stock (such as Swanson)

3 cups chopped cooked turkey (about 15 ounces)

2 (19-ounce) cans unsalted cannellini beans or other white beans, rinsed, drained, and divided

1 cup frozen whole-kernel corn

1½ teaspoons ground cumin

1 teaspoon chili powder

½ teaspoon salt

¼ teaspoon freshly ground black pepper

1 (4.5-ounce) can chopped green chiles

1 cup fat-free milk

½ cup chopped fresh cilantro

1 Melt butter in a large Dutch oven over medium-high heat. Add onion and next 4 ingredients (through garlic), and sauté 5 minutes. Add stock, turkey, 1½ cups beans, and next 6 ingredients (through green chiles), and bring to a boil. Cover, reduce heat, and simmer 15 minutes.

2 Mash remaining beans. Add mashed beans and milk to turkey mixture. Simmer, uncovered, 20 minutes or until mixture is thick, stirring frequently. Stir in chopped cilantro.

PER SERVING (serving size: 1 cup):

Food Choices: 1 Starch, 2 Lean Proteins

Calories 156; **Fat** 1.8g (sat 0.6g, mono 0.3g, poly 0.2g, trans 0g); **Protein** 18g; **Carbohydrate** 17g; **Fiber** 4g; **Sugars** 3g; **Cholesterol** 33mg; **Iron** 2mg; **Sodium** 220mg; **Potassium** 384mg; **Phosphorus** 189mg; **Calcium** 71mg

Hidden Sodium in
Broths and Stocks

Having diabetes means you're at greater risk for heart disease, so your health-care team may recommend you decrease the amount of sodium you consume, particularly if you have high blood pressure. If you have high blood pressure, check with your health-care team about your goal for sodium.

Broths are a basic pantry staple used in many recipes, and canned soups make convenient lunches and snacks, but they're also some of the foods highest in sodium. Here's how to choose low-sodium broths and soups for recipes and meals.

Be sure to check the milligrams of sodium on the label, not just the banner on the front of the package. Labeling terms for sodium can be confusing. Products labeled "low-sodium" contain much less sodium than the regular kind and are a healthier choice than those with the very similar wording "lower-sodium."

• Reduced-sodium or lower-sodium means the sodium is reduced by at least 25% per serving compared to the regular product. For broths and soups, products with this wording on the label may still be very high in sodium.

• Low-sodium means it has 140 milligrams or less per serving. This wording on the label means that the broth or soup is a heart-healthy choice.

The best way to know what is in your broth is to make your own at home. Try our recipe below for flavorful homemade chicken stock you can use in any recipe that calls for canned chicken broth. You can store the broth in the refrigerator for up to 4 days or freeze it for up to 3 months.

Chicken Stock

Hands-on Time: 15 minutes
Total Time: 11 hours, 15 minutes   **Serves:** 20

15 black peppercorns
12 fresh parsley sprigs
10 fresh thyme sprigs
8 pounds chicken backs, necks, or wings
5 carrots, chopped
5 celery stalks, chopped
4 bay leaves
3 large onions, chopped
5 quarts cold water

1 Combine all ingredients in a 12-quart stock-pot. Bring to a boil over medium-high heat. Reduce heat to low; simmer 4 hours, skimming and discarding foam as needed. Strain through a cheesecloth-lined colander into a large bowl; discard solids. Cool stock to room temperature. Cover and refrigerate 6 hours or overnight. Skim fat from surface; discard fat.

PER SERVING (serving size: 1 cup):
Food Choice: Free
Calories 11; **Fat** 0.5g (sat 0.1g, mono 0.1g, poly 0.1g, trans 0g); **Protein** 1g; **Carbohydrate** 0g; **Fiber** 0g; **Sugars** 0g; **Cholesterol** 6mg; **Iron** 0mg; **Sodium** 6mg; **Potassium** 17mg; **Phosphorus** 12mg; **Calcium** 2mg

Eggplant Sandwiches with Spinach and Fontina

Eggplant, like other nonstarchy vegetables, is full of fiber with few carbs and calories so it keeps you full longer than bread and doesn't spike blood sugar levels.

Hands-on Time: 36 minutes   **Total Time**: 36 minutes   **Serves**: 7

2 (1-pound) eggplants, peeled and cut into 28 (½-inch-thick) slices

¼ teaspoon kosher salt

1 cup water

1 (10-ounce) package fresh spinach

Cooking spray

1½ cups finely chopped red onion

½ teaspoon crushed red pepper

2 garlic cloves, minced

1 tablespoon fresh lemon juice

¼ teaspoon freshly ground black pepper

2 ounces fontina cheese, shredded (about ½ cup)

2 tablespoons grated fresh Parmesan cheese

¼ cup fat-free milk

3 large egg whites, lightly beaten

1 cup dry polenta

4 teaspoons olive oil, divided

14 lemon wedges

1 Preheat broiler. Sprinkle eggplant with ¼ teaspoon salt. Place half of eggplant on a baking sheet; broil 5 minutes on each side or until lightly browned. Repeat procedure with remaining eggplant.

2 Bring 1 cup water to a boil in a large Dutch oven. Add spinach; cover and cook 2 minutes or until wilted. Drain well. Place spinach on several layers of paper towels; cover with additional paper towels. Let stand 5 minutes, pressing down occasionally. Coarsely chop spinach.

3 Heat a medium skillet over medium heat. Coat pan with cooking spray. Add onion, red pepper, and garlic; cook 4 minutes or until onion is tender, stirring occasionally. Stir in lemon juice; cook 30 seconds or until liquid evaporates. Combine onion mixture and chopped spinach in a bowl; stir in black pepper.

4 Combine fontina and Parmesan in a small bowl. Working with 1 eggplant slice at a time, spread about 2½ tablespoons spinach mixture over each of 14 eggplant slices; sprinkle each with about 2 teaspoons cheese mixture. Cover with remaining eggplant slices, and gently press together.

5 Combine milk and egg whites in a medium bowl, stirring with a whisk. Working with 1 sandwich at a time, brush both sides of each sandwich with milk mixture, and dredge in polenta.

6 Heat a large nonstick skillet over medium-high heat. Add 2 teaspoons oil to pan: swirl to coat. Add half of sandwiches; cook 5 minutes on each side or until browned. Repeat procedure with 2 teaspoons oil and remaining sandwiches. Serve with lemon wedges.

PER SERVING (serving size: 2 sandwiches and 2 lemon wedges):

Food Choices: 1½ Starches, 2 Nonstarchy Vegetables, 1½ Fats

Calories 236; **Fat** 7.9g (sat 2.5g, mono 2.1g, poly 0.5g, trans 0g); **Protein** 11g; **Carbohydrate** 35g; **Fiber** 5g; **Sugars** 6g; **Cholesterol** 11mg; **Iron** 4mg; **Sodium** 435mg; **Potassium** 363mg; **Phosphorus** 86mg; **Calcium** 214mg

Sweet and Hot Pepper Open-Faced Egg Sandwiches

There's a great interplay of flavors here, with the tingly heat of cherry pepper and the sweetness of bell pepper. For an even spicier dish, substitute 2 tablespoons pickled jalapeño slices for the cherry pepper.

Hands-on Time: 19 minutes **Total Time**: 19 minutes **Serves**: 4

4 (1½-ounce) slices whole-grain sourdough bread

4 teaspoons extra-virgin olive oil, divided

1¼ cups thinly sliced red bell pepper

1¼ cups thinly sliced red onion

3 garlic cloves, minced

1 bottled hot cherry pepper, drained and thinly sliced

1 ounce part-skim mozzarella cheese, shredded (about ¼ cup)

1 tablespoon 1% low-fat milk

¼ teaspoon freshly ground black pepper

5 large eggs, lightly beaten

4 large egg whites, lightly beaten

¼ cup chopped fresh flat-leaf parsley leaves

1 Preheat broiler.

2 Place bread slices on a baking sheet; broil 1 minute on each side or until toasted.

3 Heat a large nonstick skillet over medium-high heat. Add 2 teaspoons oil to pan; swirl to coat. Add bell pepper, onion, garlic, and cherry pepper to pan; sauté 3 minutes or just until tender. Remove pepper mixture from pan. Return pan to medium heat. Add 2 teaspoons oil to pan; swirl to coat. Combine cheese, milk, black pepper, eggs, and egg whites in a bowl, stirring with a whisk; add to pan. Cook 2½ minutes or until eggs are set but still soft, stirring constantly. Top bread slices with egg mixture and pepper mixture; sprinkle with parsley.

PER SERVING (serving size: 1 bread slice, ½ cup egg mixture, and ¼ cup pepper mixture):

Food Choices: 1½ Starches, 2 Nonstarchy Vegetables, 2 Lean Proteins, 1½ Fats

Calories 326; **Fat** 12.9g (sat 3.6g, mono 6.1g, poly 2.1g, trans 0g); **Protein** 19g; **Carbohydrate** 32g; **Fiber** 3g; **Sugars** 6g; **Cholesterol** 237mg; **Iron** 3mg; **Sodium** 434mg; **Potassium** 364mg; **Phosphorus** 242mg; **Calcium** 132mg

Avocado BLT

A healthful avocado spread replaces the traditional mayonnaise in this sandwich loaded with bacon, gourmet greens, and juicy, ripe tomatoes.

Hands-on Time: 9 minutes **Total Time:** 9 minutes **Serves:** 4

½ **cup Creamy Avocado Spread**

8 **(1-ounce) slices thin-sliced 15-grain bread, toasted**

2 **cups gourmet** salad greens

8 **(¼-inch-thick) slices** tomato

8 **center-cut bacon slices, cooked**

1 Spread 2 tablespoons Creamy Avocado Spread over 4 bread slices. Top each with ½ cup greens, 2 tomato slices, and 2 bacon slices. Top with remaining bread slices.

PER SERVING (serving size: 1 sandwich):

Food Choices: 2 Starches, 1 Medium-Fat Protein, 1 Fat

Calories 245; **Fat** 11g (sat 2.3g, mono 6.7g, poly 1.9g, trans 0g); **Protein** 12g; **Carbohydrate** 33g; **Fiber** 7g; **Sugars** 5g; **Cholesterol** 10mg; **Iron** 2mg; **Sodium** 409mg; **Potassium** 523mg; **Phosphorus** 191mg; **Calcium** 67mg

Creamy Avocado Spread

Hands-on Time: 5 minutes **Total Time:** 5 minutes **Serves:** 4

1 **peeled ripe** avocado, **coarsely mashed**

1 **tablespoon fresh** lemon **juice**

1 **garlic clove, minced**

¼ **teaspoon salt**

⅛ **teaspoon ground red pepper**

1 Combine all ingredients in a small bowl, stirring with a fork until blended.

PER SERVING (serving size: 2 tablespoons):

Food Choice: 1 Fat

Calories 65; **Fat** 5.7g (sat 0.6g, mono 3.9g, poly 0.8g, trans 0g); **Protein** 1g; **Carbohydrate** 4g; **Fiber** 1g; **Sugars** 0g; **Cholesterol** 0mg; **Iron** 0mg; **Sodium** 74mg; **Potassium** 252mg; **Phosphorus** 28mg; **Calcium** 2mg

Choosing **Whole-Grain** Bread

Whole-grain bread is the best choice because it's made using the entire grain of wheat, leaving the healthy bran, germ, and endosperm intact. These parts of the grain provide wholesome fiber, B vitamins, zinc, iron, and antioxidants. But labels can be deceiving at times. Here's how to choose the best whole-grain bread.

• "Whole grain" on the label doesn't mean the bread is 100% whole grain. Labeling laws allow products that contain a combination of whole grains and refined grains to say "whole grain" on the label.

• Read the ingredient label. To determine if bread is 100% whole wheat, the first ingredient should be "whole-wheat flour" or "100% whole-wheat flour." If the label says "wheat flour" or "enriched flour" this means there is white flour in the bread.

• Avoid added sugars, if you can. The vast majority of major brands of whole-wheat bread contain added sugars in the form of brown sugar, honey, molasses, high fructose corn syrup, evaporated cane syrup, or other sweeteners. Read the label, and choose a brand that has these ingredients listed toward the end of the ingredient list (ingredients are listed in descending order of predominance by weight).

• Check for locally made breads. Despite the gluten-free craze, there are artisanal bakers in many communities providing sugar-free handmade loaves as a wholesome alternative to factory-produced breads.

• Look for brands with added fiber. If you look to bread for a big portion of your daily fiber, many brands boost the roughage in whole-wheat bread by adding inulin, a natural fiber extracted from the chicory plant.

• It comes as a shock to many people once they have to start watching their sodium that bread can contain a significant amount of sodium. Bread has to have some salt in it or it tastes flat and flavorless. But if you're watching your sodium, check the Nutrition Facts, and choose a brand of bread that is lower in sodium.

6 Wholesome Loaves

Bread (values per slice)	Weight (oz)	Calories	Carbs (g)	Fiber (g)	Sodium (mg)
Nature's Own 100% Whole Wheat Bread	1	60	11	2	125
Arnold 100% Whole Wheat Bread	1.5	110	20	3	150
Arnold 12 Grain Bread	1.5	110	21	3	170
Nature's Own Double Fiber Wheat Bread	1	40	10	5	150
Rudi's Organic Bakery Double Fiber Bread	1.6	90	17	6	170
Pepperidge Farm Whole Grain Double Fiber Bread	1.5	100	22	6	120

Goat Cheese and Roasted Pepper Panini

The sweetness of roasted red bell peppers is an ideal foil to the pungency of the goat cheese and kalamata olives.

Hands-on Time: 11 minutes **Total Time:** 11 minutes **Serves:** 4

2½ **ounces goat cheese, softened**

12 **pitted kalamata olives, coarsely chopped**

8 **(1-ounce) slices sourdough bread**

16 **basil leaves**

2 **cups spring mix greens**

1 **cup bottled roasted red bell peppers**

Cooking spray

1 Combine cheese and olives in a small bowl, stirring until well blended. Spread about 1 tablespoon cheese mixture over each of 4 bread slices. Divide basil leaves, greens, and bell pepper into fourths; arrange over cheese mixture on each bread slice. Top with 4 bread slices.

2 Heat a large grill pan or skillet over medium heat. Coat pan with cooking spray. Add sandwiches to pan. Cover with a sheet of foil; top with a heavy skillet. Cook 3 minutes or until lightly browned. Turn sandwiches over; replace foil and skillet. Cook 3 minutes or until golden.

PER SERVING (serving size: 1 sandwich):

Food Choices: 1½ Starches, 1 Nonstarchy Vegetable, 1 Medium-Fat Protein

Calories 206; **Fat** 8.4g (sat 2.4g, mono 2.1g, poly 0.7g, trans 0g); **Protein** 6g; **Carbohydrate** 23g; **Fiber** 2g; **Sugars** 1g; **Cholesterol** 43mg; **Iron** 1mg; **Sodium** 433mg; **Potassium** 175mg; **Phosphorus** 128mg; **Calcium** 59mg

Southwestern White Bean Pita Pockets

Processing the beans helps to hold the remaining ingredients together. For variation, try black beans in place of white ones.

Hands-on Time: 20 minutes   **Total Time:** 20 minutes   **Serves:** 4

1½ tablespoons fresh lime juice, divided

2 teaspoons extra-virgin olive oil, divided

½ teaspoon ground cumin

¼ teaspoon salt, divided

¼ teaspoon ground red pepper

2 (15-ounce) cans organic white beans, rinsed, drained, and divided

½ cup diced plum tomato

¼ cup diced red bell pepper

¼ cup diced seeded peeled cucumber

3 tablespoons diced red onion

1 tablespoon chopped fresh cilantro

1 small jalapeño pepper, seeded and minced

2 (6-inch) pitas, cut in half

4 Boston lettuce leaves

2 ounces crumbled queso fresco (about ½ cup)

4 lime wedges

1 Place 1 tablespoon lime juice, 1 teaspoon oil, cumin, ⅛ teaspoon salt, ground red pepper, and 1 cup beans in a food processor; process until smooth, scraping sides of bowl as needed.

2 Place 1½ teaspoons lime juice, 1 teaspoon olive oil, ⅛ teaspoon salt, remaining beans, tomato, and next 5 ingredients (through jalapeño) in a bowl; toss well to combine.

3 Spread about 3½ tablespoons processed bean mixture inside each pita half. Place 1 lettuce leaf, about ¾ cup tomato mixture, and 2 tablespoons cheese inside each pita half. Serve with lime wedges.

PER SERVING (serving size: 1 pita half and 1 lime wedge):
Food Choices: 2 Starches, 1 Nonstarchy Vegetable, 1 Lean Protein, ½ Fat

Calories 265; **Fat** 6.1g (sat 1.9g, mono 2.4g, poly 0.4g, trans 0g); **Protein** 14g; **Carbohydrate** 39g; **Fiber** 7g; **Sugars** 4g; **Cholesterol** 10mg; **Iron** 4mg; **Sodium** 244mg; **Potassium** 510mg; **Phosphorus** 138mg; **Calcium** 166mg

Asparagus-and-Spinach Toasts with Fontina Cheese

Fontina, known for its mild flavor and creamy texture, melts easily, which makes it a perfect choice for cheese toast.

Hands-on Time: 14 minutes   **Total Time:** 14 minutes   **Serves:** 2

1 pound asparagus spears

Cooking spray

1 cup (¼-inch) diagonally sliced green onions

⅔ cup water

4 cups chopped fresh spinach

1 tablespoon thinly sliced fresh basil

¼ teaspoon freshly ground black pepper

1 ounce fontina or mozzarella cheese, shredded (about ¼ cup)

4 (1-ounce) slices whole-wheat bread, toasted

1 Snap off tough ends of asparagus. Heat a large skillet over medium-high heat; coat pan with cooking spray. Add onions; sauté 1 minute. Add asparagus and ⅔ cup water; bring to a boil. Reduce heat, and simmer 5 minutes. Add spinach; simmer 3 minutes. Stir in basil and pepper.

2 Sprinkle 1 tablespoon cheese over each toast slice; cut each slice diagonally in half. Place 4 toast halves on each of 2 plates. Spoon 1 cup asparagus mixture over each serving.

PER SERVING (serving size: 4 toast halves):

Food Choices: 2 Starches, 2 Nonstarchy Vegetables, 1 High-Fat Protein

Calories 268; **Fat** 6.8g (sat 3.1g, mono 1.6g, poly 1.4g, trans 0g); **Protein** 15g; **Carbohydrate** 39g; **Fiber** 11g; **Sugars** 8g; **Cholesterol** 16mg; **Iron** 6mg; **Sodium** 417mg; **Potassium** 1,054mg; **Phosphorus** 354mg; **Calcium** 239mg

Succotash Burritos

Fresh soybeans (edamame) are high in protein and fiber. They take the place of lima beans in this updated succotash recipe. Look for ready-to-eat, fully cooked edamame in the produce section of your supermarket.

Hands-on Time: 15 minutes   **Total Time**: 15 minutes   **Serves**: 6

2 teaspoons olive oil

1 (10-ounce) package (about 1¾ cups) refrigerated fully cooked shelled edamame

1½ cups frozen corn, thawed

½ cup chopped red bell pepper

¼ cup chopped red onion

1 garlic clove, minced

2 cups torn spinach

½ teaspoon ground cumin

¼ teaspoon salt

¼ teaspoon freshly ground black pepper

6 (8-inch) whole-wheat tortillas, warmed

6 tablespoons salsa

6 tablespoons shredded reduced-fat Monterey Jack cheese

Cilantro sprigs (optional)

1 Heat a large nonstick skillet over medium-high heat. Add oil to pan; swirl to coat. Add edamame and next 4 ingredients (through garlic). Sauté 5 minutes or until bell pepper and onion are tender. Add spinach, cumin, salt, and black pepper.

2 Spoon about ⅔ cup vegetable mixture down center of each tortilla. Top each with 1 tablespoon salsa and 1 tablespoon cheese. Fold top and bottom of each tortilla toward center; roll up burrito-style. Garnish with cilantro sprigs, if desired.

PER SERVING (serving size: 1 burrito):

Food Choices: 2 Starches, 1 Medium-Fat Protein, ½ Fat

Calories 251; **Fat** 7.8g (sat 1.1g, mono 3.4g, poly 2.2g, trans 0g); **Protein** 16g; **Carbohydrate** 31g; **Fiber** 12g; **Sugars** 5g; **Cholesterol** 0mg; **Iron** 3mg; **Sodium** 342mg; **Potassium** 584mg; **Phosphorus** 230mg; **Calcium** 188mg

ingredient pointer

Don't let its size fool you—the tiny cumin seed is loaded with vitamins and minerals. Among them are copper and iron, which help form red blood cells, and vitamins A, B, and C. Additionally, this small kernel packs a punch of flavor. Hot and earthy, a little goes a long way.

Grilled Salmon and Avocado Pitas

Avocado adds rich flavor and hunger-staving fiber, while wasabi mayonnaise elevates the heat in this Asian-inspired sandwich.

Hands-on Time: 25 minutes **Total Time:** 25 minutes **Serves:** 4

⅓ **cup canola mayonnaise**

1 **tablespoon wasabi paste**

2 **teaspoons rice vinegar**

1 **teaspoon lower-sodium soy sauce**

½ **pound salmon or arctic char fillet**

2 **teaspoons olive oil**

Cooking spray

2 **(6½-inch) whole-wheat pita rounds**

1 **cup loosely packed arugula**

1 **ripe avocado, diced (about 1 cup)**

1 **medium tomato, seeded and diced**

1 Preheat grill to medium-high heat.

2 In a small bowl, combine mayonnaise, wasabi paste, vinegar, and soy sauce. Set aside.

3 Brush salmon with olive oil. Place salmon on grill rack coated with cooking spray; grill 3 to 4 minutes on each side or until desired degree of doneness. Remove from grill, and quickly toast pita rounds on grill, about 2 minutes, turning once.

4 Cut or flake salmon into 1-inch cubes. Cut pita rounds in half; spread wasabi mayonnaise on insides. Fill each pita half with salmon, arugula, avocado, and tomato.

PER SERVING (serving size: 1 pita half):

Food Choices: 1½ Starches, 2 Lean Proteins, 2 Fats

Calories 321; **Fat** 18.1g (sat 2.3g, mono 10.6g, poly 4.2g, trans 0g); **Protein** 16g; **Carbohydrate** 23g; **Fiber** 5g; **Sugars** 2g; **Cholesterol** 29mg; **Iron** 2mg; **Sodium** 440mg; **Potassium** 608mg; **Phosphorus** 263mg; **Calcium** 27mg

ingredient pointer

You can find prepared wasabi paste packed in a tube in the Asian food aisle of most grocery stores, or you can mix wasabi powder with just enough water to make a paste.

Open-Faced Salmon Sandwiches with Tomato and Avocado

Coarsely chop leftover salmon and combine with any remaining mayo mixture. Top toasted bread and garnish with arugula for a quick lunch.

Hands-on Time: 23 minutes   **Total Time**: 23 minutes   **Serves**: 4

4 (1-ounce) slices diagonally cut ciabatta or rustic Italian bread

2 teaspoons olive oil

4 (4-ounce) salmon fillets, skinned (about ¾ inch thick)

¼ cup canola mayonnaise

2 tablespoons water

1 tablespoon minced fresh chives, divided

1½ teaspoons Dijon mustard

4 Bibb lettuce leaves

4 (½-inch-thick) slices tomato, halved

½ peeled ripe avocado, cut into 8 slices

4 lemon wedges

1 Preheat broiler.

2 Arrange bread slices on a baking sheet; broil 1 minute on each side or until toasted.

3 Heat a large nonstick skillet over medium heat. Add oil to pan; swirl to coat. Add fillets to pan; cook 4 minutes on each side or until desired degree of doneness.

4 Combine canola mayonnaise, 2 tablespoons water, 2 teaspoons minced chives, and Dijon mustard in a small bowl, stirring with a whisk. Spread mayonnaise mixture over bread slices; top each with 1 lettuce leaf, 1 halved tomato slice, 2 avocado slices, and 1 fish fillet. Sprinkle with 1 teaspoon chives. Serve with lemon wedges.

PER SERVING (serving size: 1 sandwich and 1 lemon wedge):
Food Choices: 1 Starch, 1 Nonstarchy Vegetable, 3 Lean Proteins, 1 Fat
Calories 345; **Fat** 17.3g (sat 2.3g, mono 9.5g, poly 4.4g, trans 0g); **Protein** 27g; **Carbohydrate** 19g; **Fiber** 3g; **Sugars** 1g; **Cholesterol** 60mg; **Iron** 2mg; **Sodium** 402mg; **Potassium** 598mg; **Phosphorus** 349mg; **Calcium** 21mg

Curry Chicken Wraps with Nectarine Chutney

Add a bit of exotic flavor to a basic grilled chicken wrap by marinating the chicken in a yogurt-curry mixture and topping it with nectarine chutney.

Hands-on Time: 20 minutes **Total Time:** 2 hours, 20 minutes **Serves:** 6

1 cup plain fat-free yogurt

3 tablespoons curry powder

3 tablespoons fresh lime juice, divided

4 (4-ounce) skinless, boneless chicken breast halves

10 cilantro sprigs

6 garlic cloves, crushed

2 cups chopped nectarines

¾ cup finely sliced green onions

¼ cup low-sugar apricot jam

2 tablespoons chopped fresh cilantro

2 tablespoons chopped fresh mint

1 tablespoon grated peeled fresh ginger

1 tablespoon cider vinegar

¼ teaspoon ground red pepper

Cooking spray

6 (1.9-ounce) light whole-wheat flatbreads

24 (⅛-inch-thick) slices cucumber

1½ cups loosely packed baby arugula

1 cup vertically sliced red onion

1 Combine yogurt, curry powder, and 1 tablespoon lime juice in a large heavy-duty zip-top plastic bag; squeeze bag to mix. Cut 3 shallow slits in each chicken breast. Add chicken, cilantro sprigs, and garlic to bag, squeezing to coat chicken. Seal and marinate in refrigerator 2 hours, turning occasionally.

2 Combine 2 tablespoons lime juice, nectarines, and next 7 ingredients (through red pepper) in a bowl; toss gently. Cover and set aside.

3 Preheat grill to medium-high heat.

4 Remove chicken from bag; discard marinade. Place chicken on grill rack coated with cooking spray. Cover and grill 4 minutes on each side or until chicken is done. Let stand 5 minutes. Cut chicken across grain into thin slices.

5 Place ⅓ cup nectarine chutney in center of each flatbread. Divide chicken among flatbreads. Top each with 4 cucumber slices, ¼ cup arugula, and about 2½ tablespoons red onion; roll up.

PER SERVING (serving size: 1 wrap):

Food Choices: 2 Starches, 1 Nonstarchy Vegetable, 2 Lean Proteins

Calories 265; **Fat** 4.9g (sat 0.5g, mono 0.9g, poly 1g, trans 0g); **Protein** 25g; **Carbohydrate** 38g; **Fiber** 8g; **Sugars** 8g; **Cholesterol** 49mg; **Iron** 3mg; **Sodium** 415mg; **Potassium** 566mg; **Phosphorus** 256mg; **Calcium** 57mg

Open-Faced Chicken Sandwiches with Artichoke Pesto

Be sure to look for artichoke hearts that are canned in brine, not oil.

Hands-on Time: 20 minutes   **Total Time:** 20 minutes   **Serves:** 6

3 (8-ounce) skinless, boneless chicken breast halves

½ teaspoon freshly ground black pepper, divided

⅛ teaspoon salt

Cooking spray

6 ounces drained canned artichoke hearts

2 ounces Parmigiano-Reggiano cheese, shaved and divided (about ½ cup)

2 tablespoons pine nuts

2 tablespoons canola mayonnaise

2 teaspoons olive oil

3 garlic cloves

6 (1-ounce) slices multigrain bread

3 tablespoons chopped fresh flat-leaf parsley

1 Preheat broiler.

2 Cut each chicken breast half in half lengthwise to form 2 cutlets. Sprinkle with ¼ teaspoon pepper and salt. Heat a grill pan over medium-high heat. Coat pan with cooking spray. Add chicken to pan; cook 4 minutes on each side or until done.

3 Place artichokes, 3 tablespoons cheese, nuts, mayonnaise, oil, ¼ teaspoon pepper, and garlic in a mini food processor; pulse until coarsely ground.

4 Place bread slices on a baking sheet; broil 1 minute on each side. Spread 2½ tablespoons pesto on each slice. Slice chicken; place 3 ounces on each bread slice. Top with remaining cheese and parsley.

PER SERVING (serving size: 1 sandwich):

Food Choices: 1 Starch, 1 Nonstarchy Vegetable, 3 Lean Proteins, 1 Fat

Calories 295; **Fat** 11g (sat 2.8g, mono 4.1g, poly 2.1, trans 0g); **Protein** 31g; **Carbohydrate** 18g; **Fiber** 4g; **Sugars** 3g; **Cholesterol** 71mg; **Iron** 2mg; **Sodium** 406mg; **Potassium** 365mg; **Phosphorus** 319mg; **Calcium** 215mg

Rosemary-Chicken Panini with Spinach and Sun-Dried Tomatoes

Here's a delicious solution to the busy weeknight dinner dilemma. This excellent sandwich is loaded with fresh flavor and is guaranteed to satisfy any appetite.

Hands-on Time: 32 minutes **Total Time:** 62 minutes **Serves:** 4

4 (3-ounce) chicken cutlets

1 teaspoon chopped fresh rosemary

2 teaspoons extra-virgin olive oil

¼ cup chopped drained oil-packed sun-dried tomato

⅛ teaspoon crushed red pepper

8 garlic cloves, thinly sliced

1 (6-ounce) package fresh baby spinach

Cooking spray

⅛ teaspoon freshly ground black pepper

8 (¾-ounce) slices country-style Italian bread

2 ounces fresh mozzarella cheese, shredded (about ½ cup)

1 Place chicken in a large zip-top plastic bag; sprinkle rosemary over chicken. Seal bag, and marinate in refrigerator 30 minutes.

2 Heat a large nonstick skillet over medium-high heat. Add 2 teaspoons oil to pan; swirl to coat. Add sun-dried tomato, red pepper, and garlic; sauté 1 minute or until garlic begins to brown. Add spinach; cook 1 minute or until spinach barely wilts. Set aside.

3 Heat a grill pan over medium-high heat; coat with cooking spray. Remove chicken from bag; discard marinade. Sprinkle chicken with black pepper. Cook chicken 3 minutes on each side or until done. Remove chicken from pan; keep pan on medium-high heat.

4 Top each of 4 bread slices with 1 tablespoon cheese, 1 chicken cutlet, one-fourth of spinach mixture, 1 additional tablespoon cheese, and 4 bread slices.

5 Recoat grill pan with cooking spray. Arrange 2 sandwiches in pan. Place a cast-iron or heavy skillet on top of sandwiches; press gently to flatten. Cook 4 minutes on each side (leave pan on sandwiches while they cook). Repeat procedure with remaining 2 sandwiches. Cut each sandwich in half; serve immediately.

PER SERVING (serving size: 1 sandwich):

Food Choices: 1½ Starches, 1 Nonstarchy Vegetable, 3 Lean Proteins, 1 Fat

Calories 308; **Fat** 10.6g (sat 3.3g, mono 3.2g, poly 1.4g, trans 0g); **Protein** 26g; **Carbohydrate** 26g; **Fiber** 3g; **Sugars** 2g; **Cholesterol** 66mg; **Iron** 3mg; **Sodium** 409mg; **Potassium** 745mg; **Phosphorus** 334mg; **Calcium** 95mg

Turkey Pitas with Tahini-Yogurt Sauce

If you can't find tahini, substitute an equal amount of peanut butter to make the yogurt sauce.

Hands-on Time: 15 minutes   **Total Time:** 15 minutes   **Serves:** 4

Cooking spray
1 teaspoon ground cumin
1 teaspoon paprika
¼ teaspoon ground turmeric
⅛ teaspoon kosher salt
3 (4-ounce) turkey cutlets
4 (6-inch) whole-wheat pitas
1 cup thinly sliced cucumber
1 cup thinly sliced red bell pepper
2 tablespoons tahini (sesame seed paste)
2 tablespoons plain fat-free yogurt
1½ tablespoons fresh lemon juice
1 tablespoon water
½ teaspoon freshly ground black pepper

1 Heat a grill pan over medium-high heat. Coat pan with cooking spray. Combine cumin, paprika, turmeric, and salt in a small bowl. Rub spice mixture over turkey. Add turkey to pan; cook 3 minutes on each side or until done. Remove turkey from pan.

2 Cut off top third of each pita; reserve for another use. Add pitas to pan; grill 30 seconds on each side or until marked. Cut turkey into slices. Divide turkey, cucumber, and bell pepper among pitas.

3 Combine tahini and remaining ingredients in a small bowl, stirring with a whisk. Serve tahini mixture with sandwiches.

PER SERVING (serving size: 1 filled pita and about 1½ tablespoons sauce):

Food Choices: 2 Starches, 1 Nonstarchy Vegetable, 3 Lean Proteins

Calories 307; **Fat** 6.1g (sat 1g, mono 1.7g, poly 2.4g, trans 0g); **Protein** 29g; **Carbohydrate** 37g; **Fiber** 6g; **Sugars** 2g; **Cholesterol** 53mg; **Iron** 3mg; **Sodium** 412mg; **Potassium** 504mg; **Phosphorus** 359mg; **Calcium** 70mg

Turkey Cobb Salad Roll-Ups

The original Cobb Salad made its debut at the Brown Derby Restaurant in Hollywood. It was created as a way to use a variety of leftovers—turkey, tomatoes, onions, avocado, blue cheese, and Roquefort dressing. This is a lightened version with less fat and more fiber.

Hands-on Time: 15 minutes   **Total Time:** 15 minutes   **Serves:** 4

2 cups shredded romaine lettuce

1 cup chopped seeded tomato (1 medium)

¼ cup chopped green onions (2 medium)

3 tablespoons blue cheese–flavored yogurt dressing

½ teaspoon freshly ground black pepper

8 ounces thinly sliced roast turkey

1 ripe avocado, diced

4 (1.9-ounce) multigrain flatbreads with flax

1 Combine first 7 ingredients in a medium bowl. Spoon turkey mixture onto flatbreads; roll up.

PER SERVING (serving size: 1 wrap):

Food Choices: 1½ Starches, 1 Nonstarchy Vegetable, 3 Lean Proteins, 1 Fat

Calories 301; **Fat** 13.3g (sat 2.3g, mono 6.4g, poly 3.4g, trans 0g); **Protein** 29g; **Carbohydrate** 25g; **Fiber** 12g; **Sugars** 2g; **Cholesterol** 53mg; **Iron** 2mg; **Sodium** 381mg; **Potassium** 444mg; **Phosphorus** 146mg; **Calcium** 83mg

Greek-Seasoned Steak Sandwiches

Serve these hearty sandwiches with a side of crisp carrot and celery sticks and light ranch dressing for dipping. Make breadcrumbs with the parts of pita you cut off by pulsing in a food processor. You can freeze them for up to a couple of months.

Hands-on Time: 15 minutes   **Total Time**: 45 minutes   **Serves**: 4

3 tablespoons red wine vinegar, divided

4 teaspoons extra-virgin olive oil, divided

1 tablespoon minced fresh garlic

1 teaspoon dried oregano

1 12-ounce flank steak, trimmed

¼ teaspoon kosher salt, divided

⅜ teaspoon freshly ground black pepper, divided

Cooking spray

2 tablespoons plain fat-free Greek yogurt

¼ teaspoon Dijon mustard

4 (6-inch) whole-wheat pitas

12 small romaine lettuce leaves

4 thin red onion slices

1 cucumber, thinly sliced

1 tomato, cut into 12 slices

1 Combine 2 tablespoons vinegar, 1 teaspoon oil, garlic, and oregano in a large zip-top plastic bag. Add steak to bag; seal. Let stand at room temperature 20 minutes, turning once.

2 Heat a grill pan over medium-high heat. Remove steak from bag; discard marinade. Sprinkle ⅛ teaspoon salt and ¼ teaspoon pepper over both sides of steak. Coat pan with cooking spray. Place steak in pan; grill 5 minutes on each side or until desired degree of doneness. Remove steak from pan; let stand 10 minutes. Cut steak across grain into thin slices.

3 Combine 1 tablespoon vinegar, 1 tablespoon oil, ⅛ teaspoon salt, ⅛ teaspoon pepper, yogurt, and mustard in a bowl, stirring with a whisk.

4 Cut off top third of each pita; reserve for another use. Arrange 3 lettuce leaves, 1 onion slice, one-fourth of cucumber slices, 3 tomato slices, and one-fourth of steak in each pita; top each sandwich with 1 tablespoon yogurt mixture.

PER SERVING (serving size: 1 sandwich):

Food Choices: 1½ Starches, 1 Nonstarchy Vegetable, 2 Medium-Fat Proteins

Calories 313; **Fat** 11.9g (sat 3.3g, mono 5.8g, poly 1.2g, trans 0g); **Protein** 23g; **Carbohydrate** 29g; **Fiber** 5g; **Sugars** 3g; **Cholesterol** 51mg; **Iron** 3mg; **Sodium** 397mg; **Potassium** 484mg; **Phosphorus** 234mg; **Calcium** 132mg

Quinoa-Stuffed Kale Rolls
with Goat Cheese, page 224

Satisfying Suppers

Looking for simple and delicious ideas for diabetes-friendly dinners? From pizzas, pastas, and casseroles to stir fries and grilled meats, these tasty dishes won't disappoint.

Strawberry, Pistachio, and Goat Cheese Pizza

This dish is a refreshing departure from traditional pizza. Substitute your favorite soft cheese or greens.

Hands-on Time: 8 minutes   **Total Time:** 16 minutes   **Serves:** 6

1 pound refrigerated fresh pizza dough

2 ounces crumbled goat cheese (about ¼ cup)

1 cup sliced fresh strawberries

1 cup trimmed watercress

½ teaspoon extra-virgin olive oil

½ teaspoon fresh lemon juice

Dash of freshly ground black pepper

1 ounce Parmigiano-Reggiano cheese, shaved (about ¼ cup)

3 tablespoons shelled dry-roasted, unsalted pistachios, chopped

1 Preheat oven to 425°.

2 Roll dough into a 14-inch circle on a floured surface. Place dough on a baking sheet. Bake at 425° for 8 minutes. Remove from oven; arrange goat cheese over crust.

3 Combine strawberries, watercress, olive oil, juice, and black pepper; toss gently to coat. Arrange strawberry mixture over goat cheese. Sprinkle pizza with Parmigiano-Reggiano and nuts. Cut into 12 wedges. Serve immediately.

PER SERVING (serving size: 2 wedges):

Food Choices: 2½ Starches, 1 Medium-Fat Protein

Calories 269; **Fat** 6.9g (sat 2.3g, mono 2.5g, poly 1g, trans 0g); **Protein** 12g; **Carbohydrate** 39g; **Fiber** 6g; **Sugars** 2g; **Cholesterol** 8mg; **Iron** 1mg; **Sodium** 446mg; **Potassium** 190mg; **Phosphorus** 146mg; **Calcium** 96mg

small change, big result

Instead of piling on meat and cheese, fresh greens and strawberries make healthy, flavorful toppings for this pizza. Slivers of Parmesan add richness and pistachios add crunch, so you won't miss the typical toppings and you'll cut saturated fat and calories.

Steak Florentine

This satisfying beef dish hails from Florence, Italy. Often, this traditional recipe is made with a thick cut of rib-eye, but we've substituted filet mignon. A paste of fresh garlic, rosemary, and olive oil infuses the steaks with flavor.

Hands-on Time: 17 minutes   **Total Time:** 22 minutes   **Serves:** 4

2½ **teaspoons chopped fresh rosemary**

2 **teaspoons olive oil**

4 **garlic cloves, peeled**

½ **teaspoon freshly ground black pepper**

¼ **teaspoon salt**

4 **(4-ounce) beef tenderloin steaks (1½ inches thick), trimmed**

Cooking spray

2 **cups trimmed** arugula

2½ **cups hot cooked** brown rice

4 lemon **wedges**

Rosemary leaves (optional)

1 Preheat grill to medium-high heat.

2 Place first 3 ingredients in a blender; process until mixture forms a paste, stopping blender and scraping down sides frequently.

3 Sprinkle pepper and salt over both sides of steaks; spread garlic paste over both sides of steaks.

4 Place steaks on grill rack coated with cooking spray, and grill 5 minutes on each side or until desired degree of doneness. Remove from grill; let stand 5 minutes. Serve steak over arugula with rice. Squeeze a lemon wedge over each serving and garnish with rosemary, if desired.

PER SERVING (serving size: ½ cup arugula, 1 steak, and about ½ cup rice):

Food Choices: 2 Starches, 1 Nonstarchy Vegetable, 3 Lean Proteins

Calories 308; **Fat** 10.9g (sat 3.4g, mono 5g, poly 1g, trans 0g); **Protein** 22g; **Carbohydrate** 38g; **Fiber** 3g; **Sugars** 1g; **Cholesterol** 54mg; **Iron** 3mg; **Sodium** 196mg; **Potassium** 363mg; **Phosphorus** 266mg; **Calcium** 41mg

small change, big result

Rib-eye steaks are well-marbled, and therefore high in fat and saturated fat. By switching to lean tenderloin in this recipe, you'll save nearly 5 grams of total fat and 2 grams of saturated fat in each serving. Just be sure not to overcook this lean cut to keep it juicy and tender.

Flank Steak and Edamame with Wasabi Dressing

Wasabi paste is an intensely hot, green paste that tastes similar to horseradish and is sometimes referred to as Japanese horseradish.

Hands-on Time: 20 minutes   **Total Time:** 20 minutes   **Serves:** 4

1 (1-pound) flank steak, trimmed

2 tablespoons plus 2 teaspoons lower-sodium soy sauce, divided

½ teaspoon freshly ground black pepper

⅛ teaspoon salt

Cooking spray

2 teaspoons dark sesame oil

1 tablespoon ground ginger

2 teaspoons bottled minced garlic

1 (10-ounce) package frozen shelled edamame (green soybeans), thawed

¼ cup rice vinegar

2 teaspoons wasabi paste

1 Heat a grill pan over medium-high heat. Rub steak with 2 teaspoons soy sauce; sprinkle with pepper and salt. Coat pan with cooking spray. Add steak to pan. Cook 5 minutes on each side or until desired degree of doneness. Remove from pan; let stand 10 minutes. Cut steak diagonally across grain into ½-inch-thick slices.

2 While steak stands, heat a large nonstick skillet over medium heat. Add oil to pan; swirl to coat. Add ginger and garlic; sauté 1 minute, stirring occasionally. Add 2 tablespoons soy sauce and edamame to pan; cook 2 minutes.

3 Combine vinegar and wasabi paste in a bowl, stirring until smooth. Serve steak over edamame mixture, and drizzle with vinegar mixture.

PER SERVING (serving size: ½ cup edamame mixture, 3 ounces steak, and 1 tablespoon vinegar mixture):

Food Choices: ½ Starch, 4 Lean Proteins, 1 Fat

Calories 282; **Fat** 12.4g (sat 3.1g, mono 3.6g, poly 3.9g, trans 0g); **Protein** 32g; **Carbohydrate** 9g; **Fiber** 3g; **Sugars** 5g; **Cholesterol** 65mg; **Iron** 4mg; **Sodium** 430mg; **Potassium** 824mg; **Phosphorus** 351mg; **Calcium** 49mg

Thai Basil Beef with Rice Noodles

Sure to become a fast favorite, this flavorful Thai dish boasts multiple Power Foods. Use kitchen shears or a knife and fork to chop the rice noodles into smaller pieces, which will make them easier to toss with the curry–lime juice dressing.

Hands-on Time: 18 minutes **Total Time:** 18 minutes **Serves:** 4

8 cups water

1 (1-pound) flank steak, trimmed

1½ cups (1½-inch-long) slices fresh asparagus (about 1 pound)

4 ounces wide rice stick noodles (bánh pho)

3 tablespoons fresh lime juice

1 tablespoon fish sauce

½ teaspoon Thai red curry paste

1 cup cherry tomatoes, halved

½ cup thinly sliced fresh basil

1 Heat a large grill pan over medium-high heat.

2 While pan heats, bring 8 cups water to a boil in a large saucepan.

3 Add steak to grill pan; grill 5 minutes on each side or until desired degree of doneness. Remove from pan; let stand 5 minutes. Cut steak across grain into thin slices.

4 While steak cooks, add asparagus to boiling water; cook 2 minutes. Remove asparagus with a slotted spoon. Add noodles to boiling water; cook 3 minutes or until done. Drain; rinse well. Cut noodles into smaller pieces; place in a medium bowl.

5 While noodles cook, combine lime juice, fish sauce, and curry paste in a large bowl. Add one-half of lime mixture to noodles; toss to coat. Add steak, asparagus, tomatoes, and basil to remaining lime mixture in large bowl; toss to combine. Serve steak mixture over noodles.

PER SERVING (serving size: ½ cup noodles and 1 cup steak mixture):

Food Choices: 1½ Starches, 1 Nonstarchy Vegetable, 3 Lean Proteins

Calories 280; **Fat** 6.9g (sat 2.8g, mono 2.7g, poly 0.3g, trans 0g); **Protein** 25g; **Carbohydrate** 29g; **Fiber** 2g; **Sugars** 2g; **Cholesterol** 65mg; **Iron** 4mg; **Sodium** 421mg; **Potassium** 508mg; **Phosphorus** 220mg; **Calcium** 48mg

Horseradish-Garlic Flank Steak with Lemony Arugula

Horseradish gives grilled flank steak a tangy kick of spiciness.

Hands-on Time: 24 minutes   **Total Time**: 24 minutes   **Serves**: 4

2 tablespoons prepared horseradish

1 tablespoon extra-virgin olive oil

¼ teaspoon salt

4 garlic cloves, minced

1 (1-pound) flank steak, trimmed

Cooking spray

1 tablespoon fresh lemon juice

1 tablespoon water

1 teaspoon extra-virgin olive oil

½ teaspoon Dijon mustard

¼ teaspoon freshly ground black pepper

1 (5-ounce) bag arugula

2 cups hot cooked brown basmati rice

1 ounce Parmesan cheese, shaved (about ¼ cup)

1 Preheat grill to medium-high heat.

2 Combine first 4 ingredients in a bowl, stirring with a whisk. Spread mixture onto both sides of steak.

3 Place steak on grill rack coated with cooking spray. Grill 4 to 5 minutes on each side or until desired degree of doneness. Remove from grill; let stand 5 minutes.

4 While steak stands, combine lemon juice, 1 tablespoon water, 1 teaspoon olive oil, mustard, and black pepper in a large bowl, stirring with a whisk. Add arugula; toss to coat. Cut steak diagonally across grain into thin slices. Serve steak over arugula mixture with rice and top with cheese.

PER SERVING (serving size: 1 cup arugula mixture, 3 ounces steak, ½ cup rice, and 1 tablespoon cheese):

Food Choices: 2 Starches, 1 Nonstarchy Vegetable, 3 Lean Proteins, 1½ Fats

Calories 386; **Fat** 14.4g (sat 4.2g, mono 6.1g, poly 0.9g, trans 0g); **Protein** 31g; **Carbohydrate** 35g; **Fiber** 3g; **Sugars** 3g; **Cholesterol** 75mg; **Iron** 3mg; **Sodium** 369mg; **Potassium** 606mg; **Phosphorus** 385mg; **Calcium** 183mg

Individual Salsa Meat Loaves

Making meat loaf in single-serving portions reduces the cooking time by half and keeps the meat juicy.

Hands-on Time: 10 minutes   **Total Time:** 40 minutes   **Serves:** 4

2 large egg whites
½ cup plus 2 tablespoons
   fresh salsa, divided
⅓ cup quick-cooking oats
¼ cup ketchup, divided
1 pound ground sirloin
Cooking spray

1 Preheat oven to 350°.

2 Place egg whites in a large bowl, stirring well with a whisk. Stir in ½ cup salsa, oats, and 2 tablespoons ketchup. Add beef; mix well. Divide beef mixture into 4 equal portions, shaping each into an oval-shaped loaf. Coat a foil-lined rimmed baking sheet with cooking spray. Place loaves on prepared pan.

3 Bake at 350° for 30 minutes or until done.

4 Combine 2 tablespoons salsa and 2 tablespoons ketchup in a small bowl; spread mixture over loaves.

PER SERVING (serving size: 1 meat loaf):

Food Choices: ½ Starch, 3 Lean Proteins

Calories 190; **Fat** 6g (sat 2.1g, mono 2.1g, poly 0.7g, trans 0g); **Protein** 25g; **Carbohydrate** 11g; **Fiber** 2g; **Sugars** 5g; **Cholesterol** 60mg; **Iron** 2mg; **Sodium** 341mg; **Potassium** 472mg; **Phosphorus** 217mg; **Calcium** 7mg

ingredient pointer

Quick-cooking oats, sometimes called "1-minute oats," are rolled oats that have been chopped into tinier pieces. They're typically less chewy than the rolled kind but cook more quickly. They can easily be substituted for the rolled variety.

Soba with Marinated Beef and Tomatoes

You can substitute whole-wheat uncooked spaghetti or vermicelli noodles for the soba. Sprinkle with toasted sesame seeds and additional sliced green onions, if you like.

Hands-on Time: 15 minutes **Total Time:** 20 minutes **Serves:** 6

- **1 (1-pound) flank steak, trimmed**
- **1 teaspoon cornstarch**
- **1 teaspoon water**
- **½ teaspoon lower-sodium soy sauce**
- **10 ounces uncooked** soba **(buckwheat noodles)**
- **1 teaspoon canola oil, divided**
- **½ cup (1-inch) sliced green onions**
- **½ cup fat-free, lower-sodium chicken broth**
- **4 plum** tomatoes, **quartered (about ½ pound)**
- **1 teaspoon oyster sauce**
- **1 garlic clove, crushed**

1 Cut steak diagonally across grain into thin slices. Combine cornstarch, 1 teaspoon water, and soy sauce in a large zip-top plastic bag. Add steak; seal and toss well to coat. Marinate in refrigerator 10 minutes.

2 While steak is marinating, cook noodles according to package directions. Drain noodles, and keep warm. Remove steak from bag, discarding marinade.

3 Heat a large nonstick skillet over medium-high heat. Add 1 teaspoon oil to pan; swirl to coat. Add green onions, and sauté 30 seconds. Add steak, and cook 4 minutes or until steak loses its pink color. Remove steak from pan, and keep warm.

4 Add chicken broth and tomatoes to pan, and stir well. Cover, reduce heat, and cook 3 minutes or until thick. Stir in steak, oyster sauce, and garlic, and cook 4 minutes or until thoroughly heated. Combine beef mixture with noodles in a large bowl, and toss well.

PER SERVING (serving size: 1 cup):

Food Choices: 2 Starches, 1 Nonstarchy Vegetable, 2 Lean Proteins

Calories 286; **Fat** 5.6g (sat 1.5g, mono 1.9g, poly 0.4g, trans 0g); **Protein** 22g; **Carbohydrate** 35g; **Fiber** 3g; **Sugars** 2g; **Cholesterol** 44mg; **Iron** 3mg; **Sodium** 447mg; **Potassium** 497mg; **Phosphorus** 280mg; **Calcium** 29mg

Quick Curried Beef

This mildly spicy and slightly sweet meal will satisfy fans of Asian-inspired flavors.

Hands-on Time: 20 minutes   **Total Time:** 20 minutes   **Serves:** 4

1 (3½-ounce) bag boil-in-bag long-grain rice
1 (1-pound) flank steak, trimmed
Cooking spray
½ cup (1-inch) sliced green onions
1 garlic clove, minced
1 tablespoon ground coriander
1 teaspoon ground cumin
¼ teaspoon salt
¼ teaspoon ground turmeric
1 (14.5-ounce) can diced tomatoes, drained

1 Cook rice according to package directions, omitting salt and fat.

2 While rice cooks, cut steak diagonally across grain into thin slices.

3 Heat a large skillet over medium-high heat. Coat pan with cooking spray. Add onions and garlic; sauté 2 minutes. Add coriander, cumin, salt, and turmeric; sauté 1 minute.

4 Add steak; sauté 6 minutes or until done. Add tomatoes, and reduce heat to low. Cook 3 minutes or until thoroughly heated. Serve over rice.

PER SERVING (serving size: ½ cup rice and 1 cup beef mixture):

Food Choices: 1½ Starches, 1 Nonstarchy Vegetable, 3 Lean Proteins

Calories 289; **Fat** 6.5g (sat 2.3g, mono 2.2g, poly 0.3g, trans 0g); **Protein** 27g; **Carbohydrate** 28g; **Fiber** 3g; **Sugars** 3g; **Cholesterol** 68mg; **Iron** 4mg; **Sodium** 251mg; **Potassium** 538mg; **Phosphorus** 265mg; **Calcium** 67mg

ingredient pointer

Flank steak is a tender, flavorful, and very lean cut of beef. It is a thin steak from the abdomen of the cow and is sometimes called London broil. The trick to ensuring tenderness is to slice this steak across the grain. Look for the long fibers running lengthwise on the steak, and slice the steak across the width of the steak, not the length.

Smothered Pepper Steak

Round out the meal with a side of brown rice or a simple salad of mixed greens.

Hands-on Time: 14 minutes   **Total Time:** 29 minutes   **Serves:** 4

3 tablespoons all-purpose flour

4 (4-ounce) ground sirloin patties

¼ teaspoon freshly ground black pepper

Cooking spray

1 (16-ounce) package frozen bell pepper stir-fry

1 (14.5-ounce) can unsalted diced tomatoes with basil, garlic, and oregano (such as Hunt's), undrained

2 tablespoons lower-sodium soy sauce

1 Place flour in a shallow dish. Dredge sirloin patties in flour; sprinkle patties with black pepper. Heat a large skillet over medium-high heat; coat pan with cooking spray. Coat patties with cooking spray. Add patties to pan; cook 3 minutes on each side or until lightly browned.

2 Add stir-fry, tomatoes, and soy sauce to meat in pan; bring to a boil. Reduce heat; simmer 15 minutes or until meat is done and pepper mixture is slightly thick.

PER SERVING (serving size: 1 sirloin patty and ¾ cup sauce):
Food Choices: ½ Starch, 2 Nonstarchy Vegetables, 3 Lean Proteins
Calories 246; **Fat** 8g (sat 2g, mono 2g, poly 0.5g, trans 0g); **Protein** 25g; **Carbohydrate** 18g; **Fiber** 2g; **Sugars** 9g; **Cholesterol** 60mg; **Iron** 3mg; **Sodium** 286mg; **Potassium** 844mg; **Phosphorus** 245mg; **Calcium** 52mg

small change, big result

Typically stir-fried with a hefty amount of oil, this pepper steak is made with lean sirloin and prepared with cooking spray to cut fat and calories. Using frozen stir-fry peppers and canned tomatoes adds a generous amount of low-carb veggies—and makes it easy enough for the busiest weeknight.

Curried Beef with Peanut-Coconut Sauce

Peanuts are low on the glycemic index and are loaded with protein and fiber. Using peanut butter is a creative and nutritious way to thicken sauces and spreads. Just be sure to use it in moderation, as it's also high in calories and fat.

Hands-on Time: 25 minutes   **Total Time:** 50 minutes   **Serves:** 6

2 tablespoons water

1 tablespoon red curry paste

1 (1½-pound) boneless top sirloin steak, trimmed

1 cup uncooked jasmine rice

2 teaspoons sesame oil, divided

½ pound asparagus spears, diagonally cut into 1-inch pieces (about 2 cups)

1 cup snow peas, cut in half diagonally

½ cup shredded carrot (about 1 medium)

¾ cup fat-free, lower-sodium chicken broth (such as Swanson)

¾ cup chopped green onions

⅓ cup creamy peanut butter

⅓ cup light coconut milk

2 tablespoons fresh lime juice

1 tablespoon lower-sodium soy sauce

1 Combine 2 tablespoons water and curry paste in a large bowl; stir with a whisk until smooth. Cut steak diagonally across grain into ¼-inch-thick slices; cut slices into thin strips. Add steak to curry paste, tossing to coat. Cover and marinate in refrigerator 30 minutes.

2 Cook rice according to package directions, omitting salt and fat.

3 While rice cooks, heat a large nonstick skillet over medium-high heat. Add ½ teaspoon oil to pan; swirl to coat. Add half of steak; sauté 3 minutes or until steak is done. Remove steak from pan; keep warm. Repeat procedure with ½ teaspoon oil and remaining steak.

4 Heat pan over medium-high heat. Add 1 teaspoon oil to pan; swirl to coat. Add asparagus, snow peas, and carrot; sauté 5 minutes or until vegetables are crisp-tender. Stir in broth and remaining 5 ingredients (through soy sauce); cook 3 minutes, stirring constantly. Return steak to pan; cook 2 minutes or until thoroughly heated. Serve over hot cooked rice.

PER SERVING (serving size: about ½ cup rice and ¾ cup curried beef mixture):

Food Choices: 1½ Starches, 1 Nonstarchy Vegetable, 3 Lean Proteins, ½ Fat

Calories 301; **Fat** 9.7g (sat 3.0g, mono 4.1g, poly 1.8g, trans 0g); **Protein** 26g; **Carbohydrate** 28g; **Fiber** 3g; **Sugars** 3g; **Cholesterol** 54mg; **Iron** 3mg; **Sodium** 291mg; **Potassium** 671mg; **Phosphorus** 201mg; **Calcium** 25mg

3 Must-Have
Skillets

Skillets are the everyday workhorses of the kitchen, whether you're cooking a quick weeknight meal or preparing an elaborate holiday dinner party. Here are the only three you'll ever need:

• **Nonstick skillet.** For healthy cooking using very little fat, this is a pan you'll use all the time. You can choose a skillet with a traditional nonstick coating or an eco-friendly ceramic coating—either type works great for low-fat cooking and easy cleanup. Buy the best quality you can afford for this kitchen essential. Let the size of your family determine the size you buy: If you cook most often for two, choose a 10-inch skillet; if there are three or four in your family, a 12-inch skillet is the best bet.

• **Stainless-steel skillet.** These pans are perfect to use when you are sautéing chicken breasts or pork chops, and then making a sauce in the same pan. As with a nonstick skillet, you can cook with a stainless-steel skillet using just a small amount of oil, but the advantage of stainless steel is that it browns food better. When you're making a pan sauce, this is a plus, since you'll incorporate all the flavorful browned bits from the bottom of the skillet into your sauce. Choose a skillet with an ovenproof handle so it can go from stovetop to oven. This feature is handy when you want to brown a large piece of meat on the stovetop, and then finish it in the oven. Again, let your family size be your guide and buy the skillet that best suits your needs.

• **Cast-iron skillet.** Many cooks swear by cast iron, and for good reason. The heavy metal conducts heat evenly and holds heat better than stainless steel. Cast iron is fantastic for cooking beef or tuna steaks, salmon fillets, or beef hamburgers—any dish where you want a well-browned exterior and a moist, juicy interior. It's also perfect for baking cornbread, giving the bread a crisp, browned exterior crust. When well seasoned, a cast-iron skillet works just as well as a nonstick skillet. These inexpensive skillets are available already seasoned and require minimal care for maintaining a rust-free nonstick surface.

Orange and Mustard–Glazed Pork Chops

Marmalade provides pectin to give the glaze syrupy body and balances the sweet orange juice with a touch of pleasant bitterness.

Hands-on Time: 30 minutes **Total Time:** 40 minutes **Serves:** 4

½ cup fresh orange juice (about 2 oranges)

2 tablespoons sugar-free orange marmalade

1 tablespoon whole-grain mustard

1 tablespoon canola oil

4 (5-ounce) bone-in pork loin chops (1 inch thick)

¼ teaspoon kosher salt

¼ teaspoon freshly ground black pepper

2 rosemary sprigs

1 medium-sized red onion, cut into ½-inch wedges

2 tablespoons fresh lime juice

1 Preheat oven to 425°.

2 Combine juice, marmalade, and mustard in a saucepan over medium-high heat. Bring to a boil, reduce heat, and simmer 15 minutes or until syrupy.

3 Heat a large ovenproof skillet over medium-high heat. Add oil to pan; swirl to coat. Sprinkle pork with salt and pepper. Add to pan; cook 5 minutes or until browned. Turn pork; add rosemary and onion to pan. Pour juice mixture over pork.

4 Bake at 425° for 10 minutes or until a thermometer registers 145°. Place onion and rosemary on a platter. Return pan to medium-high heat; add lime juice. Cook 4 minutes or until liquid is syrupy. Add pork to platter; drizzle with sauce.

PER SERVING (serving size: 1 chop, about 3 onion wedges, and about 3 tablespoons sauce):

Food Choices: ½ Carbohydrate, 3 Lean Proteins, 1 Fat

Calories 210; **Fat** 9.4g (sat 2g, mono 4.3g, poly 1.7g, trans 0g); **Protein** 22g; **Carbohydrate** 10g; **Fiber** 1g; **Sugars** 4g; **Cholesterol** 66mg; **Iron** 1mg; **Sodium** 255mg; **Potassium** 530mg; **Phosphorus** 270mg; **Calcium** 31mg

Pork and Asparagus Stir-Fry

Sake, or rice wine, is fragrant and slightly sweet, a perfect addition to this simple spring stir-fry. You can also use dry sherry wine or a small splash of sherry vinegar. If using larger asparagus, cut lengthwise into slices.

Hands-on Time: 18 minutes   **Total Time:** 18 minutes   **Serves:** 4

2 tablespoons lower-sodium soy sauce, divided

2½ teaspoons cornstarch, divided

2 teaspoons sake (rice wine) or dry sherry

2 teaspoons dark sesame oil

1 (1-pound) pork tenderloin, trimmed and cut into strips

⅓ cup unsalted chicken stock (such as Swanson)

1 tablespoon canola oil

2 teaspoons minced fresh garlic

2 teaspoons minced peeled fresh ginger

1 pound thin asparagus, trimmed and cut into 2-inch pieces

1 small red bell pepper, cut into 2-inch pieces

½ small white onion, cut into thin wedges (about ¾ cup)

⅛ teaspoon salt

2 (8.5-ounce) pouches precooked rice (such as Uncle Ben's)

1 Combine 1 tablespoon soy sauce, 2 teaspoons cornstarch, sake, and sesame oil in a large bowl. Add pork; toss to coat. Combine 1 tablespoon soy sauce, ½ teaspoon cornstarch, and stock in a small bowl.

2 Heat a wok or large skillet over high heat. Add canola oil; swirl to coat. Add garlic and ginger; stir-fry 30 seconds or until fragrant. Add pork mixture to pan; stir-fry 3 minutes or until browned. Add asparagus, bell pepper, and onion; stir-fry 3 minutes or until crisp-tender. Add stock mixture and salt; bring to a boil. Cook 2 minutes or until sauce is slightly thick.

3 Prepare rice according to package directions. Serve with pork mixture.

PER SERVING (serving size: about 1½ cups pork mixture and ½ cup rice):

Food Choices: 2½ Starches, 2 Nonstarchy Vegetables, 3 Lean Proteins, ½ Fat

Calories 396; **Fat** 11.1g (sat 2g, mono 5g, poly 3.3g, trans 0g); **Protein** 32g; **Carbohydrate** 45g; **Fiber** 6g; **Sugars** 4g; **Cholesterol** 74mg; **Iron** 5mg; **Sodium** 428mg; **Potassium** 873mg; **Phosphorus** 462mg; **Calcium** 45mg

Chipotle Grilled Pork Tenderloin with Strawberry-Avocado Salsa

If pressed for time, grill the pork a day ahead, refrigerate, and serve it at room temperature; slice the pork just before serving.

Hands-on Time: 15 minutes   **Total Time:** 2 hours, 30 minutes   **Serves:** 12

Pork:
1½ cups (¼-inch-thick) slices onion
¼ cup minced chipotle chile, canned in adobo sauce
3 tablespoons fresh lime juice
2 garlic cloves, crushed
3 (1-pound) pork tenderloins, trimmed
1 teaspoon salt
Cooking spray

Salsa:
5 cups quartered fresh strawberries (about 2 quarts)
1⅓ cups chopped peeled avocado (about 1 large)
¼ cup thinly sliced green onions
¼ cup chopped fresh cilantro
3 tablespoons fresh lime juice
¼ teaspoon salt

1 To prepare pork, combine first 4 ingredients in a large zip-top plastic bag. Add pork; seal and marinate in refrigerator 2 hours, turning bag occasionally.

2 Preheat grill to medium-high heat.

3 Remove pork from bag; discard marinade. Sprinkle pork with 1 teaspoon salt. Place pork on grill rack coated with cooking spray. Grill 20 minutes or until a thermometer registers 160° (slightly pink), turning occasionally. Let stand 10 minutes; slice.

4 To prepare salsa, combine strawberries and remaining ingredients in a medium bowl; toss gently. Serve immediately with pork.

PER SERVING (serving size: 3 ounces pork and about ⅓ cup salsa):
Food Choices: ½ Fruit, 3 Lean Proteins
Calories 180; **Fat** 6.6g (sat 1.8g, mono 3.2g, poly 0.8g, trans 0g); **Protein** 23g; **Carbohydrate** 7g; **Fiber** 2g; **Sugars** 4g; **Cholesterol** 63mg; **Iron** 2mg; **Sodium** 348mg; **Potassium** 555mg; **Phosphorus** 248mg; **Calcium** 19mg

ingredient pointer

Since this recipe uses just one chile from the can, you'll end up with extra chiles in adobo sauce. Process the remaining chiles and sauce in a blender to create a paste. Store the paste in the freezer. The next time you'll need chiles in adobo, scoop out some and stir into the dish. One tablespoon of paste equals one chile.

Speedy Chicken and Cheese Enchiladas

Rotisserie chicken and prechopped vegetables speed up prep for this casserole. You can pick your degree of hotness on the enchilada sauce—mild, medium, or hot.

Hands-on Time: 12 minutes   **Total Time:** 15 minutes   **Serves:** 4

Cooking spray

1 cup prechopped white onion

1 cup prechopped red bell pepper

¾ cup enchilada sauce

2 cups chopped skinless, boneless rotisserie chicken breast (about 8 ounces)

4 ounces preshredded reduced-fat 4-cheese Mexican-blend cheese (about 1 cup), divided

½ teaspoon ground cumin

8 (6-inch) corn tortillas

¼ cup fat-free sour cream

¼ cup chopped tomato

¼ cup chopped fresh cilantro

1 Preheat broiler.

2 Heat a large skillet over medium-high heat. Coat pan with cooking spray. Add onion and pepper; sauté 2 minutes or until crisp-tender. Add enchilada sauce; bring to a boil. Cover, reduce heat, and simmer 5 minutes.

3 Combine chicken, ¾ cup cheese, and cumin, tossing well.

4 Wrap tortillas in damp paper towels; microwave at HIGH 30 seconds or until warm. Spoon ¼ cup chicken mixture in center of each tortilla; roll up. Place tortillas, seam sides down, in an 11 x 7–inch glass or ceramic baking dish coated with cooking spray. Pour sauce mixture over enchiladas; broil 3 minutes or until thoroughly heated. Sprinkle ¼ cup cheese over enchiladas, and broil 1 minute or until cheese melts. Serve with sour cream, tomato, and cilantro.

PER SERVING (serving size: 2 enchiladas, 1 tablespoon sour cream, 1 tablespoon tomato, and 1 tablespoon cilantro):

Food Choices: 1½ Starches, 1 Nonstarchy Vegetable, 3 Lean Proteins

Calories 311; **Fat** 9.5g (sat 3.2g, mono 1.8g, poly 1.1g, trans 0g); **Protein** 28g; **Carbohydrate** 30g; **Fiber** 4g; **Sugars** 6g; **Cholesterol** 63mg; **Iron** 1mg; **Sodium** 427mg; **Potassium** 488mg; **Phosphorus** 386mg; **Calcium** 329mg

Spicy Chicken and Snow Peas

A mixture of snow peas, carrots, and red bell peppers coupled with crunchy peanuts and spicy chile paste creates an amazingly tasty and quick supper. You can also serve this with brown rice—a Power Food—if you prefer.

Hands-on Time: 20 minutes   **Total Time:** 20 minutes   **Serves:** 4

1 (3½-ounce) bag boil-in-bag long-grain rice

2 tablespoons granulated no-calorie sweetener (such as Splenda)

2 tablespoons lower-sodium soy sauce

2 tablespoons rice vinegar

2 teaspoons sambal oelek (ground fresh chile paste)

1 teaspoon ground ginger

Cooking spray

1 teaspoon dark sesame oil

1½ cups matchstick-cut carrots

1 cup thinly sliced red bell pepper

2 cups snow peas, trimmed

1½ cups chopped cooked chicken breast

¼ cup unsalted, dry-roasted peanuts

1 Cook rice according to package directions, omitting salt and fat. Keep warm.

2 Combine sweetener and next 4 ingredients (through ginger) in a small bowl. Heat a large skillet over medium-high heat. Coat pan with cooking spray. Add oil to pan; swirl to coat. Add carrots and pepper to pan; sauté 2 minutes. Add peas and chicken to pan; sauté 1 minute. Transfer chicken mixture to a large bowl.

3 Return pan to heat. Add soy sauce mixture to pan; bring to a boil. Cook until reduced to ¼ cup (about 1½ minutes), stirring constantly. Serve rice with chicken mixture; drizzle with sauce and sprinkle with peanuts.

PER SERVING (serving size: ½ cup rice, 1¼ cups chicken mixture, 1 tablespoon sauce, and 1 tablespoon peanuts):

Food Choices: 2 Starches, 1 Nonstarchy Vegetable, 2 Lean Proteins

Calories 312; **Fat** 8.2g (sat 1.4g, mono 3.4g, poly 2.4g, trans 0g); **Protein** 23g; **Carbohydrate** 36g; **Fiber** 4g; **Sugars** 7g; **Cholesterol** 45mg; **Iron** 4mg; **Sodium** 410mg; **Potassium** 597mg; **Phosphorus** 251mg; **Calcium** 58mg

ingredient pointer

Sambal oelek (ground fresh chile paste) is a Chinese condiment that is often added to stews as a flavoring. It's essentially pureed fresh chiles, but some varieties have bean paste or garlic added. We prefer the basic variety. This somewhat thin sauce has intense heat. Stir it into sauces and marinades.

Chicken and Asparagus in White Wine Sauce

This tasty chicken and asparagus with white wine sauce is easy enough for a weeknight dinner but impressive enough for company. The recipe works equally well with green beans in place of asparagus, although you'll miss out on a Power Food. You can use chicken stock in place of wine, if you like.

Hands-on Time: 20 minutes   **Total Time:** 20 minutes   **Serves:** 4

4 (4-ounce) skinless, boneless chicken breast halves

½ teaspoon salt

¼ teaspoon freshly ground black pepper

2 tablespoons olive oil

3 tablespoons all-purpose flour

½ cup dry white wine

½ cup unsalted chicken stock (such as Swanson)

2 garlic cloves, minced

1 pound asparagus spears, trimmed

2 tablespoons chopped fresh parsley

1 tablespoon fresh lemon juice

1⅓ cups cooked quinoa

1 Place each chicken breast half between 2 sheets of heavy-duty plastic wrap; pound to ¼-inch thickness using a meat mallet or small heavy skillet. Sprinkle chicken breasts with salt and freshly ground black pepper.

2 Heat a large nonstick skillet over medium-high heat. Add oil to pan; swirl to coat. Place flour in a shallow dish. Dredge chicken in flour. Add chicken to pan; cook 3 minutes on each side or until done. Remove chicken from pan; keep warm.

3 Add wine, stock, and garlic to pan, scraping pan to loosen browned bits; cook 2 minutes. Add asparagus; cover and cook 3 minutes or until asparagus is crisp-tender. Remove from heat; stir in parsley and juice. Divide quinoa among 4 plates. Top with chicken; drizzle sauce over chicken. Serve with asparagus.

PER SERVING (serving size: ⅓ cup quinoa, 1 chicken breast half, about 2 tablespoons sauce, and about 5 asparagus spears):

Food Choices: 1 Starch, 1 Nonstarchy Vegetable, 4 Lean Proteins

Calories 308; **Fat** 11g (sat 1.6g, mono 5.8g, poly 1.2g, trans 0g); **Protein** 30g; **Carbohydrate** 21g; **Fiber** 3g; **Sugars** 2g; **Cholesterol** 73mg; **Iron** 3mg; **Sodium** 450mg; **Potassium** 680mg; **Phosphorus** 374mg; **Calcium** 41mg

Orange and Tomato–Simmered Chicken with Couscous

This recipe is easily customizable. Cauliflower can replace the fennel, or the couscous can be switched for a whole grain like farro or brown rice. There are plenty of vegetables in this complete dinner, but if you desire, fresh, lightly dressed greens would go well with this dish.

Hands-on Time: 25 minutes   **Total Time:** 50 minutes   **Serves:** 4

1 medium fennel bulb with stalks

2 teaspoons olive oil

8 skinless, bone-in chicken thighs (about 1½ pounds)

¼ teaspoon kosher salt

¼ teaspoon freshly ground black pepper

¾ cup prechopped onion

1 carrot, cut into ¼-inch-thick slices

¼ teaspoon ground cinnamon

¼ teaspoon ground red pepper (optional)

⅓ cup fresh orange juice

10 pitted kalamata olives, quartered

1 (14.5-ounce) can unsalted diced tomatoes, drained

1 cup water

⅔ cup uncooked whole-wheat couscous

1 Trim tough outer leaves from fennel; mince feathery fronds to measure 2 tablespoons. Remove and discard stalks. Cut fennel bulb in half lengthwise; discard core. Vertically slice fennel bulb.

2 Heat a large skillet over medium-high heat. Add oil to pan; swirl to coat. Sprinkle chicken with salt and black pepper. Add chicken to pan; cook 3 minutes on each side or until well browned. Transfer chicken to a plate.

3 Add sliced fennel, onion, and carrot to pan; cook 3 minutes. Add cinnamon and red pepper, if desired; cook 1 minute. Add orange juice, olives, and tomatoes. Increase heat to high, and bring to a boil. Add chicken and accumulated juices to pan. Reduce heat to medium, and cook 20 minutes or until chicken is done.

4 Bring 1 cup water to a boil in a medium saucepan. Stir in couscous; cover. Remove from heat; let stand 5 minutes. Fluff with a fork.

5 Serve chicken and vegetables over couscous. Top with fennel fronds.

PER SERVING (serving size: about ⅓ cup couscous, 2 chicken thighs, and about ½ cup vegetables):

Food Choices: 2 Starches, 2 Nonstarchy Vegetables, 3 Lean Proteins, 1½ Fats

Calories 400; **Fat** 14.8g (sat 3.3g, mono 5.7g, poly 2.7g, trans 0g); **Protein** 33g; **Carbohydrate** 36g; **Fiber** 6g; **Sugars** 8g; **Cholesterol** 99mg; **Iron** 3mg; **Sodium** 374mg; **Potassium** 658mg; **Phosphorus** 285mg; **Calcium** 80mg

Pan-Seared Chicken Thighs with Lemon and Tomatoes

Your family will love this speedy, succulent chicken. The tomatoes and lemon slices infuse this meal with bright flavors as well as antioxidants.

Hands-on Time: 15 minutes   **Total Time:** 15 minutes   **Serves:** 4

2 teaspoons canola oil

8 (4-ounce) bone-in chicken thighs, skinned

½ teaspoon freshly ground black pepper

¼ teaspoon salt

1 (14.5-ounce) can unsalted organic fire-roasted diced tomatoes, undrained

¼ cup sliced pimiento-stuffed olives

2 garlic cloves, minced

1 lemon, thinly sliced

1 Heat a large nonstick skillet over medium-high heat. Add oil to pan; swirl to coat. Sprinkle chicken with pepper and salt. Add chicken to pan, and cook 4 minutes on each side or until browned.

2 Add tomatoes, olives, and garlic to pan, spooning mixture over and around chicken. Place lemon slices on chicken. Reduce heat to medium-low. Cover and cook 4 minutes or until chicken is done.

PER SERVING (serving size: 2 chicken thighs and ½ cup tomato mixture):

Food Choices: 1 Nonstarchy Vegetable, 4 Lean Proteins, 1 Fat

Calories 297; **Fat** 14.4g (sat 3.1g, mono 6.5g, poly 3.4g, trans 0g); **Protein** 32g; **Carbohydrate** 7g; **Fiber** 1g; **Sugars** 4g; **Cholesterol** 175mg; **Iron** 2mg; **Sodium** 423mg; **Potassium** 605mg; **Phosphorus** 311mg; **Calcium** 37mg

small change, big result

Using skinless chicken thighs saves about 50 calories per serving in this recipe compared to using thighs with the skin on. Unlike chicken breasts, chicken thighs don't dry out as easily and stay moist and tender as they cook, so you won't miss the skin at all.

Braised Chicken with Kale

Bake chicken leg quarters in a broth mixture along with kale and tomatoes for a simple one-dish dinner.

Hands-on Time: 20 minutes   **Total Time:** 1 hour, 40 minutes   **Serves:** 4

Cooking spray

4 teaspoons canola oil, divided

4 chicken leg quarters, skinned

½ teaspoon freshly ground black pepper

1.1 ounces all-purpose flour (about ¼ cup)

5 garlic cloves, chopped

1 (16-ounce) package cut prewashed kale

1 (14.5-ounce) can unsalted fire-roasted diced tomatoes, undrained

1 (14.5-ounce) can unsalted chicken stock (such as Swanson)

1 tablespoon red wine vinegar

1 Preheat oven to 325°.

2 Heat a Dutch oven over medium-high heat. Coat pan with cooking spray. Add 1 teaspoon canola oil. Sprinkle chicken with black pepper. Place flour in a dish, and dredge chicken. Place 2 leg quarters in pan, and cook 1½ minutes on each side. Remove from pan. Repeat procedure with 1 teaspoon oil and remaining 2 leg quarters. Remove from pan.

3 Add 2 teaspoons oil to pan. Add garlic; cook 20 seconds. Add half of kale; cook 2 minutes. Add remaining kale; cook 3 minutes. Stir in tomatoes and stock; bring to a boil. Return chicken to pan. Cover and bake at 325° for 1 hour and 15 minutes. Remove chicken from pan; stir in vinegar. Serve chicken over kale mixture.

PER SERVING (serving size: 1¼ cups kale mixture and 1 leg quarter):

Food Choices: ½ Starch, 2 Nonstarchy Vegetables, 4 Lean Proteins

Calories 326; **Fat** 11.4g (sat 1.9g, mono 5g, poly 3.1g, trans 0g); **Protein** 34g; **Carbohydrate** 23g; **Fiber** 4g; **Sugars** 5g; **Cholesterol** 131mg; **Iron** 5mg; **Sodium** 237mg; **Potassium** 1,063mg; **Phosphorus** 365mg; **Calcium** 215mg

Grilled Halibut with Tomato-Avocado Salsa

Topped with a fresh and delicious tomato-avocado salsa, this grilled halibut is ideal for an easy weeknight supper or a special-occasion meal.

Hands-on Time: 14 minutes **Total Time:** 14 minutes **Serves:** 4

3½ **cups grape** tomatoes, **halved**

½ **cup diced ripe** avocado **(about 1 medium)**

2 **tablespoons chopped fresh basil**

1 **teaspoon fresh** lime **juice**

½ **teaspoon minced fresh garlic**

½ **teaspoon olive oil**

¼ **teaspoon salt**

⅛ **teaspoon freshly ground black pepper**

½ **teaspoon salt**

¼ **teaspoon freshly ground black pepper**

4 **(4-ounce) halibut fillets**

Cooking spray

4 lime **wedges**

1 Preheat grill to medium-high heat.

2 Combine first 8 ingredients in a bowl; set aside.

3 Sprinkle ½ teaspoon salt and ¼ teaspoon pepper over fish. Coat fish with cooking spray. Place fish on grill rack coated with cooking spray; grill 4 minutes on each side or until fish flakes easily when tested with a fork or until desired degree of doneness. Arrange fish on serving plates; squeeze lime wedges over fish. Spoon salsa over fish.

Note You can cook the fish on a preheated grill pan over medium-high heat, if desired.

PER SERVING (serving size: 1 fillet and about ¼ cup salsa):

Food Choices: 1 Nonstarchy Vegetable, 4 Lean Proteins

Calories 217; **Fat** 5.9g (sat 1g, mono 3.1g, poly 1g, trans 0g); **Protein** 33g; **Carbohydrate** 8g; **Fiber** 3g; **Sugars** 4g; **Cholesterol** 83mg; **Iron** 1mg; **Sodium** 344mg; **Potassium** 1,161mg; **Phosphorus** 247mg; **Calcium** 32mg

Broiled Salmon with Marmalade-Dijon Glaze

Although quick enough for a hectic weeknight, this dish will impress guests, too. Serve with a salad and roasted potatoes.

Hands-on Time: 9 minutes   **Total Time**: 17 minutes   **Serves**: 4

⅓ **cup sugar-free orange marmalade**

1 **tablespoon Dijon mustard**

½ **teaspoon garlic powder**

¼ **teaspoon salt**

¼ **teaspoon freshly ground black pepper**

⅛ **teaspoon ground ginger**

4 **(4-ounce) salmon fillets**

Cooking spray

1 Preheat broiler.

2 Combine first 6 ingredients in a small bowl, stirring well. Place fish on a jelly-roll pan coated with cooking spray. Brush half of marmalade mixture evenly over fish; broil 6 minutes. Brush fish with remaining marmalade mixture; broil 2 minutes or until desired degree of doneness.

PER SERVING (serving size: 1 fillet):

Food Choices: ½ Carbohydrate, 3 Lean Proteins, ½ Fat

Calories 200; **Fat** 8.7g (sat 2.1g, mono 3.8g, poly 2.1g, trans 0g); **Protein** 24g; **Carbohydrate** 8g; **Fiber** 0g; **Sugars** 4g; **Cholesterol** 58mg; **Iron** 0mg; **Sodium** 289mg; **Potassium** 580mg; **Phosphorus** 338mg; **Calcium** 15mg

Fresh Tuna Tacos

Let everyone assemble their own tacos for a fun, casual supper.

Hands-on Time: 15 minutes **Total Time:** 15 minutes **Serves:** 4

¾ **teaspoon chili powder**

½ **teaspoon ground cumin**

⅛ **teaspoon salt**

⅛ **teaspoon chipotle chile powder or chile powder**

1 **pound yellowfin tuna fillet (about ¾ inch thick)**

Cooking spray

8 **(6-inch) corn tortillas**

1 **cup sliced peeled avocado (about 1 medium)**

½ **cup vertically sliced onion**

¼ **cup cilantro leaves**

16 **pickled jalapeño slices**

8 **teaspoons reduced-fat sour cream**

4 **lime wedges**

1 Combine first 4 ingredients in a small bowl; sprinkle spice mixture over both sides of fish.

2 Heat a grill pan over high heat; coat pan with cooking spray. Add fish; cook 2 minutes on each side or until medium-rare or until desired degree of doneness. Cut fish into ¼-inch-thick slices.

3 Warm tortillas according to package directions. Divide fish among tortillas; top each with 2 tablespoons avocado, 1 tablespoon onion, 1½ teaspoons cilantro, and 2 jalapeño slices. Top each with 1 teaspoon sour cream. Serve tacos with lime wedges.

PER SERVING (serving size: 2 filled tacos and 1 lime wedge):

Food Choices: 2 Starches, 3 Lean Proteins

Calories 306; **Fat** 8.6g (sat 1.7g, mono 4.1g, poly 1.6g, trans fat 0g); **Protein** 30g; **Carbohydrate** 28g; **Fiber** 6g; **Sugars** 2g; **Cholesterol** 45mg; **Iron** 2mg; **Sodium** 370mg; **Potassium** 820mg; **Phosphorus** 484mg; **Calcium** 78mg

ingredient pointer

Corn flavor really shines through in corn tortillas, making them great for use in these fish tacos. To heat them, pop tortillas in the microwave for a few seconds, or if you have a little more time, heat them individually in a dry skillet over medium-high heat for 45 seconds to 1 minute on each side until they develop a few brown spots.

Scallops with Capers and Tomatoes

Always request dry-packed sea scallops. They tend to be fresher and haven't been soaked in a sodium solution to temporarily plump them up. Serve these scallops over hot cooked angel hair pasta. You can use unsalted chicken broth in place of the wine, if you prefer.

Hands-on Time: 12 minutes   **Total Time:** 12 minutes   **Serves:** 4

12 large sea scallops (about 1½ pounds)
Cooking spray
1 garlic clove, minced
½ cup dry white wine
1 tomato, seeded and diced (about 1 cup)
2½ tablespoons capers, drained
2 tablespoons chopped fresh basil
1 tablespoon extra-virgin olive oil

1 Pat scallops dry with paper towels. Heat a large skillet over medium-high heat. Coat pan with cooking spray. Add scallops to pan; cook 3 minutes on each side or until done. Remove scallops from pan; keep warm.

2 Add garlic to pan; cook 15 seconds. Add wine and next 3 ingredients (through basil) to pan. Spoon mixture over scallops; drizzle with oil just before serving.

PER SERVING (serving size: 3 scallops and ⅓ cup sauce):
Food Choices: 1 Nonstarchy Vegetable, 4 Lean Proteins
Calories 212; **Fat** 5g (sat 0.7g, mono 2.8g, poly 0.8g, trans 0g); **Protein** 29g; **Carbohydrate** 7g; **Fiber** 1g; **Sugars** 1g; **Cholesterol** 56mg; **Iron** 1mg; **Sodium** 436mg; **Potassium** 486mg; **Phosphorus** 586mg; **Calcium** 53mg

Pesto Shrimp Pasta

Pesto and tomatoes balance the more subtle flavors of juicy shrimp.

Hands-on Time: 8 minutes   **Total Time:** 15 minutes   **Serves:** 4

4 ounces uncooked angel hair pasta
6 cups water
1¼ pounds peeled and deveined large shrimp
3 tablespoons commercial pesto
1 cup halved grape tomatoes
1 ounce Parmesan cheese, shaved (about ¼ cup)

1 Cook pasta according to package directions, omitting salt and fat; drain.

2 Meanwhile, bring 6 cups water to a boil in a large saucepan. Add shrimp; cook 2 to 3 minutes or until done. Drain; toss with 2 tablespoons pesto and tomatoes. Stir in pasta and 1 tablespoon pesto. Top with cheese.

PER SERVING (serving size: 1 cup shrimp pasta and 1 tablespoon cheese):
Food Choices: 1½ Starches, 4 Lean Proteins, ½ Fat
Calories 320; **Fat** 11g (sat 2.7g, mono 6.3g, poly 1.7g, trans 0g); **Protein** 31g; **Carbohydrate** 24g; **Fiber** 2g; **Sugars** 2g; **Cholesterol** 220mg; **Iron** 5mg; **Sodium** 450mg; **Potassium** 364mg; **Phosphorus** 517mg; **Calcium** 189mg

Scallops with Capers
and Tomatoes

Broccoli-Quinoa Casserole with Chicken and Cheddar

In this updated riff on chicken-rice casserole, whole-grain quinoa stands in for the typical white rice, adding protein and a slightly crunchy texture. It's a modern interpretation that still has loads of old-school comfort-food appeal.

Hands-on Time: 20 minutes   **Total Time:** 55 minutes   **Serves:** 8

1 tablespoon canola oil, divided

1 cup uncooked quinoa, rinsed and drained

1¼ cups water

1 (12-ounce) package microwave-in-bag fresh broccoli florets

Cooking spray

12 ounces skinless, boneless chicken breast, cut into bite-sized pieces

¼ teaspoon kosher salt, divided

¼ teaspoon freshly ground black pepper, divided

1½ cups chopped onion

6 garlic cloves, minced

½ cup fat-free milk

2½ tablespoons all-purpose flour

1½ cups unsalted chicken stock (such as Swanson)

2 ounces Parmesan cheese, grated (about ½ cup)

½ cup canola mayonnaise

3 ounces reduced-fat cheddar cheese, shredded (about ¾ cup)

1 Heat a medium saucepan over medium-high heat. Add 1½ teaspoons oil; swirl to coat. Add quinoa; cook 2 minutes or until toasted, stirring frequently. Add 1¼ cups water; bring to a boil. Cover, reduce heat, and simmer 15 minutes or until quinoa is tender. Remove from heat; let stand 5 minutes. Fluff with a fork.

2 Preheat oven to 400°.

3 Cook broccoli in microwave according to package directions, reducing cook time to 2½ minutes.

4 Heat a Dutch oven over medium-high heat. Coat pan with cooking spray. Add chicken to pan; sprinkle with ⅛ teaspoon salt and ⅛ teaspoon pepper. Cook 5 minutes or until browned, turning occasionally; remove from pan.

5 Add 1½ teaspoons oil to pan; swirl to coat. Add onion and garlic; sauté 5 minutes. Combine milk and flour, stirring with a whisk. Add milk mixture, stock, ⅛ teaspoon salt, and ⅛ teaspoon pepper to pan. Bring to a boil, stirring frequently; cook 2 minutes or until thick. Remove from heat; cool slightly. Add Parmesan, stirring until cheese melts. Stir in quinoa, broccoli, chicken, and mayonnaise. Spoon mixture into a 2-quart glass or ceramic baking dish coated with cooking spray. Sprinkle with cheddar. Bake at 400° for 15 minutes or until casserole is bubbly and cheese melts.

PER SERVING (serving size: 1 cup):

Food Choices: 1 Starch, 1 Nonstarchy Vegetable, 2 Lean Proteins, 1 Fat

Calories 276; **Fat** 11.7g (sat 3g, mono 5.2g, poly 3g, trans 0g); **Protein** 20g; **Carbohydrate** 22g; **Fiber** 3g; **Sugars** 3g; **Cholesterol** 35mg; **Iron** 2mg; **Sodium** 419mg; **Potassium** 421mg; **Phosphorus** 350mg; **Calcium** 241mg

Asian Stir-Fry Quinoa Bowl

A stir-fry quinoa bowl brimming with fresh veggies and tofu is a healthy replacement for the days you just can't kick the craving for takeout.

Hands-on Time: 28 minutes   **Total Time:** 28 minutes   **Serves:** 4

8 ounces extra-firm tofu

2 tablespoons toasted sesame oil, divided

1 cup (1-inch) sliced green onions

1 tablespoon minced peeled fresh ginger

5 ounces thinly sliced shiitake mushroom caps

5 garlic cloves, thinly sliced

1 red bell pepper, thinly sliced

3 tablespoons lower-sodium soy sauce, divided

2 tablespoons rice vinegar, divided

2 cups cooked quinoa

2 cups thinly sliced napa (Chinese) cabbage

¼ cup chopped fresh cilantro

1 Arrange tofu on several layers of heavy-duty paper towels. Cover with additional paper towels; let stand 15 minutes. Cut into ½-inch-thick cubes.

2 Heat a large nonstick skillet over medium-high heat. Add 1 tablespoon oil to pan; swirl to coat. Add tofu; sauté 4 minutes or until browned. Place tofu in a bowl. Return pan to medium-high heat. Add 1 tablespoon oil to pan; swirl to coat. Add onions and next 4 ingredients (through bell pepper); stir-fry 4 minutes or just until tender. Add 2 tablespoons soy sauce and 1 tablespoon vinegar; cook 30 seconds. Add mushroom mixture to tofu.

3 Stir in 1 tablespoon soy sauce, 1 tablespoon vinegar, quinoa, cabbage, and cilantro. Toss well to combine.

PER SERVING (serving size: 1¼ cups):

Food Choices: 2 Starches, 1 Nonstarchy Vegetable, 1 Medium-Fat Protein

Calories 279; **Fat** 12.5g (sat 1.7g, mono 3.7g, poly 5.1g, trans 0g); **Protein** 12g; **Carbohydrate** 31g; **Fiber** 5g; **Sugars** 4g; **Cholesterol** 0mg; **Iron** 3mg; **Sodium** 419mg; **Potassium** 610mg; **Phosphorus** 298mg; **Calcium** 99mg

Quinoa-Stuffed Kale Rolls with Goat Cheese

Lacinato kale, also called Tuscan or dinosaur kale, has long, pliable, flat leaves perfect for stuffing.

Hands-on Time: 1 hour **Total Time:** 1 hour, 25 minutes **Serves:** 6

- **2 pounds plum tomatoes, chopped**
- **6 garlic cloves, coarsely chopped**
- **2 teaspoons chopped fresh thyme**
- **½ teaspoon kosher salt**
- **12 large Lacinato kale leaves (about 1 large bunch)**
- **2 teaspoons extra-virgin olive oil**
- **1 medium onion, chopped**
- **¾ cup uncooked quinoa, rinsed and drained**
- **1½ cups organic vegetable broth**
- **⅓ cup chopped walnuts, toasted and divided**
- **Cooking spray**
- **2 ounces goat cheese, crumbled (about ¼ cup)**

1 Place tomatoes, garlic, and thyme in a large saucepan. Cover and simmer 30 minutes or until tomatoes are very tender, stirring occasionally. Remove pan from heat. Add salt; coarsely mash with a potato masher.

2 While tomatoes cook, bring a large saucepan of water to a boil; add half of kale. Cook 1 minute. Remove kale from pan with a slotted spoon; plunge into ice water. Repeat procedure with remaining kale. Drain and pat dry. Remove center rib from each kale leaf, leaving the leaf whole and uncut at leafy end.

3 Heat a medium saucepan over medium-high heat. Add olive oil to pan; swirl to coat. Add onion to pan; sauté 5 minutes or until tender. Add quinoa; cook 2 minutes, stirring constantly. Add broth; bring to a boil. Cover, reduce heat, and simmer 15 minutes or until liquid is absorbed. Remove pan from heat; stir in 3 tablespoons walnuts.

4 Preheat oven to 375°.

5 Spread about ¾ cup tomato sauce over bottom of an 11 x 7–inch glass or ceramic baking dish coated with cooking spray. Working with 1 kale leaf at a time, place about ¼ cup quinoa mixture in center of leaf. Fold in edges of leaf; roll up, jelly-roll fashion. Repeat procedure with remaining kale leaves and quinoa mixture to form 12 rolls. Place rolls, seam sides down, in dish. Spoon remaining sauce over rolls. Cover and bake at 375° for 20 minutes. Sprinkle with remaining walnuts and cheese. Bake, uncovered, for 5 minutes.

PER SERVING (serving size: 2 rolls):

Food Choices: 1 Starch, 2 Nonstarchy Vegetables, 1 Medium-Fat Protein

Calories 220; **Fat** 9.6g (sat 2.2g, mono 2.5g, poly 4.2g, trans 0g); **Protein** 9g; **Carbohydrate** 27g; **Fiber** 5g; **Sugars** 7g; **Cholesterol** 4mg; **Iron** 3mg; **Sodium** 257mg; **Potassium** 704mg; **Phosphorus** 210mg; **Calcium** 102mg

Spinach-Artichoke Pasta with Vegetables

An appetizer favorite becomes a silky, creamy sauce for a quick pasta dinner full of cheesy, veggie, nutty goodness.

Hands-on Time: 22 minutes   **Total Time:** 22 minutes   **Serves:** 6

8 ounces uncooked rotini pasta

2½ cups (2-inch) cut asparagus

1½ cups (2 x ½-inch) cut yellow bell pepper

⅔ cup fat-free milk

1 (8-ounce) package frozen spinach-and-artichoke cheese dip (such as T.G.I. Friday's), thawed

½ teaspoon kosher salt

12 grape tomatoes, halved

¼ cup basil leaves, torn

3 tablespoons pine nuts, toasted

1 ounce Parmigiano-Reggiano cheese, shaved (about ¼ cup)

1 Cook pasta according to package directions, omitting salt and fat. During last 3 minutes of cooking, add asparagus and bell pepper to pan; drain.

2 Combine milk and spinach dip in a medium saucepan over medium heat; bring to a simmer. Reduce heat, and cook 5 minutes or until slightly thick. Combine pasta mixture, spinach mixture, salt, and tomatoes in a large bowl; toss to coat. Sprinkle with basil, pine nuts, and cheese.

PER SERVING (serving size: about 1½ cups):

Food Choices: 2 Starches, 1 Nonstarchy Vegetable, 1 Medium-Fat Protein

Calories 261; **Fat** 7g (sat 2.6g, mono 1.2g, poly 1.6g, trans 0g); **Protein** 13g; **Carbohydrate** 38g; **Fiber** 4g; **Sugars** 7g; **Cholesterol** 10mg; **Iron** 3mg; **Sodium** 384mg; **Potassium** 649mg; **Phosphorus** 576mg; **Calcium** 196mg

Farfalle with Sausage, Cannellini Beans, and Kale

Use a vegetable peeler to shave fresh Parmesan cheese on top of this rustic pasta dish featuring sun-dried tomatoes, turkey Italian sausage, and fresh kale.

Hands-on Time: 16 minutes   **Total Time**: 16 minutes   **Serves**: 8

8 ounces uncooked farfalle (bow tie pasta)

¼ cup oil-packed sun-dried tomatoes

1½ cups chopped onion

8 ounces hot turkey Italian sausage

6 garlic cloves, minced

2 cups unsalted chicken stock (such as Swanson)

1 teaspoon dried Italian seasoning

¼ teaspoon crushed red pepper

1 (16-ounce) package fresh kale

1 (15-ounce) can cannellini beans, rinsed and drained

1 ounce Parmesan cheese, shaved (about ¼ cup)

1 Cook pasta according to package directions, omitting salt and fat. Drain, reserving 1 cup cooking liquid; keep warm.

2 While pasta cooks, drain tomatoes in a small sieve over a bowl, reserving 2 teaspoons oil; slice tomatoes. Heat a large Dutch oven over medium heat. Add sliced tomatoes, reserved 2 teaspoons tomato oil, onion, and sausage to pan; cook 10 minutes or until sausage is browned, stirring to crumble. Add garlic to pan; cook 1 minute. Add stock, seasoning, and pepper to pan. Stir in kale; cover and simmer 5 minutes or until kale is tender. Stir in pasta, reserved 1 cup cooking liquid, and beans. Sprinkle with cheese.

PER SERVING (serving size: 1⅓ cups pasta mixture and 2 teaspoons cheese):

Food Choices: 2 Starches, 1 Nonstarchy Vegetable, 1 Medium-Fat Protein

Calories 241; **Fat** 5.5g (sat 0.8g, mono 1.2g, poly 0.4g, trans 0g); **Protein** 15g; **Carbohydrate** 35g; **Fiber** 4g; **Sugars** 3g; **Cholesterol** 19mg; **Iron** 3mg; **Sodium** 395mg; **Potassium** 566mg; **Phosphorus** 183mg; **Calcium** 159mg

Butternut-Kale Lasagna

Gruyère-spiked béchamel drapes over the noodles and squash to give this lasagna velvety richness. Hearty, earthy kale perfectly balances the sweet squash, and crunchy, toasted pecans crown the top of the luscious lasagna.

Hands-on Time: 25 minutes   **Total Time**: 55 minutes   **Serves**: 6

¼ cup water

1 (12-ounce) package prechopped fresh butternut squash

3 cups prechopped kale

1 tablespoon olive oil

1½ tablespoons minced fresh garlic

1.1 ounces all-purpose flour (about ¼ cup)

2¾ cups fat-free milk, divided

2 ounces Gruyère cheese, shredded and divided (about ½ cup)

1 ounce Parmigiano-Reggiano cheese, grated (about ¼ cup)

½ teaspoon salt

¼ teaspoon freshly ground black pepper

Cooking spray

6 no-boil lasagna noodles

3 tablespoons chopped pecans

1 Preheat oven to 450°.

2 Combine ¼ cup water and squash in an 8-inch square glass or ceramic baking dish. Cover tightly with plastic wrap; pierce plastic wrap 2 to 3 times. Microwave at HIGH 5 minutes or until tender; drain. Combine squash and kale in a large bowl. Wipe dish dry.

3 Heat a medium saucepan over medium heat. Add oil to pan; swirl to coat. Add garlic; cook 2 minutes or until garlic begins to brown, stirring occasionally. Weigh or lightly spoon flour into a dry measuring cup; level with a knife. Combine flour and ½ cup milk in a small bowl, stirring with a whisk until smooth. Add milk mixture and 2¼ cups milk to pan; increase heat to medium-high. Bring to a boil; cook 1 minute or until thick, stirring frequently. Remove from heat. Stir in 1 ounce Gruyère, Parmigiano-Reggiano cheese, salt, and pepper; stir until cheese melts.

4 Coat baking dish with cooking spray. Spread ⅓ cup milk mixture in bottom of dish. Arrange 2 noodles over milk mixture; top with half of squash mixture and ⅔ cup milk mixture. Repeat layers once, ending with remaining noodles and remaining milk mixture. Cover with foil; bake at 450° for 15 minutes. Remove foil; sprinkle remaining Gruyère and pecans over top. Bake, uncovered, at 450° for 10 minutes or until lightly browned and sauce is bubbly. Let stand 5 minutes.

PER SERVING (serving size: ⅙ of lasagna):

Food Choices: 2 Starches, 1 Nonstarchy Vegetable, 1 Medium-Fat Protein, ½ Fat

Calories 271; **Fat** 9.9g (sat 3.1g, mono 4.6g, poly 1.3g, trans 0g); **Protein** 14g; **Carbohydrate** 34g; **Fiber** 3g; **Sugars** 7g; **Cholesterol** 16mg; **Iron** 2mg; **Sodium** 371mg; **Potassium** 580mg; **Phosphorus** 281mg; **Calcium** 371mg

Arugula, White Bean, and Sun-Dried Tomato Cream Quesadillas

A combo of tangy goat cheese and fat-free cream cheese adds a creamy texture to these lightened vegetarian quesadillas. They also get a considerable amount of flavor, as well as antioxidants and vitamins, from the sun-dried tomatoes and peppery arugula.

Hands-on Time: 10 minutes   **Total Time**: 10 minutes   **Serves**: 2

2 ounces fat-free cream cheese, softened (about ¼ cup)

¼ cup chopped drained oil-packed sun-dried tomato halves

2 (8-inch) multigrain tortillas

½ cup rinsed and drained unsalted cannellini beans

2 ounces goat cheese, crumbled (about ¼ cup)

2 cups baby arugula

Cooking spray

1 Combine cream cheese and sun-dried tomato in a small bowl; spread over tortillas. Mash beans with a fork. Spread beans over cream cheese mixture. Top with goat cheese and arugula. Fold tortillas in half.

2 Heat a large skillet over medium heat. Coat pan with cooking spray. Place quesadillas in pan; cook 2 to 3 minutes on each side or until golden and cheese melts. Cut each quesadilla into 3 wedges. Serve immediately.

PER SERVING (serving size: 3 wedges):

Food Choices: 1½ Starches, 1 Nonstarchy Vegetable, 2 Lean Proteins

Calories 261; **Fat** 8.3g (sat 2.5g, mono 2g, poly 0.4g, trans 0g); **Protein** 19g; **Carbohydrate** 29g; **Fiber** 12g; **Sugars** 3g; **Cholesterol** 10mg; **Iron** 2mg; **Sodium** 386mg; **Potassium** 421mg; **Phosphorus** 275mg; **Calcium** 187mg

Bell Pepper Sauté,
page 245

Comfort Food Sides

From sautéed and roasted veggies to rice and pasta dishes, these easy-to-prepare sides are brimming with bright colors and fresh flavor. Enjoy these tasty accompaniments with your favorite lunch or dinner entrée.

Asparagus with Balsamic Tomatoes

This recipe is a quick and healthy side dish for a warm spring or summer night. Feta makes a good substitute for the goat cheese. The asparagus has high levels of the antioxidant glutathione, which fights free radicals that can cause diabetes, cancer, and heart disease.

Hands-on Time: 12 minutes   **Total Time:** 12 minutes   **Serves:** 4

1 pound asparagus spears

2 teaspoons extra-virgin olive oil

1½ cups halved grape tomatoes

½ teaspoon minced fresh garlic

2 tablespoons balsamic vinegar

¼ teaspoon salt

3 tablespoons crumbled goat cheese

½ teaspoon freshly ground black pepper

1 Snap off tough ends of asparagus. Cook asparagus in boiling water to cover 2 minutes or until crisp-tender. Drain.

2 Heat a large skillet over medium-high heat. Add olive oil to pan; swirl to coat. Add tomatoes and garlic; cook 5 minutes. Stir in vinegar; cook 3 minutes. Stir in salt. Arrange asparagus on a platter; top with tomato mixture. Sprinkle with cheese and pepper.

PER SERVING (serving size: ¼ of asparagus, about 3 tablespoons tomatoes, and about 2 teaspoons cheese):

Food Choices: 1 Nonstarchy Vegetable, 1 Fat

Calories 71; **Fat** 3.9g (sat 1.4g, mono 2.0g, poly 0.3g, trans 0g); **Protein** 3g; **Carbohydrate** 7g; **Fiber** 2g; **Sugars** 4g; **Cholesterol** 4mg; **Iron** 1mg; **Sodium** 179mg; **Potassium** 269mg; **Phosphorus** 61mg; **Calcium** 23mg

ingredient pointer

Grape tomatoes have a meatier texture and sweeter flavor than cherry tomatoes. They also keep longer than cherry tomatoes, making them perfect for having on hand to toss into salads, add to side dishes, and to use for snacks. For best flavor, store grape tomatoes at room temperature—they'll stay fresh for up to a week.

Asparagus and Lemon Risotto

This risotto cooks uncovered in the microwave. Be sure you are using at least a 2-quart bowl to allow plenty of room for the liquid to boil.

Hands-on Time: 18 minutes   **Total Time:** 39 minutes   **Serves:** 8

¾ **cup chopped onion**

3 **tablespoons olive oil**

2 **garlic cloves, minced**

1 **cup uncooked Arborio rice or other medium-grain rice**

3 **cups unsalted chicken stock (such as Swanson)**

⅓ **cup dry white wine**

1 **pound asparagus spears, cut into ½-inch pieces**

½ **teaspoon grated lemon rind**

1½ **tablespoons fresh lemon juice**

½ **teaspoon salt**

¼ **teaspoon freshly ground black pepper**

1½ **ounces shaved Parmigiano-Reggiano cheese (⅓ cup), divided**

1 Combine first 3 ingredients in a 2-quart microwave-safe bowl. Microwave at HIGH 3 minutes. Stir in rice; microwave at HIGH 3 minutes. Stir in stock and wine; microwave at HIGH 16 minutes, stirring for 30 seconds every 4 minutes. Add asparagus; microwave at HIGH 2 minutes. Stir in rind, juice, salt, pepper, and half of cheese. Top with remaining cheese.

PER SERVING (serving size: ½ cup):

Food Choices: 1 Starch, 2 Nonstarchy Vegetables, 1 Fat

Calories 179; **Fat** 6.4g (sat 1.3g, mono 4g, poly 0.6g, trans 0g); **Protein** 7g; **Carbohydrate** 24g; **Fiber** 2g; **Sugars** 2g; **Cholesterol** 3mg; **Iron** 2mg; **Sodium** 250mg; **Potassium** 412mg; **Phosphorus** 151mg; **Calcium** 64mg

ingredient pointer

Be sure to snap or cut off the tough ends of the asparagus spears before cooking them. To maintain freshness, wrap a moist paper towel around the stem ends, or stand the spears upright in about 2 inches of cold water.

Asparagus with Lemon-Basil Yogurt Sauce

Lemon rind and basil add a refreshing zing to the creamy yogurt.

Hands-on Time: 4 minutes   **Total Time:** 8 minutes   **Serves:** 4

1 pound asparagus **spears**

½ cup plain **fat-free Greek yogurt**

2 tablespoons chopped fresh basil

½ teaspoon grated lemon **rind**

2 tablespoons fresh lemon **juice**

¼ teaspoon salt

¼ teaspoon freshly ground black pepper

1 Snap off tough ends of asparagus. Cook asparagus in boiling water to cover 2 minutes or until crisp-tender; drain. Plunge asparagus into ice water; drain.

2 Combine yogurt and remaining ingredients in a small bowl. Serve over asparagus.

PER SERVING (serving size: ¼ of asparagus and 2 tablespoons sauce):

Food Choice: 1 Nonstarchy Vegetable

Calories 42; **Fat** 0g (sat 0g, mono 0g, poly 0g, trans 0g); **Protein** 5g; **Carbohydrate** 7g; **Fiber** 3g; **Sugars** 4g; **Cholesterol** 0mg; **Iron** 1mg; **Sodium** 156mg; **Potassium** 337mg; **Phosphorus** 111mg; **Calcium** 47mg

Broccoli with Quinoa and Bacon

Quinoa is low fat and cholesterol free. Dress it up with bacon bits and sautéed broccoli for a fresh and colorful side.

Hands-on Time: 8 minutes   **Total Time:** 21 minutes   **Serves:** 4

¾ cup uncooked quinoa, **rinsed and drained**

1 cup water

3 teaspoons olive oil, divided

2 cups fresh broccoli **florets**

2 tablespoons water

⅛ teaspoon salt

2 bacon slices, cooked and crumbled

1 Heat quinoa in a medium saucepan over medium-high heat; sauté 2 minutes. Add 1 cup water; bring to a boil. Cover, reduce heat, and simmer 13 minutes. Remove from heat; let stand 2 minutes.

2 While quinoa cooks, heat a saucepan over medium-high heat. Add 1 teaspoon olive oil to pan; swirl to coat. Add broccoli florets; sauté 2 minutes. Add 2 tablespoons water; cover and reduce heat. Cook 2 minutes. Combine quinoa, broccoli, 2 teaspoons olive oil, salt, and bacon.

PER SERVING (serving size: about 1 cup):

Food Choices: 1 Starch, 1 Nonstarchy Vegetable, 1 Fat

Calories 160; **Fat** 5.3g (sat 1.1g, mono 2.2g, poly 1.4g, trans 0g); **Protein** 7g; **Carbohydrate** 22g; **Fiber** 3g; **Sugars** 2g; **Chololesterol** 4mg; **Iron** 2mg; **Sodium** 139mg; **Potassium** 302mg; **Phosphorus** 174mg; **Calcium** 32mg

Sesame-Broccoli
Stir-Fry

Sesame-Broccoli Stir-Fry

Pair this tangy stir-fry with grilled chicken for a flavorful weeknight meal.

Hands-on Time: 3 minutes   **Total Time:** 11 minutes   **Serves:** 4

Cooking spray

1 (12-ounce) package **broccoli coleslaw**

1 teaspoon dark sesame oil

1 teaspoon toasted sesame seeds

4 teaspoons low-fat sesame-ginger dressing

1 Heat a large skillet over medium-high heat; coat pan with cooking spray. Add broccoli coleslaw; cook 7 minutes or until crisp-tender, stirring occasionally. Add oil, and cook 1 minute. Remove from heat; stir in sesame seeds and dressing.

PER SERVING (serving size: about ½ cup):

Food Choices: 1 Nonstarchy Vegetable, ½ Fat

Calories 53; **Fat** 1.7g (sat 0.2g, mono 0.7g, poly 0.7g, trans 0g); **Protein** 2.5g; **Carbohydrate** 6g; **Fiber** 3g; **Sugars** 2g; **Cholesterol** 0mg; **Iron** 2mg; **Sodium** 90mg; **Potassium** 274mg; **Phosphorus** 62mg; **Calcium** 20mg

Balsamic Broccoli Rabe

Broccoli rabe is a leafy green vegetable with a slightly bitter taste. Olive oil, vinegar, Parmesan, salt, and pepper help create a nutritious, Italian-inspired side dish.

Hands-on Time: 15 minutes   **Total Time:** 15 minutes   **Serves:** 4

1 pound **broccoli rabe, cut into 1-inch pieces**

2 teaspoons extra-virgin olive oil

2 teaspoons balsamic vinegar

¼ teaspoon kosher salt

¼ teaspoon freshly ground black pepper

1 tablespoon shaved Parmesan cheese

1 Bring a large saucepan of water to a boil. Add broccoli rabe; boil 3 minutes or until crisp-tender. Drain. Combine broccoli rabe, olive oil, vinegar, salt, and pepper in a large bowl; toss to coat. Sprinkle with shaved Parmesan cheese.

PER SERVING (serving size: about ⅔ cup):

Food Choices: 1 Nonstarchy Vegetable, ½ Fat

Calories 62; **Fat** 2.6g (sat 0.5g, mono 1.8g, poly 0.3g; trans 0g); **Protein** 5g; **Carbohydrate** 6g; **Fiber** 1g; **Sugars** 2g; **Cholesterol** 1mg; **Iron** 1mg; **Sodium** 173mg; **Potassium** 266mg; **Phosphorus** 107mg; **Calcium** 69mg

Garlicky Sautéed Kale

Kale is a powerhouse of nutrients that are linked to better bone, heart, and digestive health. Here, its natural mustardy flavor is tempered by the garlic.

Hands-on Time: 10 minutes   **Total Time:** 10 minutes   **Serves:** 4

2 teaspoons olive oil

1 tablespoon sliced garlic

8 packed cups Lacinato kale

¼ cup unsalted chicken stock (such as Swanson)

¼ teaspoon salt

¼ teaspoon freshly ground black pepper

1 Heat a large skillet over medium-high heat. Add olive oil to pan; swirl to coat. Add garlic, and cook 2 minutes or just until garlic begins to brown. Add kale; sauté 2 minutes, tossing frequently. Stir in chicken stock, salt, and pepper; cover and cook over medium heat 3 minutes or just until kale wilts.

PER SERVING (serving size: about 1 cup):

Food Choices: 3 Nonstarchy Vegetables, ½ Fat

Calories 93; **Fat** 3.3g (sat 0.5g, mono 1.9g, poly 0.7g; trans 0g); **Protein** 5g; **Carbohydrate** 14g; **Fiber** 3g; **Sugars** 1g; **Cholesterol** 0mg; **Iron** 2mg; **Sodium** 214mg; **Potassium** 622mg; **Phosphorus** 83mg; **Calcium** 187mg

ingredient pointer

Lacinato kale is sometimes called Tuscan kale or dinosaur kale. It has flat, slender blue-green leaves and is more tender than the more common curly-leafed kale. Look for it in larger supermarkets or farmers' markets. For most recipes, you can use different varieties of kale interchangeably, but keep in mind that the tougher curly kale needs to be torn into smaller pieces if eaten raw; or, if cooking it, simmer it a few more minutes to make sure it's tender.

Kale and Quinoa Pilaf

You can make this fresh and healthy side dish in a snap. This is a great use for leftover cooked brown rice and quinoa.

Hands-on Time: 12 minutes **Total Time:** 12 minutes **Serves:** 8

2 teaspoons canola oil

½ cup chopped onion

½ cup thinly sliced carrot

½ cup chopped red bell pepper

2 garlic cloves, minced

2 teaspoons curry powder

1 teaspoon chili paste with garlic

½ teaspoon grated peeled fresh ginger

7 cups torn kale

1½ cups cooked brown rice

1 cup cooked quinoa

2 tablespoons minced fresh cilantro

1 tablespoon lower-sodium soy sauce

1 (15-ounce) can unsalted chickpeas (garbanzo beans), rinsed and drained

1 Heat a large nonstick skillet over medium heat. Add oil to pan; swirl to coat. Add onion, carrot, bell pepper, and garlic; sauté 2 minutes. Add curry powder, chili paste, and ginger; sauté 1 minute. Add kale and remaining ingredients; cook 3 minutes or until thoroughly heated, stirring occasionally. Serve at room temperature.

PER SERVING (serving size: 1 cup):

Food Choices: 1½ Starches, 1 Nonstarchy Vegetable, ½ Fat

Calories 165; **Fat** 3.3g (sat 0.2g, mono 0.9g, poly 0.7g, trans 0g); **Protein** 7g; **Carbohydrate** 31g; **Fiber** 5g; **Sugars** 2g; **Cholesterol** 0mg; **Iron** 3mg; **Sodium** 193mg; **Potassium** 445mg; **Phosphorus** 135mg; **Calcium** 116mg

Baby Potatoes
with Kale and Garlic

Dress up baby potatoes with chopped kale and sautéed garlic. For variety and added color, try using a combination of white, purple, and red potatoes.

Hands-on Time: 5 minutes   **Total Time:** 20 minutes   **Serves:** 4

1 pound sliced baby potatoes

1½ tablespoons canola oil

2 tablespoons sliced garlic

3 cups chopped kale

1 tablespoon water

1 teaspoon sesame oil

¼ teaspoon salt

¼ teaspoon freshly ground black pepper

1 Place potatoes in a saucepan; cover with water. Bring to a boil. Cook 8 minutes; drain.

2 Heat a large skillet over medium-high heat. Add canola oil to pan; swirl to coat. Add potatoes and garlic; cook 3 minutes. Add kale and 1 tablespoon water. Cover and cook 3 minutes. Add sesame oil, salt, and pepper; toss to combine.

PER SERVING (serving size: ¾ cup):

Food Choices: 1 Starch, 1 Nonstarchy Vegetable, 1 Fat

Calories 167; **Fat** 6.9g (sat 0.6g, mono 3.8g, poly 2.2g, trans 0g); **Protein** 4g; **Carbohydrate** 25g; **Fiber** 3g; **Sugars** 2g; **Cholesterol** 0mg; **Iron** 2mg; **Sodium** 190mg; **Potassium** 758mg; **Phosphorus** 104mg; **Calcium** 87mg

Mashed-Potato Cakes with Onions and Kale

Friends and family will appreciate this fresh spin on potatoes, a staple starch of the dinner table.

Hands-on Time: 12 minutes   **Total Time:** 55 minutes   **Serves:** 8

12 cups water
1 bunch kale, trimmed (about 4 ounces)
2⅔ cups (1-inch) cubed Yukon gold or red potato (about 1 pound)
¾ teaspoon salt, divided
1 tablespoon olive oil
1 tablespoon butter
3 cups diced onion
2 tablespoons chopped fresh sage
¼ cup sliced green onions
¼ teaspoon freshly ground black pepper
Cooking spray
Sage sprigs (optional)

1 Bring 12 cups water to a boil in a Dutch oven; add kale. Cover and cook over medium heat 5 minutes or until tender. Remove kale with a slotted spoon, reserving cooking liquid. Chop kale, and set aside.

2 Add potato to reserved cooking liquid in pan; bring to a boil. Reduce heat, and simmer 10 minutes or until tender. Drain; partially mash potatoes. Stir in kale and ¼ teaspoon salt.

3 Preheat oven to 400°.

4 Heat oil and butter in a large nonstick skillet over medium-high heat; swirl to coat pan. Add ½ teaspoon salt, diced onion, and chopped sage. Cook 13 minutes or until browned. Combine potato mixture, onion mixture, green onions, and pepper. Remove from heat; cool slightly. Divide potato mixture into 8 equal portions, shaping each into a ½-inch-thick patty. Place patties on a baking sheet coated with cooking spray. Bake at 400° for 20 minutes.

5 Preheat broiler. Broil patties 5 minutes or until browned. Garnish with sage sprigs, if desired.

PER SERVING (serving size: 1 patty):
Food Choices: 1 Starch, 1 Nonstarchy Vegetable, ½ Fat
Calories 123; **Fat** 3.5g (sat 1.2g, mono 1.7g, poly 0.3g, trans 0g); **Protein** 3g; **Carbohydrate** 22g; **Fiber** 3g; **Sugars** 4g; **Cholesterol** 4mg; **Iron** 1mg; **Sodium** 248mg; **Potassium** 421mg; **Phosphorus** 62mg; **Calcium** 44mg

Roasted Peppers and Tomatoes with Herbs and Capers

This dish is baked just long enough to bring out the juices of the tomatoes, and then chilled. Serve it as a salad or a side dish. Keep the colors of the tomatoes and peppers the same, or vary them wildly. Campari tomatoes are commonly available at supermarkets; look for tomatoes that are smaller than the vine-ripened ones but larger than grape tomatoes (about 1½ inches wide).

Hands-on Time: 35 minutes   **Total Time:** 2 hours   **Serves:** 8

2 **red bell peppers**

2 **yellow bell peppers**

1½ **pounds Campari tomatoes, halved**

⅜ **teaspoon kosher salt, divided**

¼ **teaspoon freshly ground black pepper**

⅓ **cup flat-leaf parsley leaves**

3 **tablespoons extra-virgin olive oil**

1 **tablespoon chopped fresh oregano**

1 **tablespoon capers, rinsed and drained**

2 **teaspoons minced fresh garlic**

12 **niçoise olives, pitted and halved**

1 Preheat broiler.

2 Cut bell peppers in half lengthwise; discard seeds and membranes. Place halves, skin sides up, on a foil-lined baking sheet; flatten with hand. Broil 10 minutes or until blackened. Wrap peppers in foil; let stand 10 minutes. Peel; cut into ½-inch strips.

3 Preheat oven to 400°.

4 Combine tomatoes, ¼ teaspoon salt, and black pepper in a medium bowl.

5 Combine ⅛ teaspoon salt, parsley, and remaining ingredients in a small bowl. Place one-third of tomatoes in bottom of a 1½-quart gratin dish. Top with one-third of peppers and one-third of parsley mixture. Repeat layers twice, ending with parsley mixture. Cover and bake at 400° for 30 minutes or until vegetables are thoroughly heated. Cool to room temperature; cover and chill.

PER SERVING (serving size: ¾ cup):

Food Choices: 1 Nonstarchy Vegetable, 1 Fat

Calories 97; **Fat** 6.9g (sat 0.9g, mono 4.9g, poly 0.8g, trans 0g); **Protein** 2g; **Carbohydrate** 8g; **Fiber** 2g; **Sugars** 5g; **Cholesterol** 0mg; **Iron** 1mg; **Sodium** 222mg; **Potassium** 348mg; **Phosphorus** 39mg; **Calcium** 23mg

Spinach and Onion
Couscous

Bell Pepper Sauté

Look for multipacks of green, red, and yellow bell peppers at your grocery store; they are often less expensive than if you purchased each pepper separately.

Hands-on Time: 6 minutes **Total Time:** 11 minutes **Serves:** 5

1 teaspoon olive oil

1 large yellow bell pepper, seeded and cut into julienne strips

1 large green bell pepper, seeded and cut into julienne strips

1 large red bell pepper, seeded and cut into julienne strips

2 shallots, chopped

⅛ tablespoon salt

2 tablespoons chopped fresh parsley

¼ teaspoon freshly ground black pepper

1 Heat a large nonstick skillet over medium-high heat. Add oil to pan; swirl to coat. Add bell peppers and shallots to pan; sprinkle vegetables with salt. Sauté 5 minutes or until bell peppers are crisp-tender. Stir in chopped fresh parsley and black pepper; cook 1 minute.

PER SERVING (serving size: about 1 cup):

Food Choice: 1 Nonstarchy Vegetable

Calories 40; **Fat** 1.2g (sat 0.2g, mono 0.7g, poly 0.2g, trans 0g); **Protein** 1g; **Carbohydrate** 7g; **Fiber** 2g; **Sugars** 3g; **Cholesterol** 0mg; **Iron** 1mg; **Sodium** 62mg; **Potassium** 225mg; **Phosphorus** 135mg; **Calcium** 11mg

Spinach and Onion Couscous

Couscous adds texture and heartiness to this side.

Hands-on Time: 4 minutes **Total Time:** 11 minutes **Serves:** 4

¾ cup water

¼ cup finely chopped red onion

¼ teaspoon salt

1 (6-ounce) package fresh baby spinach, coarsely chopped

½ cup uncooked couscous

1 Combine first 3 ingredients in a medium microwave-safe bowl. Cover with heavy-duty plastic wrap, and vent. Microwave at HIGH 2 minutes.

2 Add spinach and couscous to onion mixture; cover and microwave at HIGH 2 minutes. Let stand, covered, 5 minutes; fluff with a fork. Serve immediately.

PER SERVING (serving size: ¾ cup):

Food Choices: 1 Starch, 1 Nonstarchy Vegetable,

Calories 103; **Fat** 0.2g (sat 0g, mono 0.1g, poly 0.1g, trans 0g); **Protein** 4g; **Carbohydrate** 22g; **Fiber** 3g; **Sugars** 1g; **Cholesterol** 0mg; **Iron** 2mg; **Sodium** 215mg; **Potassium** 499mg; **Phosphorus** 77mg; **Calcium** 38mg

Swiss Chard with Warm
Bacon Vinaigrette

Sautéed Spinach with Raisins and Pine Nuts

Spinach makes this tasty dish a good source of potassium.

Hands-on Time: 9 minutes **Total Time:** 9 minutes **Serves:** 4

4 teaspoons pine nuts

1 teaspoon olive oil

2 garlic cloves, minced

2 (6-ounce) packages fresh baby spinach

¼ teaspoon salt

¼ teaspoon freshly ground black pepper

⅛ teaspoon crushed red pepper

Dash of ground nutmeg

⅓ cup golden raisins

1 Heat a large nonstick skillet over medium-high heat; add pine nuts, and cook 3 minutes or until lightly browned, stirring constantly. Remove from pan; set aside.

2 Add oil to pan; swirl to coat. Add garlic; sauté 30 seconds. Add spinach; sauté 4 minutes or until spinach wilts. Remove from heat; sprinkle with salt and next 3 ingredients (through nutmeg). Add pine nuts and raisins; toss well. Serve immediately with a slotted spoon.

PER SERVING (serving size: ½ cup):

Food Choices: ½ Fruit, 2 Nonstarchy Vegetables, ½ Fat

Calories 94; **Fat** 3.1g (sat 0.3g, mono 1.5g, poly 1.2g, trans 0g); **Protein** 3g; **Carbohydrate** 15g; **Fiber** 3g; **Sugars** 9g; **Cholesterol** 0mg; **Iron** 3mg; **Sodium** 212mg; **Potassium** 600mg; **Phosphorus** 76mg; **Calcium** 91mg

Swiss Chard with Warm Bacon Vinaigrette

The sweetness of applewood-smoked bacon is the perfect balance to bitter chard.

Hands-on Time: 10 minutes **Total Time:** 10 minutes **Serves:** 4

2 applewood-smoked bacon slices

2 teaspoons cider vinegar

¼ teaspoon freshly ground black pepper

6 cups chopped Swiss chard

1 Heat a medium nonstick skillet over medium heat. Add bacon to pan; cook until crisp. Remove bacon from pan; crumble. Remove pan from heat. Add vinegar and freshly ground black pepper to pan, stirring with a whisk. Pour vinegar mixture over Swiss chard, and sprinkle with crumbled bacon; toss to combine.

PER SERVING (serving size: about ½ cup):

Food Choices: 1 Nonstarchy Vegetable, 1 Fat

Calories 39; **Fat** 2.4g (sat 0.9g, mono 0g, poly 0g, trans 0g); **Protein** 3g; **Carbohydrate** 2g; **Fiber** 1g; **Sugars** 1g; **Cholesterol** 5mg; **Iron** 1mg; **Sodium** 225mg; **Potassium** 235mg; **Phosphorus** 28mg; **Calcium** 28mg

Pile 'em on!

Unlike potatoes, green peas, or corn, nonstarchy vegetables are very low in carbohydrates and calories, yet high in vitamins, minerals, and antioxidants.

Make it your goal to incorporate at least 2 to 3 servings of these vegetables into your meals every day. A serving is 1 cup of raw vegetables or ½ cup of cooked vegetables, and each serving has about 5 grams of carbs and about 25 calories.

Here are the most common nonstarchy vegetables and some ideas for getting more of them in your diet every day.

ARTICHOKES	BRUSSELS SPROUTS	CUCUMBERS	ONIONS (GREEN ONIONS, LEEKS, SWEET ONIONS)
ASPARAGUS	CABBAGE	EGGPLANT	
BEANS (GREEN, ITALIAN, WAX)	CARROTS	FENNEL	PEAS (SNOW PEAS AND SUGAR SNAP PEAS)
BEETS	CAULIFLOWER	GREENS (COLLARDS, KALE, MUSTARD, SPINACH, SWISS CHARD, TURNIP)	PEPPERS (ALL VARIETIES)
BROCCOLI	CELERY		
		JICAMA	RADISHES
		MUSHROOMS	RUTABAGA
		OKRA	SUMMER SQUASH (PATTY PAN SQUASH, YELLOW SQUASH, ZUCCHINI)
			TOMATOES
			TURNIPS

- If vegetables are ready to eat, you'll be more likely to make them your go-to snack. Spend a few minutes once a week washing and cutting up broccoli and cauliflower florets, carrots, cucumbers, jicama, peppers, or radishes for snacks to enjoy alone or with a healthy dip.
- Roast a big batch of vegetables on the weekend to use in omelets, frittatas, soups, stews, and casseroles throughout the week.
- Drink your veggies in a smoothie or have a low-sodium tomato or vegetable juice. You can add collards, spinach, kale, celery, or fennel to your favorite fruit smoothie recipes. If you buy vegetable and fruit drinks, check the label; many of these are high in carbohydrates from fruit juice concentrate.
- Add more vegetables to foods you frequently eat. Load up sandwiches with fresh spinach and sliced cucumbers. Add more veggies to soups—even canned soups are better with a few shredded carrots, chopped bell peppers, or thinly sliced summer squash thrown in.
- Begin every meal with vegetable soup or a green salad for an easy way to add a serving of vegetables. These low-cal, low-carb starters will help you feel full and more satisfied, too.

Tomatoes Provençale

Garlic, tomatoes, and olive oil permeate Provençale cuisine. Here, they combine in a dish that pairs tender roasted tomatoes with a crisp breadcrumb topping.

Hands-on Time: 15 minutes **Total Time:** 53 minutes **Serves:** 8

8 tomatoes (about 8 ounces each)

½ teaspoon salt, divided

1 (½-ounce) slice sourdough bread

6 tablespoons chopped fresh parsley

1 ounce grated fresh Parmesan cheese (about ¼ cup)

2 garlic cloves, minced

2 teaspoons extra-virgin olive oil

Cooking spray

¼ teaspoon freshly ground black pepper

Thyme leaves (optional)

1 Preheat oven to 400°.

2 Cut tops off tomatoes; discard. Carefully seed tomatoes, leaving shells intact. Sprinkle cut sides of tomatoes with ¼ teaspoon salt. Place tomatoes, cut sides down, on several layers of paper towels; drain 15 minutes.

3 Place bread in a food processor; pulse 10 times or until coarse crumbs form to measure ½ cup. Combine breadcrumbs, 6 tablespoons parsley, cheese, and garlic in a small bowl.

4 Heat a large ovenproof skillet over medium-high heat. Add oil to pan; swirl to coat. Place tomatoes, cut sides down, in pan, and sauté 5 minutes. Remove pan from heat; turn tomatoes over. Spoon about 2 tablespoons breadcrumb mixture over each tomato. Spray breadcrumb mixture with cooking spray, and sprinkle with ¼ teaspoon salt and pepper. Wrap handle of pan with foil. Bake at 400° for 30 minutes or until breadcrumb mixture browns. Garnish with thyme leaves, if desired.

PER SERVING (serving size: 1 tomato):

Food Choices: 2 Nonstarchy Vegetables, ½ Fat

Calories 73; **Fat** 2.8g (sat 0.8g, mono 1.2g, poly 0.4g, trans 0g); **Protein** 3g; **Carbohydrate** 11g; **Fiber** 2g; **Sugars** 5g; **Cholesterol** 2mg; **Iron** 1mg; **Sodium** 234mg; **Potassium** 497mg; **Phosphorus** 78mg; **Calcium** 60mg

Grilled Zucchini Bulgur Pilaf

Bulgur's mild flavor makes it a versatile ingredient. Try it in soup or salad to add whole grains and bulk.

Hands-on Time: 9 minutes   **Total Time:** 20 minutes   **Serves:** 6

1 tablespoon olive oil

¾ cup chopped onion

⅓ cup chopped celery

2 cups water

1 cup uncooked bulgur

Cooking spray

1 zucchini

¼ cup chopped fresh parsley

½ teaspoon salt

¼ teaspoon pepper

Lemon wedges (optional)

1 Heat a large saucepan over medium-high heat. Add olive oil; swirl to coat. Add onion and celery; sauté 3 minutes. Add 2 cups water and bulgur; bring to a boil. Cover, reduce heat, and simmer 11 minutes.

2 While bulgur simmers, heat a grill pan over medium-high heat; coat with cooking spray. Quarter zucchini. Grill zucchini 5 minutes; dice. Combine bulgur, zucchini, parsley, salt, and pepper. Serve with lemon wedges, if desired.

PER SERVING (serving size: ⅔ cup):

Food Choices: 1 Starch, 1 Nonstarchy Vegetable

Calories 116; **Fat** 2.8g (sat 0.4g, mono 1.7g, poly 0.7g, trans 0g); **Protein** 4g; **Carbohydrate** 21g; **Fiber** 5g; **Sugars** 2g; **Cholesterol** 0mg; **Iron** 1mg; **Sodium** 210mg; **Potassium** 242mg; **Phosphorus** 89mg; **Calcium** 26mg

Zesty White Beans and Tomatoes

This tasty spin on navy beans is as simple as it is satisfying.

Hands-on Time: 7 minutes **Total Time:** 7 minutes **Serves:** 4

1 (16-ounce) can unsalted navy beans, rinsed and drained

½ cup quartered cherry tomatoes

2 tablespoons chopped fresh parsley

1 tablespoon chopped fresh basil

1 tablespoon fresh lemon juice

1 tablespoon extra-virgin olive oil

⅜ teaspoon salt

1 garlic clove, minced

1 Combine all ingredients in a bowl. Serve at room temperature or chilled.

PER SERVING (serving size: ½ cup):

Food Choices: 1 Starch, ½ Fat

Calories 112; **Fat** 3.9g (sat 0.6g, mono 2.5g, poly 0.7g, trans 0g); **Protein** 5g; **Carbohydrate** 15g; **Fiber** 4g; **Sugars** 1g; **Cholesterol** 0mg; **Iron** 2mg; **Sodium** 231mg; **Potassium** 258mg; **Phosphorus** 98mg; **Calcium** 39mg

Barley-Mushroom Pilaf

Mushrooms infuse the barley with delicious umami flavor.

Hands-on Time: 14 minutes **Total Time:** 20 minutes **Serves:** 12

3 cups unsalted chicken stock

⅓ cup dried porcini mushrooms, chopped (about ⅓ ounce)

1½ cups uncooked quick-cooking barley

2 tablespoons olive oil

3 cups quartered shiitake mushroom caps (about 8 ounces)

2 cups chopped onion

¾ teaspoon salt

½ teaspoon dried rosemary

1 (8-ounce) package presliced mushrooms

¼ cup dry Marsala

2 teaspoons sherry vinegar

1 Combine stock and porcini in a large saucepan. Bring to a boil; stir in barley. Cover, reduce heat, and simmer 12 minutes or until tender.

2 While barley cooks, heat a Dutch oven over medium-high heat. Add oil to pan; swirl to coat. Add shiitake, onion, salt, rosemary, and presliced mushrooms; sauté 5 minutes. Stir in Marsala; cook 1 minute. Stir in barley mixture and vinegar; cook 2 minutes or until thoroughly heated, stirring frequently.

PER SERVING (serving size: ½ cup):

Food Choices: 1 Starch, 1 Nonstarchy Vegetable, ½ Fat

Calories 137; **Fat** 2.9g (sat 0.5g, mono 1.7g, poly 0.5g, trans 0g); **Protein** 6g; **Carbohydrate** 22g; **Fiber** 5g; **Sugars** 2g; **Cholesterol** 0mg; **Iron** 1mg; **Sodium** 187mg; **Potassium** 349mg; **Phosphorus** 124mg; **Calcium** 21mg

Zesty White Beans
and Tomatoes

Quinoa with Roasted Garlic, Tomatoes, and Spinach

Quinoa contains more protein than any other grain. The tiny, beige-colored seeds have a nice crunch. It's cooked and eaten like rice and other grains. Be sure to give it a good rinse before cooking, or it may have a bitter taste.

Hands-on Time: 15 minutes   **Total Time:** 1 hour, 17 minutes   **Serves:** 4

- 1 whole garlic head
- 1 teaspoon olive oil
- 1 tablespoon finely chopped shallots
- ¼ teaspoon crushed red pepper
- ½ cup uncooked quinoa, rinsed and drained
- 1 tablespoon dry white wine
- 1 cup fat-free, lower-sodium chicken broth (such as Swanson)
- ½ cup fresh baby spinach leaves
- ⅓ cup chopped seeded tomato (1 small)
- 1 tablespoon shaved fresh Parmesan cheese
- ¼ teaspoon salt

1 Preheat oven to 350°. Remove papery skin from garlic head. Cut garlic head in half crosswise, breaking apart to separate whole cloves. Wrap half of head in foil; reserve remaining garlic for another use. Bake at 350° for 1 hour; cool 10 minutes. Separate cloves; squeeze to extract garlic pulp. Discard skins.

2 During last 10 minutes of baking garlic, heat a medium saucepan over medium heat. Add oil to pan; swirl to coat. Add shallots and red pepper to pan; cook 1 minute. Add quinoa to pan; cook 2 minutes, stirring constantly. Add wine; cook until liquid is absorbed, stirring constantly. Add broth; bring to a boil. Cover, reduce heat, and simmer 15 minutes or until liquid is absorbed. Remove from heat; stir in garlic pulp, spinach, tomato, cheese, and salt. Serve immediately.

PER SERVING (serving size: ½ cup):

Food Choices: 1 Starch, ½ Fat

Calories 118; **Fat** 2.7g (sat 0.4g, mono 1.3g, poly 0.7g, trans 0g); **Protein** 5g; **Carbohydrate** 17g; **Fiber** 2g; **Sugars** 1g; **Cholesterol** 1mg; **Iron** 2mg; **Sodium** 225mg; **Potassium** 272mg; **Phosphorus** 137mg; **Calcium** 54mg

Confetti Rice Pilaf with Toasted Flaxseed

To release the omega-3 fatty acids and fiber contained in flaxseed, the hard outer coating must be broken down. Toast the seeds and chop them in a blender before adding them to this pilaf. Flaxseed keeps best when stored in an airtight container in the refrigerator.

Hands-on Time: 10 minutes   **Total Time**: 30 minutes   **Serves**: 8

¼ **cup flaxseed**

2 **teaspoons olive oil**

1 **cup chopped onion**

1 **cup uncooked basmati or long-grain rice**

1 **(16-ounce) can fat-free, lower-sodium chicken broth (such as Swanson)**

¼ **cup chopped fresh parsley**

2 **teaspoons grated lemon rind**

1 **tablespoon fresh lemon juice**

¼ **teaspoon salt**

¼ **teaspoon freshly ground black pepper**

1 Place flaxseed in a small nonstick skillet; cook over low heat 5 minutes or until toasted, stirring constantly. Place flaxseed in a blender; process just until chopped.

2 Heat a large saucepan over medium heat. Add oil to pan; swirl to coat. Add onion; cook over medium heat 3 minutes or until tender. Add rice. Cook 1 minute; stir constantly. Stir in broth; bring to a boil. Reduce heat; simmer 20 minutes or until rice is tender. Remove from heat; fluff with a fork. Stir in flaxseed, parsley, and remaining ingredients.

PER SERVING (serving size: ½ cup):

Food Choices: 1½ Starches, ½ Fat

Calories 132; **Fat** 3.6g (sat 0.4g, mono 2g, poly 1.1g, trans 0g); **Protein** 4g; **Carbohydrate** 22g; **Fiber** 2g; **Sugars** 1g; **Cholesterol** 0mg; **Iron** 2mg; **Sodium** 201mg; **Potassium** 158mg; **Phosphorus** 50mg; **Calcium** 28mg

Spicy Brown Rice

Give brown rice a little kick by adding chile paste and sesame oil to this Asian-inspired side. Pair with fatty fish like albacore tuna to make a healthy and complete meal.

Hands-on Time: 5 minutes   **Total Time:** 5 minutes   **Serves:** 4

2 cups cooked brown rice
¼ cup chopped green onions
1 teaspoon chile paste with garlic
1 teaspoon sesame oil
¼ teaspoon kosher salt

1 Combine cooked brown rice, green onions, chile paste with garlic, sesame oil, and kosher salt.

PER SERVING (serving size: about ½ cup):
Food Choices: 2 Starches
Calories 120; **Fat** 2g (sat 0.3g, mono 0.8g, poly 0.8g, trans 0g); **Protein** 3g; **Carbohydrate** 28g; **Fiber** 2g; **Sugars** 0g; **Cholesterol** 0mg; **Iron** 1mg; **Sodium** 153mg; **Potassium** 85mg; **Phosphorus** 78mg; **Calcium** 14mg

Carrot-Cilantro Bulgur

Made with shredded carrot and chopped cilantro, this nutritious dish is high in fiber and protein and low in saturated fat.

Hands-on Time: 8 minutes   **Total Time:** 16 minutes   **Serves:** 4

¾ cup uncooked bulgur
2 cups water
¾ cup shredded carrot
2 tablespoons chopped fresh cilantro
2 tablespoons fresh lime juice
1½ tablespoons extra-virgin olive oil
⅜ teaspoon kosher salt
¼ teaspoon freshly ground black pepper

1 Combine bulgur and 2 cups water in a small saucepan; bring to a boil. Cover, reduce heat, and cook 12 minutes. Drain; rinse with cold water. Drain. Stir in carrot, cilantro, lime juice, olive oil, salt, and pepper.

PER SERVING (serving size: about ⅔ cup):
Food Choices: 1½ Starches, 1 Fat
Calories 145; **Fat** 5.5g (sat 0.8g, mono 3.7g, poly 0.7g, trans 0g); **Protein** 3g; **Carbohydrate** 23g; **Fiber** 5g; **Sugars** 1g; **Cholesterol** 0mg; **Iron** 1mg; **Sodium** 199mg; **Potassium** 185mg; **Phosphorus** 87mg; **Calcium** 18mg

Multigrain Pilaf

Pecans are rich in antioxidants and in healthy fats that lower cholesterol; however, they're also high in calories, so eat them in moderation.

Hands-on Time: 5 minutes **Total Time**: 25 minutes **Serves**: 7

1 teaspoon olive oil

1 cup chopped onion

3 garlic cloves, minced

2⅓ cups organic vegetable broth (such as Swanson)

⅓ cup uncooked kasha

⅓ cup uncooked barley

⅓ cup uncooked bulgur

⅛ teaspoon kosher salt

1 bay leaf

¼ cup chopped pecans, toasted

⅛ teaspoon freshly ground black pepper

1 Heat a 2-quart saucepan over medium-high heat. Add oil to pan; swirl to coat. Add onion and garlic to pan; sauté 3 minutes or until onion is tender.

2 Add broth and next 5 ingredients (through bay leaf) to pan; bring to a boil. Cover, reduce heat, and simmer 15 minutes or until liquid is absorbed. Remove from heat. Discard bay leaf. Fluff with a fork; stir in pecans and pepper.

PER SERVING (serving size: ½ cup):

Food Choices: 1½ Starches, ½ Fat

Calories 132; **Fat** 4g (sat 0.4g, mono 2.2g, poly 1.1g, trans 0g); **Protein** 7g; **Carbohydrate** 22g; **Fiber** 4g; **Sugars** 1g; **Cholesterol** 0mg; **Iron** 1mg; **Sodium** 221mg; **Potassium** 227mg; **Phosphorus** 112mg; **Calcium** 17mg

ingredient pointer

Kasha, a popular food in the Middle East, is the toasted and hulled kernel of buckwheat, also called groats. Like barley and bulgur, kasha has a nutty flavor and gives a dish texture.

Peanut-Sesame Noodles

While the noodles cook, make the sauce and put the veggies in a bowl. Once the noodles are done, toss everything together, and you're ready to serve lunch. This dish is typically served chilled, but it's just as tasty at room temperature. You can substitute spaghetti or linguine for the soba noodles.

Hands-on Time: 4 minutes   **Total Time:** 17 minutes   **Serves:** 5

¼ **pound uncooked** soba (buckwheat noodles)

Peanut-Sesame Sauce

½ **cup matchstick-cut carrots**

⅓ **cup julienne-cut pickling cucumber**

2 **tablespoons presliced green onions**

1 **teaspoon sesame seeds (optional)**

1 Cook soba noodles according to package directions.

2 While noodles cook, prepare Peanut-Sesame Sauce.

3 Drain noodles, and rinse under cold running water. Drain. Combine noodles, carrots, cucumber, and green onions in a medium bowl. Drizzle with Peanut-Sesame Sauce; toss gently to coat. Cover and chill, or serve at room temperature. Garnish with sesame seeds, if desired.

PER SERVING (serving size: ½ cup):

Food Choices: 1 Starch, 1 Nonstarchy Vegetable, ½ Fat

Calories 124; **Fat** 3.8g (sat 0.6g, mono 1.7g, poly 1.4g, trans 0g); **Protein** 4g; **Carbohydrate** 20g; **Fiber** 2g; **Sugars** 3g; **Cholesterol** 0mg; **Iron** 1mg; **Sodium** 127mg; **Potassium** 128mg; **Phosphorus** 106mg; **Calcium** 11mg

Peanut-Sesame Sauce

Hands-on Time: 3 minutes   **Total Time:** 3 minutes   **Makes:** 3 tablespoons

1 **tablespoon creamy** peanut butter

1 **tablespoon lower-sodium soy sauce**

2 **teaspoons dark sesame oil**

2 **teaspoons seasoned rice vinegar**

⅛ **teaspoon crushed red pepper**

½ **small garlic clove, minced**

1 Combine all ingredients in a small bowl, stirring with a whisk until smooth.

PER SERVING (serving size: 1 teaspoon):

Food Choice: Free

Calories 22; **Fat** 1.9g (sat 0.3g, mono 0.8g, poly 0.7g, trans 0g); **Protein** 1g; **Carbohydrate** 1g; **Fiber** 0g; **Sugars** 1g; **Cholesterol** 0mg; **Iron** 0mg; **Sodium** 69mg; **Potassium** 31mg; **Phosphorus** 15mg; **Calcium** 1mg

Peanut Butter
Cookies, page 278

Decadent Desserts

Enjoy the health benefits from berries, nuts, oats, milk, and yogurt in these luscious, guilt-free treats—all with 150 calories or less. These bars, cookies, parfaits, and frozen treats are the perfect sweet ending to any meal.

Mixed Berry, Flaxseed, and Yogurt Parfaits

Using plain fat-free yogurt instead of the full-fat variety cuts about 7 grams of fat.

Hands-on Time: 5 minutes **Total Time:** 5 minutes **Serves:** 2

1 cup plain fat-free yogurt

2 tablespoons sugar-free strawberry preserves

¼ teaspoon grated lemon rind

¼ cup low-fat granola without raisins

1½ tablespoons flaxseed meal

1 tablespoon sliced almonds, toasted

⅔ cup mixed fresh berries

1 Combine first 3 ingredients in a small bowl. Combine granola, flaxseed meal, and almonds in a separate small bowl. Spoon half of yogurt mixture into bottom of 2 (8-ounce) glasses; top with half of granola mixture and ⅓ cup berries. Repeat layers with remaining yogurt mixture, granola mixture, and berries.

PER SERVING (serving size: 1 parfait):

Food Choices: 1½ Carbohydrates, ½ Fat-Free Milk, ½ Fat

Calories 150; **Fat** 4.5g (sat 0.2g, mono 1.7g, poly 2g, trans 0g); **Protein** 8g; **Carbohydrate** 27g; **Fiber** 5g; **Sugars** 10g; **Cholesterol** 3mg; **Iron** 1mg; **Sodium** 83mg; **Potassium** 452mg; **Phosphorus** 253mg; **Calcium** 182mg

Warm Blackberry Sauce over Peach Sorbet

A small cookie scoop, available at discount stores, will let you portion the sorbet accurately, giving your guests just a little something sweet after the meal.

Hands-on Time: 15 minutes **Total Time:** 15 minutes **Serves:** 6

2 pints fresh blackberries, halved

2 tablespoons granulated no-calorie sweetener (such as Splenda)

2½ teaspoons grated orange rind

½ teaspoon ground ginger

1 pint sugar-free peach sorbet, sweetened with sucralose

6 sugar-free gingersnaps, crushed

1 Combine first 4 ingredients in a saucepan over medium heat; cook, stirring constantly, 5 minutes or until thoroughly heated. Serve over sorbet; sprinkle with gingersnaps.

PER SERVING (serving size: ⅓ cup sorbet, about ½ cup blackberry sauce, and about 1 tablespoon crushed gingersnaps):

Food Choices: 1½ Carbohydrates

Calories 103; **Fat** 1.2g (sat 0.2g, mono 0.1g, poly 0.3g, trans 0g); **Protein** 2g; **Carbohydrate** 27g; **Fiber** 10g; **Sugars** 8g; **Cholesterol** 0mg; **Iron** 1mg; **Sodium** 18mg; **Potassium** 216mg; **Phosphorus** 139mg; **Calcium** 29mg

Mixed Berry, Flaxseed,
and Yogurt Parfaits

Fresh Fruit with Strawberry Sauce

For a variation, try this sauce spooned over yogurt or angel food cake.

Hands-on Time: 10 minutes **Total Time:** 10 minutes **Serves:** 4

1 cup frozen unsweetened whole strawberries, thawed

2 teaspoons granulated no-calorie sweetener (such as Splenda)

¼ teaspoon grated orange rind

2 cups orange sections (about 6 oranges)

1 cup cubed peeled kiwifruit (about 3 kiwifruit)

1 Place first 3 ingredients in a blender, and process until smooth; set sauce aside.

2 Spoon ½ cup orange sections and ¼ cup kiwifruit into each of 4 small bowls; top each serving with 3 tablespoons sauce.

PER SERVING (serving size: 1 parfait):

Food Choices: 1½ Fruits

Calories 91; **Fat** 0.5g (sat 0.1g, mono 0.1g, poly 0.1g, trans 0g); **Protein** 2g; **Carbohydrate** 21g; **Fiber** 6g; **Sugars** 14g; **Cholesterol** 0mg; **Iron** 1mg; **Sodium** 1mg; **Potassium** 359mg; **Phosphorus** 37mg; **Calcium** 58mg

ingredient pointer

No-calorie sweeteners are a pantry staple for people with diabetes, giving the sweet flavor of a special treat without affecting blood sugar levels. Granular no-calorie sweetener has the added advantage that it can be measured cup for cup like regular sugar, so it's easy to substitute in recipes that call for regular sugar. Granulated sweeteners such as Splenda contain bulking agents that include small amounts of carbohydrate. (For example, Splenda contains 12 grams per ½ cup.) If enough granular sweetener is used, a measurable amount of carbohydrate can be consumed.

Summer Berry Medley with Limoncello and Mint

Limoncello (lee-mon-CHAY-low) is a lemon-flavored liqueur from Italy's Amalfi Coast. It's often savored after a meal. Store it in the freezer, and serve over ice. If you have trouble finding it, substitute an orange-flavored liqueur such as Grand Marnier.

Hands-on Time: 5 minutes **Total Time:** 25 minutes **Serves:** 6

2 cups fresh blackberries

2 cups hulled fresh strawberries, quartered

2 cups fresh blueberries

1 cup fresh raspberries

2 tablespoons granulated no-calorie sweetener (such as Splenda)

1 tablespoon grated lemon rind

2 tablespoons fresh lemon juice

2 tablespoons limoncello (lemon-flavored liqueur)

½ cup torn mint leaves

1 Combine first 8 ingredients in a bowl; let stand 20 minutes. Gently stir in mint using a rubber spatula.

PER SERVING (serving size: about 1 cup):

Food Choices: 1½ Fruits

Calories 106; **Fat** 0.8g (sat 0g, mono 0.1g, poly 0.4g, trans 0g); **Protein** 2g; **Carbohydrate** 23g; **Fiber** 7g; **Sugars** 12g; **Cholesterol** 0mg; **Iron** 1mg; **Sodium** 2mg; **Potassium** 260mg; **Phosphorus** 41mg; **Calcium** 38mg

Peach Melba Parfaits

Garnish this parfait with peeled and sliced peaches to add a pop of color and juicy flavor.

Hands-on Time: 15 minutes **Total Time:** 3 hours **Serves:** 8

4 cups vanilla sugar-free low-fat ice cream, softened

1 cup mashed peeled peaches (about ¾ pound)

1 tablespoon amaretto

1 teaspoon vanilla extract

1 (12-ounce) package unsweetened frozen raspberries, thawed

3 tablespoons granulated no-calorie sweetener (such as Splenda)

1 tablespoon Grand Marnier or other orange-flavored liqueur

1½ cups fresh raspberries

1 Combine low-fat ice cream, peaches, amaretto, and vanilla in a freezer-safe container; stir well. Freeze until firm.

2 Place thawed raspberries, sweetener, and liqueur in a blender, and process until smooth. Press raspberry mixture through a sieve, reserving puree; discard seeds. Cover and chill.

3 Spoon 2 teaspoons raspberry puree into each of 8 parfait glasses or champagne flutes. Top each with about 1½ tablespoons fresh raspberries and ¼ cup ice-cream mixture. Repeat layers, ending with 2 teaspoons raspberry puree.

PER SERVING (serving size: 1 parfait):

Food Choices: 1½ Carbohydrates, 1 Fat

Calories 149; **Fat** 3.5g (sat 2g, mono 0.1g, poly 0.3g, trans 0g); **Protein** 4g; **Carbohydrate** 25g; **Fiber** 7g; **Sugars** 9g; **Cholesterol** 10mg; **Iron** 1mg; **Sodium** 71mg; **Potassium** 277mg; **Phosphorus** 89mg; **Calcium** 118mg

Raspberry Parfaits

Raspberries give nectarous flavor to this quick and refreshing dessert.

Hands-on Time: 15 minutes **Total Time:** 20 minutes **Serves:** 4

2 (6-ounce) packages fresh raspberries, divided

2 tablespoons fresh orange juice

1 tablespoon granulated no-calorie sweetener (such as Splenda)

1 cup sugar-free vanilla frozen Greek yogurt

1 Combine 1 package raspberries and juice in a small saucepan over medium-high heat; bring to a boil. Reduce heat, and simmer 8 minutes, stirring occasionally to break up berries. Place raspberry mixture, remaining package raspberries, and sweetener in a medium bowl and toss gently to combine; cool 5 minutes in freezer.

2 Place 2 tablespoons frozen yogurt in each of 4 parfait glasses or champagne flutes. Top each serving with 3 tablespoons raspberry mixture. Repeat procedure with remaining yogurt and raspberry mixture.

PER SERVING (serving size: 1 parfait):

Food Choices: 1 Carbohydrate, ½ Fat

Calories 101; **Fat** 2.8g (sat 1.5g, mono 0.1g, poly 0.3g, trans 0g); **Protein** 3g; **Carbohydrate** 18g; **Fiber** 6g; **Sugars** 7g; **Cholesterol** 10mg; **Iron** 1mg; **Sodium** 31mg; **Potassium** 167mg; **Phosphorus** 141mg; **Calcium** 72mg

Peach Melba Parfaits

White Chocolate Mousse

Take a shortcut to deliciousness by using a few store-bought items. Simply garnish with raspberries and mint and pretend you spent all day in the kitchen. If you can't find white chocolate sugar-free pudding, you can use the chocolate sugar-free kind.

Hands-on Time: 8 minutes   **Total Time:** 2 hours, 8 minutes   **Serves:** 4

1 (1-ounce) package white chocolate sugar-free, fat-free instant pudding mix

1½ cups fat-free milk

1½ cups frozen fat-free whipped topping, thawed

2 cups fresh raspberries

Mint sprigs (optional)

1 Prepare pudding mix according to package directions, using 1½ cups milk. Fold whipped topping into pudding. Cover and chill at least 2 hours. Place pudding in each of 4 dessert dishes. Top each serving with raspberries; garnish with mint, if desired.

PER SERVING (serving size: ½ cup pudding and ½ cup raspberries):

Food Choices: 1½ Carbohydrates

Calories 131; **Fat** 0.5g (sat 0.1g, mono 0.1g, poly 0.2g, trans 0g); **Protein** 4g; **Carbohydrate** 26g; **Fiber** 5g; **Sugars** 10g; **Cholesterol** 2mg; **Iron** 0mg; **Sodium** 247mg; **Potassium** 323mg; **Phosphorus** 150mg; **Calcium** 127mg

small change, big result

White chocolate mousse is traditionally made by folding whipped cream into melted white chocolate—a rich, decadent treat loaded with sugar and saturated fat. Our version lightens up this classic dessert with a sugar-free pudding mix made with fat-free milk. Fat-free whipped topping stands in for whipped cream to give the mousse its light, airy texture. It's just as satisfying with a fraction of the carbohydrates and saturated fat.

Cantaloupe Sherbet

This easy five-ingredient melon sherbet is a great way to transform fresh cantaloupe into a low-sugar frozen dessert.

Hands-on Time: 24 minutes **Total Time:** 5 hours, 24 minutes **Serves:** 5

1 large ripe cantaloupe, peeled and finely chopped (about 5 cups)

⅓ cup granulated no-calorie sweetener (such as Splenda)

2 tablespoons fresh lemon juice

2 teaspoons unflavored gelatin

¼ cup cold water

1 (8-ounce) carton vanilla fat-free yogurt sweetened with aspartame

Mint sprigs (optional)

1 Place cantaloupe, sweetener, and lemon juice in a blender or food processor; process until smooth. Transfer mixture to a medium bowl.

2 Sprinkle gelatin over ¼ cup cold water in a small saucepan; let stand 1 minute. Cook over low heat, stirring until gelatin dissolves, about 4 minutes. Add to cantaloupe mixture, stirring well. Add yogurt, stirring until smooth.

3 Pour mixture into an 8-inch square metal baking pan; freeze until almost firm.

4 Transfer mixture to a large bowl; beat with a mixer at high speed until fluffy. Spoon mixture back into pan; freeze until firm.

5 Scoop sorbet into 5 dishes. Garnish with fresh mint, if desired.

PER SERVING (serving size: 1 cup):

Food Choice: 1 Fruit

Calories 93; **Fat** 0.5g (sat 0.2g, mono 0g, poly 0g, trans 0g); **Protein** 5g; **Carbohydrate** 19g; **Fiber** 1g; **Sugars** 16g; **Cholesterol** 1mg; **Iron** 0mg; **Sodium** 50mg; **Potassium** 513mg; **Phosphorus** 65mg; **Calcium** 0mg

Peanut Butter Ice Cream Sandwiches

Stir peanut butter into no-sugar-added ice cream and spread between sugar-free gingersnaps for an easy, lower-carbohydrate frozen treat. Wrap individually in plastic wrap, and store in an airtight container in the freezer. Then you'll have single servings ready for an easy pre-made snack.

Hands-on Time: 5 minutes   **Total Time:** 3 hours   **Serves:** 8

3 tablespoons natural creamy peanut butter

2 cups vanilla no-sugar-added, fat-free ice cream, softened

16 (2-inch-diameter) sugar-free gingersnaps

1½ tablespoons finely chopped unsalted, dry-roasted peanuts

1 Swirl peanut butter into ice cream. Place in freezer 30 minutes or until firm enough to spread.

2 Spread ¼ cup ice-cream mixture onto each of 8 gingersnaps. Sprinkle with chopped peanuts. Top with 8 gingersnaps. Place sandwiches on a 15 x 10–inch jelly-roll pan; freeze until firm. Wrap sandwiches in plastic wrap, and store in freezer.

Note To soften ice cream in the microwave, remove top and liner (if any) of carton. Microwave at HIGH in 10-second intervals, checking in between, until ice cream reaches desired consistency.

PER SERVING (serving size: 1 sandwich):
Food Choices: 1 Carbohydrate, 1 Fat
Calories 109; **Fat** 6.5g (sat 2.1g, mono 0.4g, poly 0.3g, trans 0g); **Protein** 3g; **Carbohydrate** 12g; **Fiber** 1g; **Sugars** 3g; **Cholesterol** 6mg; **Iron** 0mg; **Sodium** 48mg; **Potassium** 147mg; **Phosphorus** 57mg; **Calcium** 47mg

ingredient pointer

Check the labels carefully when you buy ice cream or frozen yogurt. Depending on the brand and the flavor, calories and carbohydrates in a serving can vary widely. Always choose low-fat or fat-free versions. Choose a brand with 15 grams of carbohydrate or less in a ½-cup serving (1 Carbohydrate Choice has 15 grams of carbohydrate and about 70 calories).

The Power of Sugar

Sweet treats made with sugar are a delicious and enjoyable way to end a meal or celebrate a special occasion. But when you have diabetes, desserts should be enjoyed only occasionally and with proper meal planning. See "Minimize Added Sugars" on page 10 to learn how to incorporate a dessert into your meals.

You'll find the Peanut Butter-and-Jelly Sandwich Cookies on page 276 are made using real sugar instead of artificial sweeteners. Sugar does lend sweetness to desserts, but that's not the only reason it is a crucial ingredient in cooking and baking. Here are some surprising properties sugar lends to sweets:

• Sugar helps add volume and tenderness. Rising takes place in a cake or muffin when the small spaces created by gases formed from the action of baking powder or baking soda are trapped by protein in the flour. Sugar tenderizes the protein, allowing it to expand further, and thus make a tall, light-textured dessert. Without sugar, cakes and muffins are flat and have a tough, dense texture.

• Browning starts with sugar. A chocolate chip cookie with a crisp brown edge, a slice of pound cake with a lovely burnished crust, or a fruit cobbler with a golden biscuit topping—they all get their appeal from the magic of sugar. When sugar heats as it bakes, it caramelizes, creating the eye-appeal and caramelized flavor of the desserts we all love.

• Sugar helps retain moisture. More moisture means cakes and brownies are appealingly moist, not dry and crumbly. And the additional moisture retention makes baked goods stay fresh-tasting longer.

• Sugar balances flavor. Sugar plays an important role in flavor, even in sweets like puddings, custards, and ice cream that are not heated at a high enough temperature for sugar to caramelize. Sugar lends a roundness and balance of flavor that makes sugar-sweetened versions of these dishes taste spectacular and artificially-sweetened versions seem dull and bland.

• Sugar is the secret to creamy ice cream. Sugar lowers the freezing point of ice cream, frozen yogurt, and sorbet, which makes the ice crystals smaller. This property gives these refreshing desserts their soft, velvety texture.

• Small changes to sugar make different forms. Light brown and dark brown sugars have the same basic functional properties as white sugar when used in recipes; the only difference is that brown sugar has had some of the molasses added back that was removed in processing. Dark brown sugar has more molasses added and a stronger taste than light brown sugar, but both types lend a rich flavor to robust desserts like gingerbread, mincemeat pie, and butterscotch pudding. Powdered sugar is simply regular white sugar that is more finely ground, with a small amount of cornstarch added to prevent it from clumping. Its powdery texture is perfect when making frostings and meringues.

Blackberry–Cream Cheese Crepes

Blackberries are a great source of antioxidants, which fight free radicals that damage cells and make the body susceptible to chronic diseases. Incorporating this sweet fruit into dishes is a tasty and easy way to build up your cellular defense.

Hands-on Time: 36 minutes   **Total Time:** 66 minutes   **Serves:** 8

8 Blender Crepes

5 cups fresh blackberries, divided

¾ cup water, divided

2 tablespoons granulated no-calorie sweetener (such as Splenda)

1 tablespoon fresh lemon juice

1 tablespoon brandy

2 teaspoons cornstarch

¼ teaspoon ground cinnamon

1 tablespoon butter

4 ounces fat-free cream cheese, softened (about ½ cup)

1 Prepare Blender Crepes; set aside.

2 Place 1 cup blackberries and ½ cup water in a blender. Process about 1 minute or until smooth. Strain blackberry mixture through a sieve; discard solids.

3 Combine blackberry purée, ¼ cup water, sweetener, lemon juice, brandy, cornstarch, and cinnamon in a small saucepan; bring to a boil. Cook 1 minute over medium heat, stirring constantly. Remove from heat; stir in butter.

4 Spread 1 tablespoon cream cheese over each crepe, and top each with 2 teaspoons sauce and ¼ cup blackberries. Fold each crepe in half, then in quarters. Spoon sauce on each of 8 dessert plates; top with crepes and blackberries.

PER SERVING (serving size: 2 tablespoons sauce, 1 crepe, and ¼ cup blackberries):

Food Choices: ½ Starch, 1 Fruit, ½ Fat

Calories 130; **Fat** 2.7g (sat 1.2g, mono 0.7g, poly 0.5g, trans 0g); **Protein** 6g; **Carbohydrate** 20g; **Fiber** 5g; **Sugars** 6g; **Cholesterol** 29mg; **Iron** 1mg; **Sodium** 132mg; **Potassium** 244mg; **Phosphorus** 142mg; **Calcium** 110mg

Blender Crepes

Hands-on Time: 10 minutes   **Total Time**: 40 minutes   **Makes**: 8 crepes

3 ounces all-purpose flour
  (about ⅔ cup)
¾ cup fat-free milk
1 teaspoon granulated
  no-calorie sweetener
  (such as Splenda)
1 large egg
Cooking spray

1 Weigh or lightly spoon flour into dry measuring cups, and level with a knife. Place flour, milk, sweetener, and egg in a blender; cover and process until smooth. Pour batter into a bowl; cover and chill 30 minutes.

2 Place an 8-inch crepe pan or skillet over medium heat until hot. Coat pan with cooking spray. Remove pan from heat. Pour a scant ¼ cup batter into pan; quickly tilt pan so batter covers pan with a thin film. Cook about 1 minute.

3 Carefully lift edge of crepe with a spatula to test for doneness. The crepe is ready to turn when it can be shaken loose from the pan and the underside is lightly browned. Turn crepe over; cook 10 seconds on other side.

4 Place crepe on a towel; cool. Repeat until all batter is used, stirring batter between crepes. Stack crepes between layers of wax paper or paper towels to prevent sticking.

PER SERVING (serving size: 1 crepe):

Food Choice: ½ Starch

Calories 55; **Fat** 0.7g (sat 0.2g, mono 0.2g, poly 0.2g, trans 0g); **Protein** 3g; **Carbohydrate** 9g; **Fiber** 0g; **Sugars** 1g; **Cholesterol** 24mg; **Iron** 1mg; **Sodium** 19mg; **Potassium** 56mg; **Phosphorus** 47mg; **Calcium** 33mg

Peanut Butter-and-Jelly Sandwich Cookies

Peanut butter cookies make the perfect base for a layer of strawberry spread. Serve these sweet-and-salty cookies for an afternoon snack or a brown-bag treat.

Hands-on Time: 20 minutes **Total Time:** 36 minutes **Serves:** 20

¼ cup butter, softened

¼ cup natural creamy peanut butter

½ cup granulated no-calorie sweetener (such as Splenda)

¼ cup sugar

2 large egg whites

1 teaspoon vanilla extract

7.9 ounces all-purpose flour (about 1¾ cups)

1 teaspoon baking soda

⅛ teaspoon salt

Cooking spray

¾ cup all-fruit strawberry spread

1 Preheat oven to 350°.

2 Beat butter and peanut butter with a mixer at medium speed until creamy. Gradually add sweetener and sugar, beating well. Add egg whites and vanilla; beat well. Weigh or lightly spoon flour into dry measuring cups; level with a knife. Combine flour, baking soda, and salt in a small bowl, stirring well. Gradually add flour mixture to creamed mixture, beating well.

3 Shape dough into 40 (1-inch) balls. Place balls 2 inches apart on baking sheets coated with cooking spray. Flatten cookies into 2-inch circles using a flat-bottomed glass. Bake at 350° for 8 minutes or until lightly browned. Cool slightly on pans; remove, and cool completely on wire racks.

4 Spread about 1½ teaspoons strawberry spread on bottom of each of 20 cookies; top with remaining cookies.

PER SERVING (serving size: 1 sandwich cookie):

Food Choices: 1 Carbohydrate, ½ Fat

Calories 97; **Fat** 4g (sat 1.8g, mono 1.4g, poly 0.6g, trans 0g); **Protein** 3g; **Carbohydrate** 13g; **Fiber** 1g; **Sugars** 8g; **Cholesterol** 0mg; **Iron** 0mg; **Sodium** 104mg; **Potassium** 52mg; **Phosphorus** 26mg; **Calcium** 0mg

Peanut Butter Cookies

For best results with these delicious cookies, use regular stick butter instead of a reduced-calorie or tub-style margarine.

Hands-on Time: 12 minutes   **Total Time:** 24 minutes   **Serves:** 24

¾ **cup plus 2 tablespoons natural creamy** peanut **butter**

2 **tablespoons butter, softened**

3.4 **ounces all-purpose flour (about** ¾ **cup)**

⅓ **cup granulated no-calorie sweetener (such as Splenda)**

1 **large egg, lightly beaten**

¼ **teaspoon vanilla extract**

1 Preheat oven to 350°.

2 Beat peanut butter and butter with a mixer at medium speed until blended.

3 Weigh or lightly spoon flour into dry measuring cups; level with a knife. Combine flour and sweetener in a medium bowl. Add flour mixture to peanut butter mixture, beating well. Add egg and vanilla; beat well.

4 Shape dough into 24 (1-inch) balls. Place balls, 2 inches apart, on ungreased baking sheets; flatten cookies in a crisscross pattern with a fork. Bake at 350° for 12 minutes. Cool completely on baking sheets.

PER SERVING (serving size: 1 cookie):

Food Choices: ½ Carbohydrate, 1 Fat

Calories 84; **Fat** 5.9g (sat 1.7g, mono 2.6g, poly 1.4g, trans 0g); **Protein** 3g; **Carbohydrate** 5g; **Fiber** 1g; **Sugars** 1g; **Cholesterol** 9mg; **Iron** 0mg; **Sodium** 63mg; **Potassium** 68mg; **Phosphorus** 42mg; **Calcium** 6mg

Chocolate-Almond Cookies

Enjoy one of these low-sugar chocolate cookies with a steaming cup of chocolate-flavored coffee.

Hands-on Time: 5 minutes **Total Time:** 21 minutes **Serves:** 12

1 (8-ounce) package sugar-free chocolate-flavored snack cake mix
1 large egg, lightly beaten
2½ tablespoons water
1 tablespoon almond extract
½ teaspoon vanilla extract
Cooking spray
48 almond slices, toasted (2 to 3 tablespoons)

1 Preheat oven to 350°.

2 Combine first 5 ingredients in a bowl, stirring until blended.

3 Drop dough by level teaspoonfuls onto baking sheets coated with cooking spray. Press 1 almond slice into top of each cookie. Bake at 350° for 8 minutes. Transfer cookies to wire racks, and cool completely.

PER SERVING (serving size: 4 cookies):

Food Choice: 1 Carbohydrate

Calories 82; **Fat** 1.1g (sat 0.2g, mono 0.5g, poly .2g, trans 0g); **Protein** 2g; **Carbohydrate** 16g; **Fiber** 0g; **Sugars** 10g; **Cholesterol** 16mg; **Iron** 0mg; **Sodium** 159mg; **Potassium** 114mg; **Phosphorus** 55mg; **Calcium** 19mg

Chewy Date-Apple Bars

Crunchy walnuts and syrupy-sweet dates are a mouthwatering combination that doesn't need a bit of added sugar.

Hands-on Time: 5 minutes **Total Time:** 35 minutes **Serves:** 14

2½ cups whole pitted dates
1 cup dried apples
½ cup walnuts, toasted
½ cup old-fashioned rolled oats
¼ teaspoon ground cinnamon

1 Preheat oven to 350°.

2 Place first 3 ingredients in a food processor; process until fruit and nuts are finely chopped. Add oats and cinnamon; pulse 8 to 10 times or until moist and oats are chopped. Spoon mixture into a lightly greased 9 x 5–inch loaf pan, pressing into an even layer with plastic wrap.

3 Bake at 350° for 15 minutes. Cool completely in pan on a wire rack. Cut into 14 bars.

PER SERVING (serving size: 1 bar):

Food Choices: 1 Starch, 1 Fruit

Calories 139; **Fat** 2.5g (sat 0.3g, mono 0.4g, poly 1.8g, trans 0g); **Protein** 2g; **Carbohydrate** 30g; **Fiber** 3g; **Sugars** 23g; **Cholesterol** 0mg; **Iron** 1mg; **Sodium** 48mg; **Potassium** 243mg; **Phosphorus** 40mg; **Calcium** 18mg

References

Top 20 Power Foods, pages 20-31

ASPARAGUS

California Asparagus Commission. http://www.calasparagus.com/ConsumerInformation/NutritionalInformation/index.html

GSS. Genetics Home Reference: Your Guide to Understanding Genetic Conditions. http://ghr.nlm.nih.gov/gene/GSS

Asparagus. The Old Farmer's Almanac. http://www.almanac.com/plant/asparagus

Guide to Asparagus. *Cooking Light.* http://www.cookinglight.com/food/in-season/in-season-asparagus

AVOCADOS

California Avocado Commission. http://www.californiaavocado.com/avocado-nutrients/

Kruse M. Top 25 Power Foods for Diabetes. Diabetic Living. 2013. http://www.diabeticlivingonline.com/food-to-eat/nutrition/top-25-power-foods-diabetes?page=3

BEANS: BLACK, GARBANZO, KIDNEY, PINTO, WHITE

Bennink M, Rondini, E. An Overview of the Status of the Science on Dry Beans and Human Health. The Bean Institute. http://beaninstitute.com/wp-content/uploads/2010/01/Bennink-and-Rondini-article.pdf

BERRIES: BLUEBERRIES, RASPBERRIES, STRAWBERRIES

The Journal of Nutrition. http://jn.nutrition.org/content/140/10.toc

California Strawberry Commission. http://www.calstrawberry.com

BROCCOLI

Vasanthi HR, Mukherjee S, Das DK. Potential health benefits of broccoli- a chemico-biological overview. National Center for Biotechnology Information. 2009. http://www.ncbi.nlm.nih.gov/pubmed/19519500

Broccoli: Nutrition, Selection, Storage. Fruits and Veggies– More Matters. http://www.fruitsandveggiesmorematters.org/broccoli

CITRUS: GRAPEFRUIT, LEMONS, LIMES, ORANGES

Sunkist Citrus...A Superfruit that's also a Superfood. Sunkist Nutrition Bureau. 2012. http://www.sunkist.com/healthy/superfood-brochure/

Economos C, Clay WD. Nutrition and Health Benefits of Citrus Fruits. Food and Agriculture Organization of the United Nations. http://www.fao.org/docrep/x2650T/x2650t03.htm

FATTY FISH: ARCTIC CHAR, SALMON, TUNA

Fish 101. The American Heart Association. 2015. https://www.heart.org/HEARTORG/GettingHealthy/NutritionCenter/HealthyEating/Fish-101_UCM_305986_Article.jsp

Seafood– A Smart Choice for Diabetes. My Food Advisor: Recipes for Healthy Living. American Diabetes Association. http://www.diabetes.org/mfa-recipes/tips/2012-08/seafood-a-smart-choice-for.html

FLAXSEED

Flaxseed. WebMD. http://www.webmd.com/vitamins-supplements/

Magee E. The Benefits of Flaxseed. WebMD. 2011. http://www.webmd.com/diet/benefits-of-flaxseed

GREENS: KALE, LEAFY GREENS, SPINACH

Harvard T.H. Chan School of Public Health. Vegetables and Fruits http://www.hsph.harvard.edu/nutritionsource/what-should-you-eat/vegetables-and-fruits

Arthritis Diet. Arthritis Foundation. http://www.arthritis.org/living-with-arthritis/arthritis-diet/

Hendrick B. Green Leafy Veggies May Cut Diabetes Risk. WebMD Health News. http://www.webmd.com/diabetes/news/20100819/green-leafy-veggies-may-cut-diabetes-risk

MELON: CANTALOUPE, HONEYDEW

Brolly M. Intriguing Links Between Diabetes and Cancer. The University of Texas MD Anderson Center. 2010. http://www.mdanderson.org/publications/network/issues/2010-fall/links-between-diabetes-cancer.html

MILK, FAT-FREE

American Dairy Association and Dairy Council. Health and Wellness. Dietary Guidelines. Don't Ditch Dairy from Diabetic Diet. 2014. http://www.adadc.com

Improve Diet Quality with 3 Daily Servings of Dairy.

National Dairy Council. 2011. http://www.adadc.com/Documents/health-wellness/improve-diet-quality-with-dairy.pdf

Why LACTAID Brand? LACTAID. https://www.lactaid.com/lactaid-difference/enjoy-lactaid

NUTS

Hernandez-Alonso. Ah, Nuts! Pistachios May Lower Diabetes Risk in Those With Prediabetes. American Diabetes Association. 2014. http://www.diabetes.org/research-and-practice/patient-access-to-research/ah-nuts-pistachios-may.html

Regular Consumption of Nuts is Associated With a Lower Risk of Cardiovascular Disease in Women with Type 2 Diabetes. American Diabetes Association. 2009. http://professional.diabetes.org/ResourcesForProfessionals.aspx?cid=71436

Protect Your Heart: Choose Healthy Fats. American Diabetes Association. http://professional.diabetes.org/admin/UserFiles/2014%20CMR%20English/Choose%20Healthy%20Fats.pdf

Long-Term Effects of Increased Dietary Polyunsaturated Fat From Walnuts on Metabolic Parameters in Type II Diabetes. American Diabetes Association. 2009. http://professional.diabetes.org/News_Display.aspx?TYP=9&CID=71229

OATS

Whole Grains A-Z. Whole Grains Council. http://wholegrainscouncil.org/whole-grains-101/whole-grains-a-to-z

Health Benefits of Oats. Whole Grains Council. http://wholegrainscouncil.org/whole-grains-101/health-benefits-of-oats

Campbell A. Getting to Know Fiber. Citrucel and Oats. Diabetes Self-Management. 2011. http://www.diabetesselfmanagement.com/blog/getting-to-know-fiber-citrucel-and-oats/

PEANUT BUTTER

Is Peanut Butter Healthy? Yes, says the Harvard Heart Letter. Harvard Healthy Publications. http://www.health.harvard.edu/press_releases/is-peanut-butter-healthy

Magee E. Nutty About Peanut Butter. WebMD. 2007. http://www.webmd.com/food-recipes/nutty-about-peanut-butter

Health and Nutrition Research: Disease Prevention.

The Peanut Institute. http://www.peanut-institute.org/health-and-nutrition/disease-prevention/

QUINOA

Khan, A. Fiber in Quinoa. 2014. http://www.livestrong.com/article/380474-fiber-in-quinoa/

RED BELL PEPPERS

Bell Peppers. The World's Healthiest Foods. http://www.whfoods.com/genpage.php?dbid=50&tname=foodspice

Brody B. Pepper Power: Nutrition and Other Benefits. WebMD. 2014. http://www.webmd.com/diet/peppers-health-benefits

Vitamin A. National Institutes of Health. 2013. http://ods.od.nih.gov/factsheets/VitaminA-HealthProfessional/

SOY

Friedman M, Brandon D. Nutritional and Health Benefits of Soy Products. Journal of Agriculture and Food Chemistry. 2001. http://pubs.acs.org/doi/full/10.1021/jf0009246

TOMATOES

Magee E. Health Properties of Tomatoes. WebMD. http://www.webmd.com/food-recipes/health-properties-tomatoes

Godman, H. Lycopene-rich tomatoes linked to lower stroke risk. Harvard Health Publications. 2012. http://www.health.harvard.edu/blog/lycopene-rich-tomatoes-linked-to-lower-stroke-risk-201210105400

WHOLE GRAINS: BARLEY, BROWN RICE, BULGUR, WHEAT

Diabetes Superfoods. American Diabetes Association. 2015. http://www.diabetes.org/food-and-fitness/food/what-can-i-eat/making-healthy-food-choices/diabetes-superfoods.html

Enriched flour. Wikipedia. http://en.wikipedia.org/wiki/Enriched_flour

YOGURT, FAT-FREE

Magee E. Answers to Your Questions about Probiotics. WebMD. 2009. http://www.webmd.com/diet/answers-to-your-questions-about-probiotics?page=1

The Benefits of Yogurt. WebMD. http://www.webmd.com/diet/benefits-of-yogurt?page=2

Metric Equivalents

The information in the following charts is provided to help cooks outside the United States successfully use the recipes in this book. All equivalents are approximate.

COOKING/OVEN TEMPERATURES

	Fahrenheit	Celsius	Gas Mark
Freeze Water	32° F	0° C	
Room Temp.	68° F	20° C	
Boil Water	212° F	100° C	
Bake	325° F	160° C	3
	350° F	180° C	4
	375° F	190° C	5
	400° F	200° C	6
	425° F	220° C	7
	450° F	230° C	8
Broil			Grill

LIQUID INGREDIENTS BY VOLUME

¼ tsp	=					1 ml		
½ tsp	=					2 ml		
1 tsp	=					5 ml		
3 tsp	=	1 Tbsp	=	½ fl oz	=	15 ml		
2 Tbsp	=	⅛ cup	=	1 fl oz	=	30 ml		
4 Tbsp	=	¼ cup	=	2 fl oz	=	60 ml		
5⅓ Tbsp	=	⅓ cup	=	3 fl oz	=	80 ml		
8 Tbsp	=	½ cup	=	4 fl oz	=	120 ml		
10⅔ Tbsp	=	⅔ cup	=	5 fl oz	=	160 ml		
12 Tbsp	=	¾ cup	=	6 fl oz	=	180 ml		
16 Tbsp	=	1 cup	=	8 fl oz	=	240 ml		
1 pt	=	2 cups	=	16 fl oz	=	480 ml		
1 qt	=	4 cups	=	32 fl oz	=	960 ml		
				33 fl oz	=	1000 ml	=	1l

DRY INGREDIENTS BY WEIGHT

(To convert ounces to grams, multiply the number of ounces by 30.)

1 oz	=	1/16 lb	=	30 g
4 oz	=	¼ lb	=	120 g
8 oz	=	½ lb	=	240 g
12 oz	=	¾ lb	=	360 g
16 oz	=	1 lb	=	480 g

EQUIVALENTS FOR DIFFERENT TYPES OF INGREDIENTS

Standard Cup	Fine Powder (ex. flour)	Grain (ex. rice)	Granular (ex. sugar)	Liquid Solids (ex. butter)	Liquid (ex. milk)
1	140 g	150 g	190 g	200 g	240 ml
¾	105 g	113 g	143 g	150 g	180 ml
⅔	93 g	100 g	125 g	133 g	160 ml
½	70 g	75 g	95 g	100 g	120 ml
⅓	47 g	50 g	63 g	67 g	80 ml
¼	35 g	38 g	48 g	50 g	60 ml
⅛	18 g	19 g	24 g	25 g	30 ml

LENGTH

(To convert inches to centimeters, multiply the number of inches by 2.5.)

1 in	=					2.5 cm		
6 in	=	½ ft	=			15 cm		
12 in	=	1 ft	=			30 cm		
36 in	=	3 ft	=	1 yd	=	90 cm		
40 in	=					100 cm	=	1 m

Nutritional Information

HOW TO USE IT AND WHY

Glance at the end of any Cooking Light recipe, and you'll see how committed we are to helping you make the best of today's light cooking. With chefs, registered dietitians, home economists, and a computer system that analyzes every ingredient we use, Cooking Light gives you authoritative dietary detail. We go to such lengths so you can see how our recipes fit into your healthful eating plan.

Here's a helpful guide to put our nutritional analysis numbers into perspective. Remember, one size doesn't fit all, so take your lifestyle, age, and circumstances into consideration when determining your nutrition needs.

IN OUR NUTRITIONAL ANALYSIS, WE USE THESE ABBREVIATIONS

sat	saturated fat	trans	trans fat
mono	monounsaturated fat	g	gram
poly	polyunsaturated fat	mg	milligram

The nutritional values used in our calculations either come from The Food Processor, Version 10.4 (ESHA Research), or are provided by food manufacturers.

Index